Learning
While Black

Learning
While Black

Creating Educational Excellence
for African American Children

Janice E. Hale

THE JOHNS HOPKINS UNIVERSITY PRESS
Baltimore & London

The Johns Hopkins University Press
2715 North Charles Street
Baltimore, Maryland 21218-4363
www.press.jhu.edu

Library of Congress Cataloging-in-Publication Data

Hale, Janice E.
   Learning while Black : creating educational excellence for African American children /
Janice E. Hale.
       p.   cm.
Includes bibliographical references and index.
   ISBN 0-8018-6775-4 (hard : alk. paper) — ISBN 0-8018-6776-2 (pbk. : alk. paper)
   1. African American children—Education.   2. Discrimination in education—United
States.   3. Educational equalization—United States.   I. Title.
   LC2771 .H35 2001
371.829'96073—dc21
2001000582

A catalog record for this book is available from the British Library.

Illustrations by Walter Allen Bailey

To my parents,

Cleo Ingram Hale and Phale D. Hale Sr.,

and to my son,

Keith A. Benson Jr.

We won't let them throw the book at our children.

Let's open it and teach them!

—NAACP Voter Education Fund

Contents

Foreword

Given the racialized treatment of African Americans in the United States, learning while black can be as dangerous to one's mental and physical well-being as driving while black. Over the past few years, both Republican and Democratic politicians have vigorously denounced racial profiling, the police practice of arbitrarily stopping African American and Hispanic drivers for no other reason than that they fit a police officer's mental picture of persons likely to break the law. These same politicians have also complained bitterly about the declining levels of academic achievement in predominantly black public schools. Unfortunately, in the case of both driving while black and learning while black, most politicians have demonstrated a persistent unwillingness to "do the right thing" and to institute the necessary sanctions—accompanied by adequate financial resources—to make sure that public servants provide their services to all citizens on a nondiscriminatory basis.

In *Learning While Black: Creating Educational Excellence for African American Children,* Janice Hale describes the conditions that have contributed to the high levels of academic failure among low-income children in predominantly black public schools. Persistent shortages of and high turnover rates among urban public school teachers, the large numbers of children being raised in households headed by single women, inadequate educational materials and facilities, and the lack of accountability among school administrators are among the factors contributing to the serious deficiencies in the academic performance of poor black children. Hale clearly demonstrates that the racialized treatment of African Americans helps account for the low levels of academic achievement among black children from middle- and upper-income families, as well. Educational expectations for black boys and girls are generally lower across all social and economic backgrounds.

Hale presents a detailed description and analysis of the obstacles she encountered as a single mother attempting to ensure that her son received equal treatment in an exclusive, predominantly white private school. She documents the steps she had to take to counter the teachers' low expectations for her son, despite the presumption that all the children in the school were gifted. If Hale, a professor of education, experienced formidable difficulties in navigating the educational journey for her child, then how much more difficult must it be for single black mothers who do not possess advanced degrees in education and psychology?

Hale uses her experience as a single mother and well-respected educational consultant to chart a more positive educational future for poor black children. "Learning while black" need not be a negative experience, and Hale provides parents, teachers, and school administrators with a model for a "culturally appropriate pedagogy" to insure more-positive educational outcomes for African American children.

In an earlier book, *Black Children: Their Roots, Culture, and Learning Styles* (1986), Hale argued that the distinctive cultural background of African Americans must be taken into account in developing effective educational programs for their children. In *Unbank the Fire: Visions for the Education of African American Children* (1994), she described how, in the past, the similarities in the educational objectives posited by African American cultural institutions—the churches, schools, and communities—served to guarantee the effective training of black children. Building upon these earlier insights, she now presents specific pedagogical strategies for improving the academic performance of poor and working-class black children.

Many times the models offered by educational reformers to improve the educational outcomes for low-income children depend heavily on increased parental participation in the educational process. Indeed, the degree of success for these educational reforms is measured in terms of the additional amounts of time, energy, and financial resources that low-income parents are willing to expend toward their children's education. Hale argues that these types of educational reforms place an excessive burden on single mothers, many of whom are the sole breadwinners for their families. The responsibility for the children's academic success or failure is thus shifted away from the classroom teachers and principals and onto the already overburdened parents.

Hale's model for educational change focuses on the classroom and the all-important interactions between the teacher and the child. She emphasizes "artistic teaching" that utilizes culturally relevant material, encourages collaboration, and provides children with choices and alternative strategies for achieving specific educational outcomes. To increase motivation levels, she advocates instruction in small groups, oral literature (reading out loud), and activities that encourage physical movement.

In Hale's model, individual classroom teachers receive ongoing assistance in implementing their instructional plans through the creation of structures of accountability within the school under the direction of the principal, who serves as the "instructional leader." The formation of an instructional accountability infrastructure, made up of classroom teachers, parent and community volunteers, and an "in loco parentis committee" for each classroom, helps to insure that no child is left behind. Through strategic liaisons with neighborhood civic associations, fraternal groups, and religious institutions, the school principal draws upon external resources to support an ongoing program of cultural enrichment for the children in his or her school.

Hale's model highlights the positive role that religious institutions can play in the education of children in urban public schools. Too often, participation in church-sponsored youth programs is limited to the children of church members. Hale calls upon public school principals to reach out and challenge local religious leaders to expand their missions. Within the school the principal's role is crucial in creating what Hale calls the Family; outside the school, creating the Village becomes a major objective.

Cultural enrichment activities are extremely important for African American children from low-income families. In the past the interactions within large extended families served as vehicles for socialization, providing young children with the social skills and moral training needed for the development of positive character traits. At the present time, many poor children raised by single parents and with few siblings come to school without the social training needed to interact positively with fellow students and teachers. The cultural enrichment component of Hale's model is meant to remedy these deficiencies through a wide range of social and cultural activities sponsored by the school. Trips and excursions planned by the cultural enrichment committees broaden the social experiences of these children, introducing them to people, places, and things outside their immediate environment. Specialized training in social skills and nonviolent conflict resolution is made available, along with mentoring and tutoring programs, to ensure that the children develop a broad repertoire of social proficiencies at an early age.

As children mature, they are provided with opportunities to engage in community service programs. Involvement in activities sponsored by local church groups and social welfare institutions allows children to learn that they can make important contributions to the overall improvement of the quality of life in their neighborhoods. Exposure to institutions dedicated to the preservation of their cultural heritage is extremely important in the development of positive self-image and a sense of pride. Concerts, lectures, visits to museums, and other cultural enrichment activities should be considered an integral part of the learning process and a central element in the school program.

In making the case for the broad implementation of her model for educational change, Hale calls upon African Americans who have achieved middle-class status to recognize and accept their responsibility to assist their brothers and sisters who have not been able to take advantage of the social, economic, and political changes that have occurred since the civil rights era of the 1950s and 1960s. Although many upper-status African Americans are better able to deflect the negative impact of white racism on their own present circumstances, they remain in a vulnerable position and may not be able to protect their children from the racist beliefs and practices woven into the fabric of American society.

Janice Hale presents specific prescriptions for remedying the debilitating conditions that now cripple the educational performance of poor black children in many urban public schools. Her recommendations are based on decades of experience as a teacher, educational researcher, consultant, and professional advocate for improvements in the social welfare of African American children. Hale calls for the formation of coalitions among educators, parents, and middle-class black professionals not merely to close the academic achievement gap between black and white students but also to prepare African American children for their leadership role among African peoples throughout the world in the twenty-first century. Hale brilliantly demonstrates that, contrary to many popular perceptions, "learning while black" can be a stimulating and rewarding intellectual experience.

—V. P. Franklin, Professor of History and Education,
Teachers College, Columbia University

Preface

Every child counts.
— MICHIGAN ANTI-VOUCHER CAMPAIGN

In this book I am going on the record with realities that are usually unspoken when issues of school reform arise, especially as those issues concern lower-income African American children. By speaking these realities, I am breaking two silences. I am breaking the first silence by asserting that school reform will not be successful until we, as educators, are willing to forsake the mantras we hold near and dear. Second, I am breaking the silence about the hidden racism in education.

First, the mantras. If you were to listen to educators talk among themselves, you might believe that everything that is wrong with the education of lower-income African American children is the fault of their parents. The school reform projects that obtain quick funding are those on which everyone can agree. If the project proposes that education can be improved merely by demanding that the parents be something that they are not, the project is embraced.

In a large midwestern urban school district, when the board of education was under threat of a takeover by the governor, it proposed a ten-point program of school reform. Nine of the ten points had to do with assignments for the parents. One young mother in the meeting broke the silence I am attempting to break, pointing out that they are passing all of the school reform back to the parents. She raised the question I am raising: What assignments are being given to the people who are *paid* to teach the children? I am asking educators to reflect upon the words of the spiritual,

It's me, it's me, it's me, oh Lord,
Standing in the need of prayer.

In this book, I have woven the themes of my earlier scholarship into a model of school reform. In *Black Children: Their Roots, Culture, and Learning Styles* (Hale 1986), I sought to identify features of African and African American culture that shape how African American children behave in academic settings and approach academic tasks. In *Unbank the Fire: Visions for the Education of African American Children* (Hale 1994), I explored the issue of upward mobility, an essential component of the education of African Americans. I also attempted to continue to push the frontier of cultural elements that underlie the psychology and education of African Americans. In the last chapter of *Unbank the Fire*, I began to delve into the kind of pedagogy that is appropriate for helping African American children achieve their potential.

Now, after twenty-six years of careful thought and reflection, I am ready to state that many of the solutions that have been presented to close the "achievement gap" between African American and white children are misguided. Many of the paths that are being pursued will not take us anywhere.

The people who say that teachers need to be better trained are wrong. The people who say that we need a national teaching credential (as a means to remedying the problems in schools that serve poor children) are wrong. The people who say that the solution lies in changing the parents are wrong. These are some of the mantras we need to let go.

I believe we already know how to train people to be good teachers. I believe we can already identify good teachers of any population of children. I believe we can identify good teaching when we see it. I also believe that students in teacher education programs are taking enough courses and having enough field experiences, observations, and evaluations.

I also believe that teachers know how to teach and are able to teach effectively the children whose education is of importance to them. They are willing to teach their own children effectively, as well as the children who are in "the club." However, school reform for lower-income African American children will not be effective until we construct a supervisory and evaluative support system within the school that reinforces teachers of African

American children in their efforts to deliver to our children what they deliver to white children in white settings.

African Americans are not going to solve this problem by creating "our own schools." We are not going to solve this problem with magnet schools, charter schools, school vouchers, private schools, or church-sponsored schools. The majority of African American children attend public schools, and so the answer will not be found in bypassing the public schools. The reality is that lower-income children *need* the public schools. In addition, lower-income parents cannot afford to transport their children to schools of choice. We must change the way the public schools operate for the children who need them the most.

There is no morally correct solution to this problem unless quality education is extended to every child in America, regardless of his or her family background or income level. Creating a public school system that would promote upward mobility for the children of unskilled and uneducated parents was a golden concept at the turn of the twentieth century, when those parents were essentially white European immigrants. However, those whites who benefited from public education created a game of hide-and-seek when it came to African American children. Essentially, white Americans have hidden quality education, and African Americans have been seeking it for more than a century.

It is not enough to create teacher certification standards and assign teachers who are paid $70,000 a year to classrooms of lower-income African American children to assure that quality education will ensue. The American system of education proceeds on the assumption that the parents supervise the teacher to obtain quality services for their children. However, that system breaks down when the parents are not connected to what Lisa Delpit identifies as the "culture of power" (1988, 1995). It is my contention that for school reform to truly benefit lower-income African American children, there must be an instructional leader within the building who stands in the place of the parents, monitoring the progress of each child and assuring that the grade-level outcomes for each child are achieved.

We do not need any new blue-ribbon committees to establish standards. We already know what grade-level performance is. We do not need any more studies to be conducted to tell us what children need to know. There is nothing mystical about required competencies: why not start with reading on grade level in the first grade? Most of the reports on school reform announce that every child should be reading by the third grade. No middle-class parent is going to allow his or her child to perform below grade level in reading up to the third grade, so why is such a goal being set forth by politicians and educators as reasonable?

A superintendent in a large midwestern school district, in announcing his school reform agenda, stated that the children would be tested each year to ensure that they are working at grade level. An editorial in the local news-paper observed that the new school reform sounded just like the old school reform. The question raised by the editorial, which also just happened to be the question in my mind, was "What is he going to do when he finishes test-ing the children?" We already know that the children do not know what they are supposed to know. What did he propose to do when he had veri-fied that information, once again, beyond the shadow of a doubt? How did he plan to bring them up to grade level? That is the school reform that is missing.

This book is intended to answer that question. This book points a fin-ger where no one seems to want to point it: at the classroom. In attempt-ing to obtain funding of my research, I once spoke to a foundation execu-tive who said that his foundation focused on school management issues in education. I argued that surely the basic unit of education is the teacher and the child—the activity in the classroom. He agreed with me but stated that that element was hard to "get at." This book is an attempt to "get at" the interaction between teacher and child.

This book is also written to raise the question of accountability in schools that serve lower-income African American children. It is my contention that those of us in the African American middle class must use our con-siderable clout in the interest of the children in our community who are less fortunate than our own.

The civil rights movement in the United States was embraced by the African American middle class and the masses alike. Lower-income blacks have always been dependent on highly educated professional elites to de-velop the strategies and lead the organizations in bringing about the change they all needed. Separate issues of educational inequality affect African Americans of the middle and lower economic classes, as this book points out. However, the masses are still dependent upon highly educated professional elites to be their voice.

Who will serve as the voice for lower-income African Americans who lack the resources to move their children to suburban and private schools? Who will speak for lower-income African Americans who are disconnected from the "culture of power"? Who will speak for lower-income African Americans who do not know how to access magnet schools, charter schools, and schools of choice? Who will represent lower-income African Americans who lack the resources to supplement school vouchers? Who will represent African Americans who do not know how to negotiate parent conferences with social workers, psychiatrists, and counselors to refute special education placements, prescriptions for Ritalin, and diagnoses of attention-deficit disorder, behavioral and emotional disturbance, and other LWB—learning while black—designations? The term DWB—driving while black—has recently gained popularity; it denotes the "offense" African American motorists are guilty of when stopped by the police for imaginary traffic infractions. It is now time for us to begin to talk about LWB offenses, which teachers and psychologists use to stop African American children and take them off the pathway to success. This book is written to be the voice for African American children. I call upon African American psychologists, educators, and civil rights leaders to join me in being that voice.

To his credit, Rev. Jesse Jackson has called together leading educators to conferences in Chicago to obtain input for the formulation of a civil rights education agenda. However, the major civil rights bandwagon of late has been the issue of school financing. I am certainly not denying that school financing is inadequate wherever African Americans are found. That is a given.* However, I am challenging African American educators to look beyond the obvious and acknowledge strategies we can employ to improve the quality of instruction for lower-income children, strategies that go be-

---

* In general, school financing in high-poverty districts lags behind that in other districts, even with federal and state supplementation, but this is true regardless of their racial makeup. With poverty level controlled, predominantly African American districts, nationwide, tend to be funded at least at the level of predominantly white districts. However, the inequality is still present, because 40 percent of African American children live in households that are at the poverty level.

yond issues of money to issues of teaching excellence and achievement accountability.

The second silence I am breaking is to bring to public attention the hidden racism in education. That hidden racism has two components. Teachers impinge upon the life chances of African American children in what some would describe as "unconscious" discrimination. The term was used by physicians themselves, in a study of comparative treatments of heart attack victims, to identify their motivation in prescribing more heroic treatment for white male actors than African American actors. The African American females had received the worst treatment—40 percent poorer in quality compared with the white males (Lienert 2000).

The second component of hidden racism is the expectation of privilege among upper-class white Americans. In this book I relate some incidents of discriminatory treatment that my African American son and I experienced in an elite private school. I include examples of what the psychologist Margaret Spencer has described as the expectation of privilege among upper-class white Americans (Spencer 1999). Inferior educational outcomes are tolerated for African American children day in and day out, in inner-city, suburban, and private school settings.

At my son's school, grades are not given to the children until they are in the seventh grade. The parents receive ten-page progress reports that describe exactly how the children are faring. In inner-city school districts that serve mostly African American children, in contrast, the children's school records look like college transcripts, with children being given grades of A through F in the first grade. A child in primary school should not be given a failing grade. All we need to assess is mastery: do they have the skills, information, and abilities appropriate for their grade levels? If they do not, then we need to help them achieve these.

I was astounded to learn that in the middle and high school of the elite private school my son attends, no grade lower than a C is given. A child who does not earn a C is given "No Credit" and repeats the course. These affluent parents are not paying $15,000 a year to have their children bring home Fs. Privilege.

While doing postdoctoral work at Yale, I discovered it was next to impossible to flunk out of an Ivy League School. A student might lose a scholarship because of poor academic performance, but it is next to impossible to flunk out. The school does not want to admit that it made a mistake in admitting the child. Difficult to get in, almost impossible to flunk out. Given the origins of the Ivy League as training ground for the white elite, is this not, again, white American privilege?

Although there may be more minority students today than when the Ivy League schools were created, the culture of those schools were crafted to serve an elite white upper-middle-class student population. Although some African American students attend elite selective schools, most statistics on the minority population are misleading. The numbers of Asian American students may have increased, but the proportion of African Americans has stagnated and decreased. This is especially true of African American males.

It is my contention throughout this book that the harshest educational treatment is borne by those at the bottom of the social hierarchy. Real change in achievement for African American children will come when we extend to them the love and support that white upper- and middle-class families legislate for their children to give them an edge. African American middle-class families join the race for "success" by running after white Americans for the fruits our society offers without thinking about how to change this society for everyone. We need a healthy sense of outrage over strategies parents employ to create an uneven playing field for their children, strategies that have an adverse effect on other children. An example of this is discussed in detail in chapter 4. This is the practice of delaying entry to kindergarten for one's child to give him or her an edge over the other children without thinking about the effect that has on the classroom as a community. One danger in this practice is that, over time, kindergarten becomes more like first grade, and children who are five years old begin to be perceived as immature in comparison with children who are older than grade level.

In a column in the *Detroit Free Press*, Brian Dickerson notes the willingness of the electorate to tolerate inferior schools for African American and poor children. "The real problem is that the privileged minority that dominates the country's political life has little or no incentive to provide the kind of educational opportunity that enables poor and working-class children to rise above their station. Perhaps the real reason Johnny can't read is that—particularly in the eyes of those whose children enjoy alternatives to failing public schools—Johnny already reads well enough" (2000, 1B).

HAVING BROKEN THE SILENCES OF TREASURED MANTRAS and racism in education, I propose, in this book, a new definition of the function of the school in the lives of African American children. My brother, Phale D. Hale Jr., has noted that there are many services for children in our communities but no coordination of services. I suggest here that the school become the coordinator of community support for children. The school should take the leadership in inviting religious, social, and fraternal organizations to create cultural enrichment experiences for African American children. Evelyn Moore, president of the National Black Child Development Institute, has called for strategies to move African American children from remediation to enrichment.

In this book, I am calling for the school to improve traditional instructional practices and create culturally salient instruction that connects African American children to academic achievement. The instruction should be so delightful that the children love coming to school and find learning to be fun and exciting.

We need to eliminate the bell-curve mentality of evaluation for all children. Elementary and secondary schools need to emphasize mastery. The trumpet call of Marian Wright Edelman, to "Leave no child behind," should be the theme song of every school. Many times, any child who does not respond to the limited amount of time a teacher is willing to invest is moved into special education, which is an academic dead end. The learning disabilities that afflict white middle-class children, such as dyslexia, are "decriminalized"; they are almost prestigious. The schools readily make adjustments, and the children stay on the path to success.

THIS BOOK CALLS FOR DEVELOPING THE CONCEPT OF BEING in the Family, creating the Village, and striving for the Beloved Community. Once a child enrolls in my school, that child is in the Family, and no matter what it takes, his or her educational fortunes will never be allowed to fall behind. This calls for the creation of an instructional accountability infrastructure within the school that delivers educational excellence to the children.

The concept of the Family applies to any entity that supports and nurtures children, such as the school and the church. The concept is operational whenever there is a membership or enrollment or whenever the concept of an in-group or out-group applies.

Children who are within the walls, as members or clients, are in the Family. Children who are outside the school or church are in the Village. Adults, businesses, organizations, or agencies in the community are members of the Village who can assist the school or church in achieving their missions for children.

Striving for the Beloved Community conceptualized by American philosopher Josiah Royce (1914) and evoked by Rev. Martin Luther King Jr. entails embracing the values that will bring Heaven on earth for everyone. Creating the Beloved Community means striving to achieve for every child the goals of the Children's Defense Fund—to leave no child behind and to ensure every child a healthy start, a head start, a fair start, a safe start, and a moral start in life and successful passage to adulthood with the help of caring families and communities (www.childrensdefense.org/).

Finally, rather than endorsing calls for better teacher training, this book calls for colleges of education to improve the training and functioning of principals as instructional leaders in their buildings. What happens to teachers before they enter the classroom is not the problem. What happens to them while they are in the classroom can make the critical difference.

Part 1 of this book, "Breaking the Silence," is a statement of the problem. It is an attempt to look at the failure of African American schoolchildren from the inside out. In part 2, "Creating the Village," recommendations are made for all segments of society to join hands in creating the Beloved Community for the support of the children. In chapter 1, "Mastery and Excellence versus the Bell Curve," I argue that educators need to create a new model of partnership between home and school to close the achievement gap of African American children. I suggest that we need to deepen our understanding of the dynamics of African American families at all income levels, to be realistic about the intellectual and social development of the children upon school entry, and to create an educational delivery system that meets the children and families where they are and achieves the nonnegotiable outcomes that are the birthright of every child in this country.

In chapter 2, "Playing by the Rules," I document the achievement gap in terms of how the academic outcomes of African American children compare with those of white children. A never-ending debate revolves around the issue of what part of the gap can be attributed to social class and what part can be attributed to racialized treatment. My discussion is designed to contribute to that dialogue.

I also review the vulnerable financial situation of the African American middle class, for two reasons. One is for educators to use the tools of sociologists in understanding the dynamics of African American families that impinge on the achievement of their children in school. The other is to clarify that my call for action is directed to the organizations controlled by middle-class African Americans, not to beleaguered individuals themselves.

In chapter 3, "African American Goals and Closed Doors," I focus attention on the achievement gap of African American males. I argue that the social problems that consume our attention, such as the incarceration rate of black men, can be eradicated if we connect African American boys to academic achievement at an early age. I further develop my argument that African American children come to school ready to learn and that the outcomes we see are not the result of what happens to them in families but, rather, the result of what happens to them in the schools they attend.

Children come to school with greater or lesser advantages depending upon whether their families are affluent or impoverished. No claim is made that all children come to school with identical cognitive configurations. All of my work, in fact, has been devoted to documenting cultural patterns in school readiness and school achievement that educators should consider. In chapter 4, "Down the Up Escalator," I share experiences I encountered in trying to achieve equal educational outcomes for my son in an elite private school. The episodes I describe shed light on an issue I have often pondered: why do some African American children fare poorly in elite private schools, when the educational and income levels of their parents would not predict difficulty negotiating those environments? I have noticed a pattern among these children: parents' moving them from school to school, nervous disorders, displays of hostility, and pleas to be returned to the public schools. However, not having attended those schools myself, I did not know exactly what the problem was.

I decided to follow in the footsteps of Jean Piaget, the Swiss psychologist, in reporting my son's journey through the primary grades in an elite private school. Because it remains difficult for African American scholars to achieve funding for our research proposals to study issues in which the dominant society has little stake, we often have to draw meaning from the episodes that cross our personal paths. These insights guide us in designing meaningful questions that can be empirically explored. Piaget was criticized, at first, for using observations of his own children to formulate his theories. Because he did, however, our understanding of how children's intelligence develops has grown enormously.

In chapter 5, "Twenty-First-Century Education Project: Report and Recommendations," I share insights gained in working with a small rural school district in Mississippi, trying to improve the educational outcomes for its children. These observations are shared because of their applicability to other settings and as an example of a setting in which all of the artificial boosters of achievement, such as computer programs to improve test scores, teaching to the test, and high teachers' salaries, have been tried—all to no avail.

In chapter 6, I describe in detail the model of school reform, the foundation for which is laid in the earlier chapters. This model of school reform has three essential components:

1. *An instructional model that encompasses information presented in my earlier books about African American learning styles:* This discussion pushes the frontier further by addressing additional instructional issues that need to be considered in opening the classroom doors and getting teachers to work together in creating the Village.

2. *A model for creating an instructional accountability infrastructure within the school:* This component ensures academic excellence for all students, regardless of the cultural level of the parents.

3. *A model of cultural enrichment that is designed to move African American children from remediation to enrichment:* This component seeks to transform the traditional notion of the sphere of influence of the school. The school is conceptualized as a coordinator of services for children who are part of the Village.

In chapter 7, "The Role of the African American Church in Creating the Village," the church is highlighted as a key player in the creation of the

Village. In this chapter, I review the distinguishing role the church has historically played in the lives of African Americans. I also recommend ways in which the school can capitalize on current trends of African American churches, including adopting schools in their communities, coordinating mentoring programs for African American boys, and creating rites of passage programs for boys and girls.

In chapter 8, "Where Do We Go from Here? A Call to Action," I make recommendations to parents, civil rights leaders, foundation executives, activists, and educators about strategies that should guide our efforts in achieving upward mobility for African American children. At a staff meeting I attended at the Martin Luther King Jr. Center for Non-Violent Social Change in 1970, the historian Vincent Harding observed that African Americans are engaged in a struggle that began long before we were born and will extend long after our deaths. Our task as activists is to make our small contribution to that struggle at our moment in time. This book is written to fine-tune our efforts so that the contribution we make in our lifetime is on the cutting edge of the struggle of African Americans for quality education. I believe that we can achieve quality education for all African American children if we work together in the creation of the Village.

An appendix, titled "The Church's Educational and Advocacy Mission with African American Children: Cognitive, Affective, and Religious Context," is directed at African American Christian churches. In this section, I draw upon my master's degree in religious education to speak to African American churches about how they might conceptualize their mission to children and youth theologically, to create Christian education programs that complement the model I propose for academic achievement among African American children. The church is urged to join hands with the school to create the Village.

Acknowledgments

This book was made possible by contributions to my personal and professional life from many people. I am deeply grateful to Assistant Dean Sharon Elliott and Dean Paula Wood of the College of Education at Wayne State University for creating a productive climate and being wonderful people to work for. Without their support and encouragement, this book would have been impossible.

I thank my mother, Cleo Ingram Hale, and my father, Rev. Phale D. Hale Sr., for their support and encouragement.

I am thankful to Professor V. P. Franklin for writing the foreword. I am deeply grateful for his advice and editing. Our conversations were so stimulating and his questions so penetrating that I wish I could share the discussions that brought this book to fruition with the world. In a real sense, this is as much his book as it is mine.

I thank my former professors in the Early Childhood Education Department at Georgia State University for their friendship, advice, and support, especially James Young, Martha Abbott Shim, and Joanne Nurss. I have received support and encouragement from mentors and colleagues such as Professors Michael Cole, Edmund Gordon, James Comer, Sandra Scarr, and Asa Hilliard; Evelyn Moore, Vicki Pinkston, Carol Brunson Day, Burnece Brunson, J. D. Andrews, Steve Minter, Marilyn Smith, Professor Hakim Rashid, Ed Green, Maurice Sykes, Kenneth Burnley, and Kay Royster.

Countless friends have been supportive throughout the years, and they were acknowledged in previous books. I would like to acknowledge friends who have been particularly supportive while I was working on this book: I thank Godfrey Dillard, Keith Godfrey, and my mother, Cleo Ingram Hale, for reading the entire manuscript and giving me advice and research assistance; Rosemary and Lawrence Schenden, Agnes Clements, Aurelia Webb, Monica Kaufman, B. J. Hampton, Mae Carter Danzy, Pamela Hayling Hoffman, Jacqueline McCutcheon, Janis Prince, Carolyn Stallworth, Dan Durich, Gigi and Melvin Moore, Francesca Dinuto, Drs. Lauren Barton, Linda Higginbotham, Ramada Smith; and Josephine Johnson, Margo Edwards, Gail Smith, Judith Whittaker, Dr. Linda Scales, Denise Page Hood, Karen Overstreet, Alveda King, Toni Humber, Luella English, Rita Clark-Chambers, Barbara House, Steve Bullock, and Betty Pinkney; Linda Graves, Jerome Reide, Robert Byrd, and all of my buddies at Flood's; Anita and John Dortch, Darryl Dyer, Carolyn and James Miller, David Ellison, the late Sallie Ellison, and my siblings, Phale D. Hale Jr., Marna Hale Leaks, and Hilton Ingram Hale; my brother-in-law Emanuel Leaks; my nephews, Richard Pace and Deandre and Deante George; my uncle and cousins, Raymond, Ralph, Vinnette, and Renée Grier; and my former pastor and his wife, Edwina Moss and Rev. Otis Moss Jr., of Cleveland, Ohio. I am also grateful to Rev. Jeremiah Wright, of Chicago, for being my cheerleader.

I wish to thank all of my son's teachers from the fourth grade to the present (seventh grade) for their high expectations for him and their artistic teaching. The fact that they did their jobs made it possible for me to do mine—the writing of this book.

I especially thank my pastor, Rev. Charles G. Adams, and his wife, Agnes Adams, of Hartford Memorial Baptist Church. I am grateful for his spiritual guidance. His sermons, inspiration, and counsel have made it possible for me to survive the many challenges I have faced.

I am grateful to my secretary Renee Konarzewski for the loving support she has given me at Wayne State University.

Finally, I thank Jacqueline Wehmueller, executive editor at the Johns Hopkins University Press, for her patience, encouragement, and support as I prepared this manuscript.

THE FOLLOWING GAVE PERMISSION TO QUOTE previously published material: A. Wade Boykin, "Psychological Behavioral Verve in Academic/Task Performance: Pretheoretical Considerations." *Journal of Negro Education* 47, no. 4 (1978): 343–54; "The Triple Quandary and the Schooling of Afro-American Children," in *The School Achievement of Minority Children*, edited by Ulric Neisser (Hillsdale, N.J.: Lawrence Erlbaum Associates, 1986); and "A Talent Development Approach to School Reform," paper presented at the annual meeting of the American Educational Research Association, April 1994, New York; A. Wade Boykin and O. A. Miller, "In Search of Cultural Themes and Their Expression in the Dynamics of Classroom Life," paper presented at the annual meeting of the American Educational Research Association, March 1997, Chicago; Constance M. Ellison, A. W. Boykin, D. P. Towns, and A. Stokes, "Classroom Cultural Ecology: The Dynamics of Classroom Life in Schools Serving Low-Income African American Children," Report 44 (May) (Washington, D.C.: Howard University, Center for Research on the Education of Students Placed at Risk, 2000); Charles R. Foster, "Elements of a Black Youth Ministry," in *Working with Black Youth: Opportunities for Christian Ministry*, edited by Charles R. Foster and Grant S. Shockley (Nashville, Tenn.: Abingdon Press, 1989); and Ja J. Jahannes, "Just Because," originally published in the 1987 calendar of the National Black Child Development Institute.

Grateful acknowledgment is made to Walter Allen Bailey, an educator in the Detroit Public Schools (African Heritage High School and Cultural Center), who created the cover art and chapter illustrations throughout the book. His artwork is drawn from a curriculum packet titled "The Whole Story," which contains prints of paintings, suitable for classroom display, illustrating African and African American history from ancient to modern times and presenting futuristic depictions of events through the year 2030.

PART 1

Breaking the Silence

CHAPTER 1

Mastery and Excellence
versus the Bell Curve

Our society works remarkably well for people who go to good schools and can score well on the SAT [Scholastic Aptitude Test]. The people for whom it works least well are those at the unacceptably bad lower end of the public-education system. For them, the only reliable way to guarantee a good education that confers the basic skills for a decent life—what they're not getting now, in other words—would be to make sure that all our schools meet a minimum standard of quality.

—NICHOLAS LEMANN

There has been growing alarm about the multitude of problems in the African American community that have circumscribed the life chances of African American children: crime, violence, teen pregnancy, poor school performance, and early termination of education, to name but a few. These maladies are apparently symptoms of a complex web of social and historical problems that have festered for centuries. Many of the underlying causes are both difficult and expensive to address.

This book comes at midpoint in my career, as a clarification of terms. I have spent nearly twenty-six years attending conferences, reading treatises, listening to diatribes about the causes of and solutions to the educational maladies of African American children. My scholarship during these years has centered on an analysis of the learning styles and educational issues affecting African American children; observations from supervising student

teachers and teaching in inner-city, suburban, and private schools; and experience in negotiating the schools as the parent of an African American
male child.

It seems to me that the majority of the analyses of problems with the education of African American children have come from newspaper columnists and politicians. I am not suggesting that everything they have said is
wrong. Some have made good points; and some of those points are noted
in this book. However, their ability to create a comprehensive solution has
been limited by their not being educators.

Some architects of educational policy have advocated school vouchers,
charter schools, longer school days, longer school years, mandatory summer school, school uniforms, teacher testing, the creation of a national test,
transformation of public education into military-style boot camps, and variations along those lines. The time has now come, it seems to me, for a cri-
tique to emerge from an African American educator. Many of those who
have been searching for a solution remind me of the three blind men, each
of whom is touching a different part of an elephant—the trunk, the tail, a
leg—and trying to piece together an accurate image of the animal. The cri-
tique I offer in this book analyzes the problem; but I also offer a clear working plan and solution, for there is work for all of us to do.

The model of school reform presented in this book, if implemented, will
improve the educational future for African American children. It is a comprehensive model of school reform that features a coordinated effort on the
part of parents, churches, community volunteers, and teachers and focuses
on learning styles and teacher strategies for children from preschool
through elementary school; the implications for secondary education are
clear. Specific strategies are presented that involve the whole village in raising the child.

I offer a solution that places the school at the center of the effort to
achieve upward mobility for African American children. The school is the
appropriate focal point because everyone is required to attend school. Not
everyone has a functional family, not everyone attends church, not everyone participates in the YMCA or YWCA, but everyone *is required* to attend
school.

The Black Community Crusade for Children, which was designed by
Marian Wright Edelman, is commendable. Every component of it makes

sense. However, Edelman is going to find that unless it is centered in the school, her program will continue to miss the children everyone is trying to reach. I was the first chairperson of ACT-SO (Afro-Academic, Cultural, Technological, and Scientific Olympics), a youth achievement project of the National Association for the Advancement of Colored People (NAACP) in Atlanta. We found that the children who enrolled and won the competitions were overwhelmingly middle-class children. It is middle class even to hear about a new program. It is middle class to pick up an application and get it in on time. It is middle class to design the project, pay the entry fee, and get to the competition on time. We rarely reach the children we most need to reach with such programs. If we wish to have access to the children who are the hardest to reach, the school offers us the most access because all children, including these children, are required to attend school.

The assumptions that underlie the philosophical relationship between the schools and families must change if schooling is going to meet the needs of children and families today. Schooling in twentieth-century America has proceeded on the assumption that Ozzie and Harriet are at home. The reality is that Ozzie and Harriet are not only not at home, they are dead! We as educators *need* Ozzie and Harriet. Most of our efforts at school reform consist of conducting wakes, lamenting the loss of Ozzie and Harriet, or conducting revival meetings, trying to bring them back to life.

I know Ozzie and Harriet, because I lived the "Ozzie and Harriet" life when I was in elementary school. My family lived about three blocks from every school I attended from kindergarten through high school in Columbus, Ohio. My father was the pastor of a church, and my mother was a homemaker.

My father went to his office early in the morning; he returned home about 8:00 A.M., and we had breakfast together as a family. My father also came home at noon, and we all had lunch together. In those days, there were no school cafeterias, and everyone attended neighborhood schools, so we went home for lunch.

When we arrived home from school at 3:15, my mother had just arisen from her afternoon nap and was seated in the living room drinking a cup of coffee. She greeted us and listened to everything we wanted to share about our day.

My father arrived home at 5:30, and we all had dinner together at 5:45. Dinner was a time for discussing the great issues of our time. My father was active in civil rights, politics, and community service. We were probably more intellectually stimulated from our dinnertime conversations than from anything we were ever exposed to in school. I know "Ozzie and Harriet," because I lived "Ozzie and Harriet."

My son is certainly not living the "Ozzie and Harriet" life, and neither are most other American children. Teachers have been trained in the rhetoric that the schools work in partnership with the families in educating children. This perspective sounds perfectly reasonable on the face of it. However, the attempts to make this concept concrete have produced school success only for some children: those who have middle-class mothers who do not work outside of their homes and have the skills, the time, and the inclination to supplement their children's education; the financial resources for tutoring; connection to the "culture of power" to the extent that they can carve out a path for school success for their children regardless of what the teacher does in the classroom. In a social climate in which only 23 percent of American children are growing up in two-parent families and 85 percent of African American children are in single-parent families (Schomburg Center 1999, 320), it is difficult for families to fulfill the expectations of family life generated in the 1950s.

My brothers and sister and I attended de facto segregated schools, which were arguably the worst schools in Columbus. However, because the family was strong many achievers emerged from those schools. Having a mother who was a college graduate and also a homemaker gave us a full-time overseer who could guide our journey through those schools. My parents also sent us to elite colleges and universities out of state.

Although at the time those schools may have been among the worst in the city, they do not look so bad in comparison with many schools today. First, we had African American teachers and administrators who lived in our community and knew from whence we came and where we needed to go. Second, when we had substitute teachers, they were my mother's friends, and they knew my name. A day with a substitute was not a day to act out! We grew up in an extended family within a coherent community.

The degree of specialized expertise and insight required of me to negotiate my son's early-childhood schooling still amazes me. I left parent-teacher conferences wondering whether one has to have a doctorate and be a full professor in a college of education to be a mother! I listen to my friends who are physicians, attorneys, and bankers express frustration as they try to cut through the "psychobabble" they hear from teachers about their children. They have the intellect, the interest, and the commitment to achieve quality educational outcomes, but they do not have the training in education that would enable them to cut through teachers' attempts to project their own incompetence back onto the child. How much worse must be the outcomes for children whose parents do not understand the path, blindly trust the professional judgment of the teachers or do not know how to challenge it, and are overwhelmed by what it takes to keep their heads above water emotionally, psychologically, and financially?

Schooling will proceed more smoothly for all children, and specifically for African American children, when the schools improve the "goodness of fit" between their efforts and the role that parents can reasonably be expected to play in their children's education. Achievement data show outstanding performance in school districts that serve children who are white with high average family incomes. These data are sometimes used to argue that African American children are genetically inferior or that the quality of education in schools that serve African American children is inherently deficient.

From my experience in negotiating my son's education in an upper-income private school and in observing in inner-city and suburban schools, these results are not achieved because white children are inherently smarter or because teachers in the upper-income school districts are working harder. These outcomes are a reflection of the efforts of parents in negotiating schooling for their children. Parents who are connected to the "culture of power" know the path because they have traveled that path of achievement themselves. They have the resources to purchase homes in affluent school districts; to pay for private education; to threaten to withdraw their children and educate them at home; and to devote time to volunteering in classrooms and on committees and school boards. By their efforts, they can change, even transform, their schools.

An administrator of a prominent midwestern school district told me that the schools work well for upper-income families. I countered that it is not that the schools work well for upper-income families; rather, their children succeed because they know how to work the system or work outside of the system to produce outcomes for their children *in spite of* what the schools are doing. The success of children should not be interpreted as evidence that an upper-middle-class school system works.

When I complained, in personal conversations with the associate superintendent of one school district and the superintendent of another, about the work I was having to do to create a smooth passage for my son through school, I received the same response from both: "If you were in my school district, I would route you through my best schools and my best teachers." The superintendent said that was his practice for the children of school board members. I was appalled. These statements were made casually, with no concern about what happens to the children who do not have parents on the school board or parents like me.

When I walk into some inner-city schools, I note a look on the faces of some of the staff that conveys this message: "This is the best job I can get for the amount of money I am being paid, so I am not going anywhere. The children are not going anywhere, either. So, we are just fighting it out for six hours a day."

It is widely known that a key difference in educational outcomes hinges on the activity of parents. Therefore, architects of popular models of school reform attempt to transform schools by transforming parents, trying to get them all to function as white middle-class parents do. My perspective is not designed to discourage those efforts; in fact, I wish them all of the luck in the world. Although this path toward school reform may benefit groups of children here and there, however, it will not significantly improve the educational fortunes of great numbers of African American children—particularly given that the parents of these children tend to be young single women and grandmothers.

The overwhelming majority of African American children come from single-parent households. African Americans work longer hours for less money than whites earn (Toppo 2000); often, they are minimally educated and have substantial constraints on their time. Parental involvement programs that work for white middle-class families will not be effective with these parents. This is not to say that these programs would not be good if they worked. But what is to be done when these traditional programs fail? I want to offer an analysis and to provide a new tool to teachers, principals, and parents.

Certainly, some African American children and their families will respond well to the traditional programs. However, the result is hit or miss. Because these programs are centered on the individual families, their effectiveness is not uniform, and they will not result in an elevation of all of the children in the school. The most reliable path, in my opinion, is to center school reform on the school and, more specifically, on the relationship between teacher and student—the basic building block of education.

I call part 1 of this book "Breaking the Silence" in part because it is controversial for an education insider to assert the obvious: that the most important activity in school is the interaction between the teacher and the child. The teachers—not the parents—are being paid to teach children. When my son was in the second grade, I often wondered why he was sent home with a wheelbarrow's worth of material so that I could teach him to read at 7:30 at night, when he was with her from 8:15 until 3:15, five days a week. In my son's classroom, there were eighteen children and two full-time teachers—a teacher-student ratio of one-to-nine.

Parents whisper among themselves, expressing their frustration with this situation, but it is never brought into the dialogue on school reform. My son's teachers had attended a workshop at the University of Chicago to receive training in teaching a mathematics program. Yet, they sent him home with a workbook filled with practice problems, for which I had to introduce multiplication and fractions. I had not been to the Chicago workshop; I had no teacher's manual, no manipulatives, no teaching aides. Yet his educational fortunes in that math class depended on me, and I had to scrounge around at a local toy store for some workbooks with pictures and graphs so that I could teach him the concepts. When I pointed this out to his teachers and the director of the school, they looked at me as if I were a troublemaker.

The rhetoric on parental involvement used by educators and politicians sounds great on the surface. However, I contend that it masks some important realities. First, parental involvement as it is being espoused calls for a high degree of sophistication on the part of the parents. I am convinced that a child's success in school today is a matter not so much of how smart a child is but rather how smart a child's mother is.

Furthermore, when one is speaking of the responsibility of the family in the African American community, one is generally speaking of the responsibility of a single woman. If she has any help, it is likely to come from her mother. African American single women are under a tremendous amount of pressure, as I know from personal experience.

Even if individual mothers rise to the occasion every now and then, the inconsistency with which the majority can function according to white middle-class expectations will continue to produce the all-too-familiar outcomes. Children who enter school on public assistance will, as adults, reproduce the status of their parents. We will see upward mobility for the masses of African American children only when the outcomes they achieve as adults no longer rest primarily on the cultural level of their parents. We will see a difference in the outcomes for African American children only when the educational professionals and members of the community find ways to compensate for backgrounds that do not prepare parents and children to negotiate the schools in a sophisticated manner. This group is not limited to the poor but includes middle-class families who are not educators or do not have expertise in negotiating the schools.

One of the recommendations I make in this book is the establishment of an Educational Aide Society, modeled after the Legal Aide Society, to assist parents in negotiating the schools for their children. This society could be sponsored by an organization such as the Urban League. This proposal is addressed in greater detail in chapter 8.

Learning While Black is a call to action for the African American middle class. The impetus of the civil rights movement from 1609 to 1865 was freedom from slavery, and from 1866 to 1964, citizenship, voting rights, equal access to public facilities, and school desegregation. The defining struggle from 1964 to the present has been closing the economic gap between African Americans and whites, using strategies such as affirmative action.

It is my contention that the African American middle class must stop for a minute and come to grips with our responsibility to provide a voice for the masses of African American people. We must acknowledge that the masses of African Americans are the wind beneath our wings. As we continue our quest for upward mobility by pushing the frontiers previously closed to us, such as suburban and private schools, it is incumbent upon us to stop, turn around, and give our voice to the struggle for a decent education for inner-city children.

In my father's generation, before *Brown v. Board of Education*, African American professionals were tied to the fortunes of the African American masses because they depended upon them to get paid (see Hale 1994, 25–79). My father depended upon the African American community to put his income in the collection plate at church. African American doctors depended for their livelihoods on the lower and working classes, as well as the more well-to-do. In the absence of Medicaid and health maintenance organizations, the patient paid the doctor. Similarly, African American lawyers represented the entire community of African Americans, including the lower classes, as clients. The children of the pre-*Brown* professionals, like me, understood that every meal we ate had its source in the masses of African American people.

Before *Brown*, all African Americans were victimized by the same legal segregation and discrimination in American society. They shared a common lot. It is more difficult for middle-income blacks of the post-*Brown* era to recognize this bond. Some middle-class African Americans who took a working-class route to the middle class do not have that same sense of interdependence, obligation, and responsibility to the black masses.

Most middle-class African Americans have a sensitivity to the plight of the larger community (that is why our voting patterns do not align with those of whites of similar income levels). However, that sensitivity perhaps comes from the memory of humble beginnings and the knowledge of the difficulties encountered by family members and friends in the community of origin—not from a sense of gratitude and interdependence.

Some middle-class African Americans do not see the relationship between the positions they hold, which they feel they have achieved through hard work, and the miseries of most of our people. Some middle-class African Americans do not see the blood that has been shed for the minority set-aside programs they benefit from. Some middle-class African Americans do not recall the origins of the "minority top-off" that enhances their salaries for the high positions they hold. Some middle-class African Americans who escaped the corporate knife during downsizing so that "minority hiring goals" were not sacrificed do not make the connection between where they are now and the community they come from.

The following passage is an excerpt from a novel that speaks to the experience of the middle-class African American of the post-civil-rights era who is paid by the corporation, the HMO, or the university rather than by the African American community. This excerpt is not offered as a primary example of interactions between middle- and lower-class blacks. Nor is it offered as a primary example of interactions between black brothers and sisters. This is one fictional account that expresses some of the underlying conflicts that have developed in the post-civil-rights era between middle-income African Americans, who have benefited from the social and economic changes that have occurred recently, and lower-income blacks, who remain at the bottom of the socioeconomic ladder.

In her critically acclaimed novel, *Brothers and Sisters*, Bebe Moore Campbell graphically outlines for us this tension between the achieved African American middle class and the African American underclass. Humphrey Boone, one of the main characters, is a bank president who came from humble beginnings. His sister, a single mother of teenaged boys, is a welfare recipient who constantly needs him to "ride in on his checkbook and save them." Throughout the book, the reader is led to be judgmental toward the sister for the mistakes she has made, and she is depicted as a thorn in the side of her high-achieving brother.

Campbell artfully shocks us, however, with the following passages, which are a wake-up call to all high-achieving African Americans who look only after their own upward mobility, denying the benefits they have received from being a part of a suffering community and disavowing any responsibility to give back to that community:

Humphrey put on his coat. "I have helped you. Nobody told you to have all these kids by that sorry-a−s dude. It's not my fault."

"What you saying? I shoulda killed my kids?" she screamed, rushing toward her brother, her arms flailing. "That what you saying? I shoulda killed my kids? If you'da been a woman, the same sh−t coulda happened to you, motherf−−−−r."

"If I had been a woman, I wouldn't have had any children that I couldn't take care of. I mean, you ever hear of birth control, Chontelle?"

"Oh, yeah, Mr. Perfect. Got it all wrapped up tight, dontcha? You think you so high and mighty, just because you got you a piece of a job. You talk white. You act white. But you know one thing. You ain't white, Humptey.

You got with white folks and want to act like you don't understand what it's like to be black no more."

"Being black is not synonymous with being a poor single mother on welfare, except in your head. To me, being black is working hard and moving on up to that deluxe apartment in the sky or any other da–n place I want to be. Being black is living well, driving a good car, and taking a vacation to Hawaii when I feel like it. Why can't you see that? Don't try to guilt-trip me because I don't buy into the misery you've created for yourself, Chontelle. Why do I have to pay for your life?"

Chontelle waved her hands in her brother's face. "Sh–t. I'm paying for *yours*. Oh, I guess you can't see that. You so da–n smart, you don't even understand the real deal. Ni———r, *you where you are because folks like me threw bricks and set fires last April.* Can you dig that? You think Martin Luther King set you free? Ni— rs burning down Detroit, Chicago, and Watts set your a–s free. You can't relate to my problems? They beneath you? You think I ain't sh–t because I got married and had kids and the marriage didn't work out. You so disgusted with me, huh, Humptey? But when them white folks knock you on your a–s, I bet you'll begin to relate then. One of these days, you gone remember exactly what it's like to be a ni———r, and I hope I'm around to see it." (Campbell 1994, 312–13; italics added)

Although I am writing this book primarily as a call to action to public school districts, I have included chapters that outline what African American churches, civil rights groups, and African American parents can do. When I was a child, I was told to "pray like everything depends on God and work like everything depends on you." I address each of these groups with a passion that instructs readers to work as if everything depends on their efforts. Because that may well be the case.

CHAPTER 2

Playing by the Rules

A white man with a million dollars is a millionaire, a black man with a million dollars is a nigger with a million dollars.

—DAVID DINKINS, FORMER MAYOR OF NEW YORK CITY

Many Americans are of the opinion that those African Americans who have achieved success have made it the old-fashioned way, playing by the rules and advancing through the educational system. This perspective, advocated mostly by white Americans, is popularly known as "bootstraps" among African Americans. Rather than addressing public policies that would elevate the masses of African American people, this approach focuses on the success of upwardly mobile individuals who pull themselves up by their own bootstraps.

The Problems with the Bootstraps Perspective

America likes success stories. As Ellis Cose notes in his book *The Rage of a Privileged Class* (1993), Americans like to think that our country is on the road to being color blind. The predicament of the black underclass seems so hopeless that many find it comforting to concentrate instead on those who are doing well. As an example, Cose discusses the media response to a short section on the African American middle class in William Julius Wilson's book, *The Declining Significance of Race* (1978). Wilson argues that the life chances of individual blacks have more to do with their economic class position than with their day-to-day encounters with whites and observes that more blacks than ever before have been moving into middle-class employment positions. However, as Cose notes, Wilson has little to say about what happens to them once they get into those jobs—whether they move up the ladder or ever managed to achieve any kind of income equity with their white counterparts.

The examination of such matters is not, however, Wilson's focus. His major point is that the problems of the black underclass cannot be attributed to race alone but are largely the consequence of certain economic developments. He wrote another book, *The Truly Disadvantaged* (1987), because he felt that the critics had been so preoccupied with his remarks about the improving condition of the black middle class that they ignored his more important arguments about the deteriorating conditions of the black underclass. As Cose observes,

> Formidable though the difficulties of the so-called underclass are, Americans can hardly afford to use the plight of the black poor as an excuse for blinding itself to the difficulties of the black upwardly mobile. For one thing, though the problems of the classes are not altogether the same, they are in some respects linked. . . . Whatever one believes about the relative merits of the grievances expressed by the different economic classes, clearly the troubles of one do not cancel out the concerns of the other. (1993, 8)

The only hope for upward mobility for the black underclass is to travel the "road that with tears has been watered." It is the black middle class that opens doors to employment, provides scholarship assistance, supports historically black colleges and universities, and engages in civil rights agitation and legislative advocacy. The bumps in the road that the black middle class encounter are significant because, if not smoothed out, they will continue to impede the progress of the black underclass and their children.

The school my son attends gives scholarships to children whose parents cannot afford the tuition, and some of my dismay over his experience through the primary grades was concern about how a less-skilled parent would deal with the issues we confronted. The "better chance" these white parents and philanthropists hope to provide to the underprivileged remains out of reach as long as the environment is too difficult for the average black parent to negotiate.

White Americans who believe in the strength of the bootstraps do not understand the underbelly of black middle-class success. As Andrew Hacker points out in *Two Nations*, "While there is now a much larger black middle class, typically, the husband is likely to be a bus driver earning $32,000, while his wife brings home $28,000 as a teacher or a nurse. A white middle-class family is three to four times more likely to contain a husband earning $75,000 in a managerial position" (1992, 33).

Given this income differential within the middle class, the stress placed upon the African American family (especially women) in trying to conform to the ideal of parental involvement in their children's schools is enormous, especially when the structure of the African American family does not meet the assumptions of that model. The average African American mother must bear the burden of contributing either all or more than half of the income required for her family to meet its needs. She is poorly positioned to match the involvement that a white middle-class mother can provide.

The sociologists Joe Feagin and Melvin Sikes (1994) report that they have found no empirical research data to support the widespread belief among white Americans that employment discrimination in the American workplace is no longer a serious problem. As Cose notes,

> in lieu of scientific research, we are offered speculation and conjecture, self-congratulatory theories from whites who have never been forced to confront the racial stereotypes routinely encountered by blacks, and who—judging themselves decent people, and judging most of their acquaintances decent as well—find it impossible to believe that serious discrimination still exists. Whatever comfort such conjecture may bring some whites, it has absolutely no relevance to the experiences of blacks in America. (1993, 3)

In his conversations with people who had every accoutrement of success, Cose heard the same plaintive declaration, followed by the same question:

> I have done everything I was supposed to do. I have stayed out of trouble with the law, gone to the right schools, and worked myself nearly to death. *What more do they want?* Why in God's name won't they accept me as a full human being? Why am I pigeonholed in a "black job"? Why am I constantly treated as if I were a drug addict, a thief, or a thug? Why am I still not allowed to aspire to the same things every white person in America takes as a

birthright? Why when I most want to be seen am I suddenly rendered invisible? (ibid., 1)

An emerging body of literature (Cose 1993; Feagin and Sikes 1994; Barrett 1999) challenges white America's belief in "bootstraps." Notable is the story of Lawrence D. Mungin, an African American attorney who sued his employer, a large corporate law firm, for racial discrimination. His story is presented in *The Good Black*, written by his white former roommate at Harvard Law School, Paul Barrett (1999).

Larry Mungin was a poor kid who grew up believing that if he played by the rules and worked hard, he would succeed; and, for a while, succeed he did. Mungin's pursuit of the American Dream took him from a Queens, New York, housing project to Harvard Law School and to the Washington, D.C., office of Katten Muchin, a blue-chip Chicago law firm, where he worked toward achieving a coveted partnership. After some years, everything was in place: he had spent his whole life preparing to make it in the white world, and now he was ready to reap the rewards. But instead of becoming a partner, Mungin became the plaintiff in a racial discrimination suit that would rock the legal world and turn his life into a struggle for survival.

For Larry Mungin, the journey began in a fourth-floor walk-up in the all-black Bedford Stuyvesant section of Brooklyn. Bused, with his older sister, to a predominantly white school in nearby Queens, he was taught by his mother to ignore the taunts and insults of the white gangs, to believe, as the book's dust jacket notes, that he was "a human being first, an American second, and a black third." It was a credo he carried with him into the world—and into a fast-track career as a bankruptcy attorney.

Just a few years later, this man, who had wanted to show that he was "one of the good blacks," felt marginalized: brushed off by senior partners, given scut work, and passed over for a partnership. Angry and ready to do battle, Mungin hired an up-and-coming black firm to sue his employer. Katten Muchin mounted the best defense money could buy. A Washington, D.C., jury ruled in Mungin's favor, and the verdict made headlines from coast to coast. The final ruling on appeal was more startling, however. An all-white, three-judge panel overturned the verdict and ruled in favor of the law firm.

"The gulf separating white and black views of the Mungin case demonstrates that his story is more than a good courtroom yarn," Barrett remarks.

It dramatizes the current dilemma of race in the middle and upper reaches of American society. Openly racist behavior is uncommon these days in business and professional life. But distrust and resentment are rife. Mungin was unusual in that he had the audacity and stamina to mount a serious lawsuit. But his story reflects the experiences of countless other blacks who do not sue—people who overcome obstacles, work hard, achieve some success, yet still feel thwarted. They have the graduate degree, the leather briefcase, and the right sort of suit, but they end up estranged and embittered. They ask: What more do I have to do to be treated with respect? (Barrett 1999, 5)

The Good Black is an unapologetic examination of race and racism in America. Barrett describes Mungin as a person who defined himself largely in terms of his professional success. He spent his whole life trying to show people, mostly whites, that he was not one of *those* blacks—one of the dangerous ones, the bad ones. Nor was he one of the complainers who demand "special treatment." Mungin assumed that to get ahead, he had to distance himself from the negative stereotypes of inner-city African American men. "By the time of his lawsuit he was no longer proud of all the time and energy he had spent reassuring whites. 'To be honest,' he confessed, with a self-deprecating bite to his words, 'I wanted to show that I was like white people: Don't be afraid. I'm one of the *good* blacks.' But that hadn't been enough" (ibid., 6).

Much of the racism experienced by lower-income African Americans is de facto, institutionalized, racism; they have little contact with whites in the course of their everyday lives. However, one of the inevitable consequences of integration is that middle-class blacks encounter whites more often, and the possibility for conflict is bound to increase. Barrett suggests that middle-class African Americans are more sensitive to race-related signals because this sensitivity enables them to decipher white society—to learn the rules, in effect, that they must play by. According to Barrett, the Mungin story illustrates "the paradox of integration" (ibid., 292).Progress in race relations made it possible for Mungin to rise from humble beginnings to an enviable level of accomplishment. Only fifteen years earlier, his very presence in a corporate law firm would have been astounding. However, his success made possible the relationships with whites that led to his frustration at Katten Muchin.

Some blacks will see in Mungin's tale all the proof they need that white racism is increasing. Many whites will perceive in Mungin, and others like him in the black middle class, a tendency to embrace victimhood, a lack of gratitude for what they have. Each side's emotion fuels the other's resentment. [Mungin] could be criticized for being naive in expecting smooth enforcement of the bargain his mother made so much of: get your education, follow the rules, and the system will treat you right. But he felt the expectation earnestly. He expected to succeed in the white world and become a part of it. At Katten Muchin, he failed and it was devastating. (ibid., 282)

Financial Vulnerability of the African American Middle Class

I am not opposed to affirmative action. I am not opposed to policies that disproportionately benefit the black middle class. When opportunities are provided across the spectrum, the members of the middle class will be those who are prepared to immediately walk through the door. Additionally, black penetration of the upper echelon of the opportunity structure will create a network of economically privileged African Americans who can subsequently open doors for later generations of achievers. Creating educational and employment opportunities for middle-class African Americans enriches and uplifts the African American community; here, at least, there is a definite "trickle-down" effect.

The model of affirmative action created through the efforts of Atlanta, Georgia, mayor Maynard Jackson was presented at a symposium held at Wayne State University in 1992 and sponsored by the College of Urban, Labor, and Metropolitan Affairs, as an example for Detroit, Michigan. Jackson and the Atlanta Board of Education required contractors to form joint ventures with minority firms to bid for city and school district contracts. The minority firms selected were able to obtain experience in working on public contracts, which they could use in successfully bidding for contracts in the private sector—an arena in which they had previously been unable to compete. Those minority firms created more jobs for the hard-core unemployed in the inner city than had been created by majority contractors. In addition, African Americans who have benefited from advanced educational and employment opportunities give back to the African American community by supporting historically black colleges and universities and by contributing to scholarship funds for children from less fortunate families, to African American churches and their outreach efforts, to charitable organizations, such as the Black United Fund, volunteering to mentor youth, and so forth.

So, even if affirmative action programs benefit middle-class African Americans on the first round, the benefit ultimately passes to the total African American community. In the educational arena, however, no trickle-down effect is equal to the benefit derived by individuals in obtaining a quality education themselves. In education, every child must count. Advocacy activity should not focus upon those who are pushing the frontier to the exclusion of those who are left behind.

Many African American professionals feel resentment at being expected to accept responsibility for the forward movement of the underclass. Isabel Wilkerson, the Chicago bureau chief of the New York Times, argues that "many whites put entirely too much responsibility and burden on the black middle class for the structural and institutional racism we all inherited. It's not our responsibility. . . . It's the entire country's responsibility. Why should the onus be on . . . the (black) working couple who are just trying to make ends meet, who (themselves) are just one step away from poverty?" (quoted in Cose 1993, 105).

My argument is with the contemporary civil rights agenda that does not focus appropriately on educational quality for the majority of African American children—not with the African American middle class itself. I am calling for an acknowledgment that the cutting edge of the agenda we have set, which has encompassed attacks on legal segregation of housing and public accommodations, discriminatory voting practices, school segregation, and employment discrimination, has created gains for the middle class but not yet for the African American community as a whole.

The black middle-class family has been able to escape from the most heinous aspects of inferior schools because of our purchasing power. I am not saying that the African American middle class is responsible for financing the educational liberation of the African American masses; but the civil rights movement has some unfinished business. I am suggesting that the vision, the leadership, the advocacy, the agenda, and the voice for liberation must come not from beleaguered individuals but from the African American middle class.

I am also not saying that individuals in the African American middle class do not "give back" with volunteer efforts to help those who are less fortunate. Ulric Haynes, the dean of Hofstra University's business school, is an example.

> Among my circle of black friends, who by anybody's standards would be overachievers, every one of us is concerned for the so-called underachievers and, in some way or another, is involved in helping. . . . I have gotten our school of business involved in a partnership relationship with the Hempstead school district—which is overwhelmingly black and Latino, and is horribly poor in terms of quality—in curriculum redesign, in trying to get them computer equipment to upgrade their business education program, in one-on-one relationships. (quoted in ibid., 95)

Cose points out that certainly African American professionals can, and do, get involved in the lives of the less fortunate and that in individual cases their efforts can make a huge difference. However, volunteer work among the disadvantaged is hardly the solution to the deep-rooted problems of the masses of African American people and are not the sole responsibility of the African American middle class (ibid., 106).

Academic Achievement

The sociologist Dalton Conley has noted that more than half of all African American children under the age of six live in poverty. This is three times greater than the proportion in the white community. As we move up the age ladder, the news gets better before it gets worse again. The high school completion rates for blacks and whites are essentially the same among adults aged twenty-four to thirty-four (85 percent of African Americans and 88 percent of whites) (Conley 1999, 10). Nevertheless, there is still a 50 percent dropout rate in many inner-city schools. Many of these students are temporary dropouts who complete high school or obtain a certificate of General Educational Development (GED) later in life (Herrnstein and Murray 1994, 151). The profile of temporary dropouts is discussed in more detail in chapter 3.

The proportion of adults in this same age group who receive some college education (both those who attain degrees and those who do not) is higher for blacks than for whites: 32 percent for blacks and 28 percent for whites. However, when we examine college completion rates, we find that African Americans are only about half as likely as whites to complete bachelor's degrees: the rates are 14 percent for blacks and 28 percent for whites (Conley 1999, 10). By 1994, the college enrollment rate for whites aged eighteen to twenty-four was 43.6 percent, while the rate for African Americans was 35.5 percent (ibid., 56). Most African American college students are in two-year institutions, and one-third of those students are enrolled in programs that do not necessarily give credit toward the baccalaureate degree (Hale 1986, 178).

Conley (1999) suggests that the real story in racial differences lies in the college completion data measured in absolute rates of completion and in terms of the time it takes to complete the degree. Earnings are significantly higher for college graduates than for those with only a high school diploma, and so anything that delays completion of college reduces the length of time a person can be working at a higher income level over the lifetime. Data on students who move directly from high school to college show that in 1994, 50.8 percent of black students who graduated from high school that year were enrolled in college; the corresponding figure for white students was 64.5 percent. Given that the 1977 percentages were almost equal, these figures reflect a large gap and contradict commonly held notions that things have improved in the past thirty years. Those African Americans who do get degrees take substantially longer than whites in attaining them — on average, 7.19 years longer.

> This is a substantial opportunity cost for black students to bear in terms of lost postgraduate earnings. This longer period of time, combined with the finding that blacks are less likely to start college right after high school, makes the mean age at college completion higher, perhaps making these graduates less attractive to potential employers. The story is even worse when we consider graduate and professional degrees: African Americans hold only 3.1 percent of doctoral degrees, about a quarter as many as one would expect, given the population percentages. (Conley 1999, 57)

The National Urban League's (2000) annual overview on the state of black America notes that the number of black people in college has surged by 43 percent since the 1970s, to 1.5 million in 1997, but black women have outpaced black men in academic settings. Between 1976 and 1986 the percentage of college-aged black males enrolled in college declined from 35 to 28 percent (Conley 1999, 57); and from 1986 to 1994, among African Americans, twice as many women as men completed college (Hale 1994, 196). Between 1977 and 1997, the number of bachelor's degrees awarded to black men increased 30 percent to 32,697, while for black women the increase was 77 percent, to 59,228 (Shepard 2000). The president of the Urban League, Hugh Price, has remarked that the gap between black women and men is troublesome for the future of the black family: "As the economic gap widens, questions of whether black women will find black men who can carry their share in the household will become more evident" (quoted in ibid.).

Ellis Cose translates these statistics into human terms, citing his interviews with highly successful African Americans. Basil Paterson, the former deputy mayor of New York, remarks, "Every day I realize that I'm further ahead than I ever thought I would be in my life, yet, by any standard that is uniquely American, I'm not successful. It's too late for me to get rich because I spent too much time preparing for what I've got. . . . Most of us are ten years behind what we should have been. We couldn't get credentials until we were older than other folks." Paterson is not sure that the next generation will have it much better. He had recently received a resumé from a black graduate of a prestigious law school who was interested in international commerce. "She can't get international commerce [experience] working for me," Paterson said, speculating that she had come to him because she saw few opportunities elsewhere (quoted in Cose 1993, 84).

Conley raises the question of how to interpret the strong positive effect of being black on the odds of completing high school, especially given the absence of formal affirmative action programs at the high school level. He suggests two possible explanations. First, the schools that African American students attend are, on average, "easier" than comparable schools attended by white students. Evidence for this notion is found in the test scores and other cognitive measures that suggest that African American high school students are less well prepared than their white counterparts. This speaks to the issue of quality of education toward which this book is directed. Second, African Americans put great stock in education as a route to upward mobility, and so the families and the communities exert great effort in getting children through high school by any means necessary: thus the strong push for high school completion (Conley 1999, 75).

Cose questions whether this much-vaunted black progress in education is as qualitatively genuine as it might quantitatively seem. He cites a study of higher education conducted by the Southern Education Foundation, which finds that though the number of blacks in college overall is up, the number of black first-time, full-time freshmen is not (Cose 1999, 39). He also reports that in virtually all of the twenty-six states that now require high school seniors to pass competency exams before being allowed to graduate, a disproportionate number of those who fail to graduate because of their performance on the exam are students of color. He concludes that the exit exams essentially punish poor students and those of color for attending substandard schools (ibid., 39).

The cover story of the June 7, 1999, issue of *Newsweek* addresses the underachievement of middle-class African American children in the affluent and integrated community of Shaker Heights, Ohio, where achievement outcomes for blacks and whites would be expected to be equal (ibid.). This matter is revisited in an article in *Education Week* that appeared on March 15, 2000 (Johnston and Viadero 2000). These articles go round and round trying to shed light on a complicated issue: why do middle-class African American students fail to achieve academic success?

Some of the confusion results from the use of the term "middle class." Much contemporary writing on the subject assumes that all people living in a given community share the same social class, in every sense of the word. Most African American families living next door to white families, however, have arrived there by a different route, and their economic resources may not be comparable. As Andrew Young once stated in a television interview, "When an African American family is living in their dream house, everyone in the house is working to pay for it!" In addition, it may be that a considerable number of African Americans whose children attend Shaker Heights schools are renters rather than home owners. Many others live in neighborhoods that are technically in the city of Cleveland but entitle them to attend school in the Shaker Heights district. It is also difficult to count the children who give as their residence the address of their grand-parents or other relatives so that they can attend superior schools.

It is assumed, as well, that neighbors share a common economic and cultural history: the same linkages to the culture of power, the same information and skills to prepare their children for school and to negotiate the culture of the school, the same amount of time and energy to devote to that enterprise. Educators are confused because they lack the sociological tools to understand the dynamics of families and the manner in which those dynamics are mediated by race.

Another factor that is often missed in discussions of the black educational achievement gap is the ease with which African American children — especially boys — can silently fall through the cracks in integrated classrooms. The episodes I cite of my son's experiences shed some light on the differences in the quality of schooling delivered within the same schools. Cose expresses the belief that the test scores illuminate a real difference in academic achievement and that this difference should not be dismissed as cultural bias:

> Anyone who has spent much time in predominantly black public schools knows that education is not always a priority in such institutions. In some places, things are much as they were when I was a schoolboy and heard one teacher say that blacks have "lazy tongues," and another announce that he didn't care anyway, and yet another explain, when challenged over handing out *brain-deadening assignments*, that kids like us were incapable of handling difficult material. . . . Legions of black kids still have it instilled in them that they are not particularly intelligent; and at least partly as a result of such indoctrination, many give up on academic achievement at a very young age. (1993, 162; italics added)

In a *Newsweek* article titled "Living with the Test," Cose notes that black students who score twelve hundred or higher on the SAT test have taken high school calculus and honors English (Cose 1998, 65). The issue of quality of education provides the missing link in the problem of black academic underachievement, the one that sociologists cannot explain with statistics.

The Labor Market

Quality of education is more important than quantity of education. The payoff for increased rates of high school graduation and enrollment in college for African American children is challenged further as they move out of school and into the labor market. The gap in wages between blacks and whites at all educational levels has reportedly begun to widen since the 1980s. "Labor force participation and unemployment differentials have also increased. For example, in 1994 the unemployment rate for blacks was 13.9 percent, whereas it was only 6.2 percent for non-Hispanic whites" (Conley 1999, 10).

Among college graduates, the black unemployment rate is typically twice that for whites (Cose 1999, 144). Furthermore,

> even when African Americans are able to land a job, it is likely to be a less desirable position. In 1997, only 16 percent of employed African Americans held professional or managerial jobs, compared to 31 percent of employed whites. By contrast, black workers were overrepresented in the service sector, with its lower wages: 26 percent of employed African Americans worked in service industries in 1997, while only 15 percent of their white counterparts held jobs in this sector. (ibid., 11)

The labor market difficulties African American men continue to encounter have repercussions in many areas. The black-white wealth gap, Conley contends, is even wider than the income difference. Other areas of life are affected as well. For example, in 1997 only 46 percent of black families were made up of a married couple, compared with 81 percent of white families. The low marriage rate seems to be related in part to a shortage of well-employed men.

Conley cites income trends that reflect the occupational position of black workers. The median income of black families in 1997 was 55 percent that of white families ($26,522 and $47,023, respectively); in that same year, 26 percent of black families lived below the poverty level, compared with only 6 percent of white families (ibid., 11). Educational differences, he asserts, do not fully explain these income gaps. "Although American society may be moving closer to educational parity between blacks and whites (at least in terms of quantity of schooling) for some reason this progress is not translating into occupational (and earnings) success for blacks relative to whites" (ibid., 86). When Conley speaks of educational parity, he refers to quantitative measures—years spent in school. Because his expertise is not in the area of educational quality, he is unable to explain the disparity. Taken together, Conley's statistics and Cose's testimony support the thesis that educational differences in quality and racialized treatment in obtaining employment, higher salaries, raises, and promotions combine to produce these effects.

Conley documents his assertion that years of education do not produce equality in occupational success and earnings outcomes between blacks and whites. Among individuals who are high school graduates but have not completed additional education, median incomes are $14,881 for blacks and $18,446 for whites. However, among men with no education beyond a high school diploma, the income disparity widens. In 1997, black male high school graduates earned a median income of $18,898, compared with $26,028 for similarly educated white males. African American male high school graduates earned seventy-three cents for every dollar earned by white male high school graduates, and the wage ratios for more educated groups were not much better (Conley 1999, 11).

Even black men with bachelor's degrees earn only seventy-six cents on the dollar of white men with similar education. College-educated black women do better (ninety-seven cents on the dollar) relative to white women, but this is largely because of depressed wages among women in general. Conley reports that "twice as many well-off as poor African Americans describe insufficient pay or challenge as the feature of their job that bothers them the most. . . . It is the most highly educated who feel racial inequality the most acutely" (ibid., 86).

I do not agree that the most highly educated experience racial inequality most acutely. Each class experiences racial inequality in its own way. Rather, it is the African American middle class that most intimately experiences the paradox implicit in the American gospel that if you play by the rules you will be rewarded by equality of treatment and outcomes.

According to Cose, the real issue is white racism. "And it's very hard to call people on that, because nobody wants to think they're prejudiced. They reject it. They reject it instantly. So, we wind up doing this whole rationalization thing, where we're winding up talking about dismantling affirmative action. . . . But affirmative action is a bridge to get us over racist attitudes. . . . It's a necessary mechanism. And it's not about past days . . . from history. This is everyday reality" (ibid., 123). Moreover, Conley states, the higher an African American attempts to rise in the occupational hierarchy, the more discrimination he or she faces (1999, 9).

Joe Feagin, a sociologist who has extensively studied the black middle class, writes about the subtle displays of prejudice that account for the employment discrimination behind the statistics presented here. "Modern discrimination more often takes the form of tracking, limiting, or blocking promotions, harassment, and other differential treatment signaling disrespect" (Feagin and Sikes 1994, 35). The result, Feagin notes, is that middle class blacks are restricted, isolated, and ostracized in predominantly white workplaces. They find that they are not a part of the same networks that link together not only white co-workers but also white supervisors and clients.

Cose gives us some insight into the intangible factors that impinge upon the success of African Americans despite the assumption of meritocracy in the corporate world. Although there is widespread belief that good work can be rewarded at any time during a career, early job assignments and early promotions designate "fast starters" who do significantly better throughout their careers than others, regardless of their actual ability or performance. These determinations of who will end up on the fast track are made early in the career. This system includes no mechanisms for bringing former losers back into the competition for top positions. If there is to be true equality in a corporation, "employees must know the rules of the game, they must start at similar positions, and they must be allowed to begin the tournament when they are ready to compete" (1993, 88).

Cose points out that "if in fact the real reasons for advancement have less to do with ability than with attributes one is *a priori* assumed to possess, then it is only to be expected, given certain widespread racial assumptions in America, that very few blacks, however accomplished, manage to get near the top of the corporate hierarchy." Furthermore, if whites get ahead because of assumptions that they will fit in and that they have certain capabilities, then they will get the early high-profile job assignments, mentors within the corporation, and wide latitude to fail—but also to triumph (ibid., 89).

According to the testimonies of the high-achieving African Americans presented by Cose, blacks almost automatically lose ground because of the time it can take for a corporation to grow comfortable with them. By the time the corporation finally acknowledges their abilities, the fast-trackers have already moved up, and even the most talented blacks often end up in slower lanes. "When someone like Basil Paterson says, 'It's too late for me,' he is not speaking for himself alone, but for thousands of other blacks who wonder how much better they would be doing in a fairer world" (ibid., 89–90). Black executives inevitably compare themselves with their white peers, and no matter how well the blacks are doing, they never feel they are doing as well as their white counterparts. "In fact, when blacks compare themselves with whites in virtually any arena, the picture is unsettling" (Cose 1999, 40).

Each year, *Business Week* magazine publishes a list of the chief executive officers of the thousand largest corporations in the United States. In 1994, African Americans held exactly two of those slots, and "there are no serious signs that the other 998 firms are grooming black executives for eventual top jobs" (Hacker 1992, 113). The better jobs in America are, obviously, not held by African Americans. Only 9 percent of black men made more than $50,000 in 1997, compared with 24 percent of white men. Cose reports that although "black median income (for a family of four) reached a record high of $34,644 in 1997, that was still $21,378 less than the average for whites" (1999, 40).

Blacks at the other end of the economic spectrum are also faring much worse than whites. In 1997, the unemployment rate for whites was 4 percent; for blacks it was almost triple that rate, at 11 percent (DeBarros and Bennett 1998, 103). In the thirty-four years from 1960 and 1993, the black-to-white unemployment ratio dipped below two-to-one in only six of those years (Hacker 1992, 109). Conley argues that "this unemployment gap is not explained by different education levels; in fact, it is among male college graduates that the unemployment gap is the greatest" (1999, 83). High unemployment rates for black teens are particularly distressing: "only 40 percent of black males between 16 and 19 are in the labor force compared with 57 percent of their white counterparts" (Cose 1999, 40). Cose states that "for all of the well-documented success stories and for all of the heartwarming statistics, African Americans remain a race apart in America, a race admired, even emulated, yet held at arm's length" (ibid.).

The other debate that is seemingly never ending revolves around whether race or social class is a greater determinant of life chances and success for African Americans. William Julius Wilson (1978) argues that class has eclipsed race as the most important factor determining the life chances for African Americans. Cose finds support for this claim in terms of occupational mobility both within and across generations. However, he finds race to be the most salient predictor of earnings for given education levels and for net worth (1999, 12).

Some theorists, in trying to explain the labor market difficulties of African Americans, have suggested that while the quantity of education attained by blacks and whites has more or less equalized, racial disparities in the quality of education continue to exist, resulting in a skills mismatch that is particularly significant in our increasingly technological economy. Quality of education is, however, notoriously difficult to measure (Conley 1999, 88).

Defining quality of education, and understanding why African American children are not receiving it, is the daunting task of this book. Just as "all roads lead to Rome," so the inferior quality of education that African American children receive leads to perpetual economic inequality.

The Accumulation of Wealth

According to Dalton Conley, in 1994 the median white family held assets worth more than seven times those of the median nonwhite family. Even when black and white families are compared at the same income level, whites enjoy a huge advantage in wealth. An African American family with an income of less than $15,000 a year had no assets, while an equivalent white family held $10,000 worth of equity. At the upper income levels, white families with incomes greater than $75,000 a year had a median net worth of $308,000, almost three times the median net worth of $114,600 of an African American family at that income level (Conley 1999, 1). Conley asserts that to understand a family's well-being and the life chances of its children—its class position—we must consider not only income, education, and occupation but also accumulated wealth (property, assets, and net worth). He maintains that educational inequality leads to employment inequality, which in turn leads to income inequality, which leads to inequality of wealth, and thus the cycle continues into the next generation. He calls attention to the way wealth distribution has historically occurred and its impact on racial inequality in America.

At all income, occupational, and education levels, black families on average have significantly lower levels of wealth than similar white families. Wealth accumulation is an important indicator because it reflects support from previous generations who provide gifts, informal loans, and inheritances and passes on in the same forms to the next generation. Therefore, the concept of net worth can pick up the dynamics of the present generation and also reflect past inequalities that may be obscured in simple measures of income, occupation, or education (ibid., 6).

Conley links the discrimination African Americans have historically experienced in American social policy to the inequalities they experience today. The American welfare system, for example, originated with the Social Security Act, which was signed into law by President Franklin D. Roosevelt in 1935. Conley maintains that this legislation bifurcated the welfare state along racial lines. The original welfare system included programs like old-age insurance (under Social Security) and unemployment insurance, and Medicare health insurance was added in the 1960s. "These programs became sacrosanct, with almost unanimous support because of their universal nature. But they were not so universal when it came to African Americans. To a great extent, blacks were initially excluded from these programs because the programs did not cover the agricultural or service industries in which African Americans were predominantly represented. These industries were excluded in part as an attempt to keep southern Democrats in the New Deal coalition" (ibid., 135).

In my second book, *Unbank the Fire*, I note that in 1935 most of my father's family were agricultural workers, and most of my mother's family were domestic service workers, so both sides of my family were excluded from the Social Security Act as it was originally written. More than 77 percent of southern African Americans were sharecroppers in 1948, when the sharecropping system ended, so it is safe to say that the vast majority of African Americans were effectively denied social security coverage.

Although a group of African Americans made progress in a number of socioeconomic areas, the base from which they were starting in the 1960s was dismally low. In 1964, only 9.4 percent of blacks held professional or managerial positions, compared with 14.7 percent of whites. The median family income in the black community was less than half that in the white community. By 1969, 41.2 percent of black children were living in poverty, compared with only 9.9 percent of white children. "Even when we compared blacks and whites with similar educational credentials, African Americans suffered from lower incomes and worked in less prestigious occupations than their white counterparts" (Conley 1999, 9).

Numerous mechanisms have created inequality in wealth accumulation among African Americans. One tenacious mechanism is the practice of charging differential mortgage interest rates to white and black borrowers. Another is the practice known as steering, in which real estate agents avoid disclosure of certain properties on the market to qualified African American home buyers. The practice of redlining, by which banks withhold mortgage funds for neighborhoods considered poor economic risks, makes it next to impossible for many blacks to become home owners. The intergenerational part of the equation is that black parents who were born poor early in the century are less likely to have amassed enough wealth to lend their children the money for a down payment on a home or to cosign a loan for them.

The sociologists Douglas Massey and Nancy Denton, in their book *American Apartheid,* further elucidate the evils implicit in racial segregation in housing:

> Middle-class households—whether they are black, Mexican, Italian, Jewish, or Polish—always try to escape the poor. But only blacks must attempt their escape within a highly segregated, racially segmented housing market. Because of segregation, middle-class blacks are less able to escape than other groups, and as a result are exposed to more poverty. At the same time, because of segregation, no one will move into a poor black neighborhood except other poor blacks. Thus, both middle-class and poor blacks lose compared with the poor and middle-class of other groups: poor blacks live under unrivaled concentrations of poverty and affluent blacks live in neighborhoods that are far less advantageous than those experienced by the middle class of other groups. (1993, 52)

Conley argues that racial segregation and the existence of dual housing markets cannot be explained by class. For most minority groups, segregation declines steadily as socioeconomic status rises. However, segregation between blacks and whites does not vary significantly as the social class status of black families improves. Conley cites a study conducted by the Department of Housing and Urban Development in St. Louis that found that African Americans paid 15 to 25 percent more than whites for similar housing. "Since housing quality was controlled in this study, any difference in price would be a result of race, not class. If this pattern were to hold across the entire country, we should expect a contemporary effect of race on wealth levels, net of parental assets, and other socioeconomic measures" (Yinger et al. 1978).

The Race-Class Debate

Dalton Conley traces the notion of equality that prevails in public discourse — equality of opportunity — to the French Revolution. "Under this concept, equality would be achieved if each individual in a society enjoyed the right to compete in a contest unimpaired by discrimination of any kind" (Conley 1999, 7). Equality of opportunity is the least threatening type of equality to the white majority, who feel that all should have a place at the starting gate. This fits with the gamelike imagery many Americans use to describe the capitalist system.

Conley maintains that equality of opportunity served as the underlying philosophy that drove the triumphs of the civil rights movement of the 1950s and early 1960s, which were capped by the 1964 Civil Rights Act and the Voting Rights Act of 1965. "In theory, after 1965, discrimination in hiring, housing, and other aspects of life was illegal" (ibid., 8). (Discrimination in federally funded housing was not banned until the Civil Rights Act of 1968.)

However, William Julius Wilson (1978) maintains that at this point an overt phase of racial oppression ended in the United States and was replaced by economic subordination. Although the civil rights movement created legal equality of opportunity, and some income gains were achieved, institutionalized racism persisted, and the scars of centuries of overt repression remained. "A second type of equality had yet to be realized: *equality of condition* — more progressive and less ideologically acceptable to the American public than equality of opportunity" (Conley 1999, 8).

Although African Americans have made notable gains since the passage of civil rights legislation, upward mobility for the masses has not been one of them. Perhaps, as Conley contends, the locus of racial inequality lies no longer primarily in the labor market but rather in class and property relations that in turn affect other outcomes. "While young African Americans may have the *opportunity* to obtain the same education, income, and wealth as whites, in actuality, they are on a *slippery slope* (italics added), for the discrimination their parents faced in the housing and credit markets sets the stage for perpetual economic disadvantage" (ibid., 152).

Conley's overall thesis is provocative, but I disagree with the assertion that young African Americans have the opportunity to obtain anything close to the same education as whites, regardless of their educational setting. Certainly, it is true that because of the economic position of their parents, it is more difficult to purchase quality education or purchase homes that will allow them to attend quality public schools.

Jonathan Kozol (1991) has written extensively about the inferior education African American children receive in de facto segregated schools. This book supplements his work by unveiling practices that create differences for African American children in quality of schooling, even when they are being educated in classrooms alongside white children. This state of affairs constitutes the unfinished business of the civil rights movement.

CHAPTER 3

African American Goals and
Closed Doors

*You and this young, so-called lawyer have proven you know what they are,
they're Africans—Congratulations. What you don't know, and as far as
I can tell haven't bothered in the least to discover, is who they are. What
is their story?*

—JOHN QUINCY ADAMS TO THE AFRICAN AMERICAN
ABOLITIONIST THEODORE JOSEPH, PLAYED BY MORGAN FREEMAN, IN
THE FILM *AMISTAD*

The most critical issue facing the African American community and
American society as a whole is improving the futures of African American males. It is amazing to watch the evening news and take note of
programs that promise to take a bite out of crime, such as the gun buy-back
programs, by which corporations give coupons to individuals who turn in
their guns. Insiders know that people do not mind turning in their guns because they have three more at home—or they know that they can get another one in fifteen minutes. Recently, people were offered tuition rebates
to college for turning in guns—with no thought given to whether those individuals can even gain admission to college. These efforts are essentially
photo opportunities for chiefs of police and free advertisement for corporations. Many Americans are genuinely concerned about the problems created by a disadvantaged African American male population, but little
thought is devoted to designing long-term solutions.

At this writing the state of Michigan spends $35,000 a year to incarcerate one African American male. For maximum-security incarceration, the cost to the state is about $65,000 a year, and to the federal government, about $75,000. Compare those costs with the $8,000 it costs to enroll an African American male child in a two-year Head Start program or the $9,000 tuition cost to enroll an African American male at Morehouse College.

Voluminous data have been gathered about the changed lives that have resulted throughout the life span of children after just two years of Head Start. Morehouse College has a Phi Beta Kappa chapter. Ninety-five percent of all Morehouse College graduates go on to earn graduate degrees. Yet, Jonathan Kozol (1991) charges, libraries are being torn down to build prisons.

As I was signing books after an address in New York City, an African American mother told me that her son had recently graduated from Morehouse College. She lamented the fact that she had not been able to find any help in paying her son's education costs—but if he had gotten into trouble and been sent to prison, there would have been no limit to the amount the society was willing to spend to incarcerate him.

In the 1920s and 1930s, no more than 20 percent of the people in prisons were African Americans, including women. Today, 54 percent of the inmates admitted to federal and state prisons are African American, according to the U.S. Department of Justice (cited in Miller 1997). Jerome Miller (1997) has projected that by 2010, a majority of African American men aged eighteen to thirty-nine will be behind bars. Eventually, he predicts, few people will come in daily contact with young adult African American men. Today we find that one in three African American males are either in prison, on probation, or on parole.

Miller notes that federal housing policy for the poor and minorities has become, in effect, prison building (ibid.). In the 1980s and early 1990s the nation tripled the number of prison cells while at the same time reducing housing appropriations for the poor by more than 80 percent. Only one in four eligible poor families can now get government-sponsored housing. As Ellis Cose has pointed out in an article in *Newsweek*, "More black men than ever languish in prisons. Black academic achievement still lags that of whites. And suicides among young black men have risen sharply, reflecting a deep sense of hopelessness" (1999, 31).

Many causes have been identified for this phenomenon. Congressional Representative Carolyn Cheeks Kilpatrick (D-Michigan), who was chairwoman of the corrections subcommittee of the Michigan House Appropriations Committee for ten years, has pointed out that more than 60 percent of the inmates in state prisons are there for drug-related offenses. A *Detroit Free Press* article cites race-based discrepancies in drug sentencing as the reason that a large number of African American men are serving long prison terms (Eversley 1998).

While I was writing this book, the film *Life* was released, starring Eddie Murphy and Martin Lawrence, two African Americans who are among our funniest comedians. The film, a comedy, depicts events in the life sentences served by two African American men who were falsely accused in the 1930s by the white sheriff of a rural Mississippi town of the murder of another African American man, a murder that the sheriff himself had committed. When I read about the movie, I wondered what could be funny about this plot. When I watched the movie, I laughed at the punch lines, but at the same time I wondered why I was laughing at the tragedies and injustices these men had experienced. The screening ended with candid shots of funny things that had happened during the filming, to keep moviegoers laughing as they walked out—a ploy that effectively distracted us from realizing that we were being seduced into laughing about the greatest tragedy of present-day African American life.

The unjust incarceration of African American men is essentially a modern form of slavery. Angela Davis has called attention to the fact that once these men are released as felons, they cannot vote, which significantly reduces the voting population of African Americans (Avery 1998). The fact that these men are incarcerated during their teen and young adult years also reduces their ability to reproduce and reduces the overall population of African Americans. Cose estimates that "70 percent of young black men in Watts—those between the ages of 16 and 25—are on 'some kind of paper,' meaning they're in jail, on parole, or on probation. One million four hundred thousand black men, or 13 percent of the total, are disenfranchised because of felony convictions" (1999, 39).

An attempt was made in 1998 to get the African American community to swallow a situation comedy about slavery (*The Secret Diary of Desmond Pfeiffer*). So much protest was organized that the sponsors withdrew. On the heels of that insult, we were next presented with *Life*, which was marketed as "Eddie Murphy's project." If this is Eddie Murphy's project, I say to him "pull up." This film followed an earlier Murphy project, the television show *The PJ's*, which has been criticized for its depiction of life in the housing projects.

Mary Frances Berry notes that "the 'prison industrial complex' . . . creates jobs for one part of the economy at the expense of freedom and opportunity for another. Communities profit from running prisons. The rural and predominantly white areas in which most prisons are located also increase their share of federal grants and political representation by adding the prisoners to their census figures. Meanwhile, the urban communities these prisoners leave behind lose funds and representation" (1999, 194).

In a 1998 address to the National Urban League, Rev. Jesse Jackson noted that

> despite the unprecedented growth, wealth, and prosperity in America, millions are being left behind. For the poor, the floor has been removed. The shrinking middle class is anxious, facing merger mania, downsizing, outsourcing, and loss of benefits. Millions of people in urban and rural America are treading water, hoping to find land before the storms come.
>
> We must change the course and even the playing field while removing the roof for creative possibilities lest we be haunted by the continuation of first-class jails and second-class schools that impede us from achieving a more perfect union. (Jackson 1998, 48)

At one time most Americans agreed that it was better to pay now for public schools than to pay later for prisons. That is no longer the case, especially since there is no longer a need for black manual laborers. Because African Americans are now viewed as potential competitors to European Americans for the limited employment and educational opportunities, those who are not perceived as "the good blacks" are considered worthy prospects for the penitentiary system. An old adage advises, "Educate the best, shoot the rest." It is critical to stress the connection between inadequately funded public schools and strong support for building more prisons.

A recently released report by the Leadership Conference on Civil Rights (2000), a Washington civil rights coalition, points out that blacks who are convicted of killing whites are sentenced to death twenty-two times more often than blacks convicted of killing other blacks. The findings also make note of the wide disparities in the juvenile justice system. A black youth is six times more likely than a white youth to be locked up, even when charged with similar crimes and when neither has a prior record.

It is important to state here that most black males are not involved in violent crimes. Blacks account for about 45 percent of those arrested for America's violent crimes, but it is not true that most black males are violent.

FBI statistics show that blacks were arrested 245,437 times in 1991 for murder, forcible rape, robbery, and aggravated assault. The country's total population then was just under 249 million, including nearly 31 million blacks and roughly 14 million black males. If we assume that each arrest represents the apprehension of a separate individual, blacks arrested for violent crimes made up less than 1 percent of the black population in 1991—and just under 1.7 percent of the black male population (less, in fact, since the aggregate figure of 245,437 includes crimes committed by females). In other words, less than one-tenth of a percent of the population—not 6 percent—is committing 45 percent of violent crimes. (Cose 1993, 94)

While many experts call for education, training, and employment opportunities in addition to "apple pie, two-parent families, and Sunday School," what is needed is a more precise and insightful analysis of the problem and more understanding of the special needs of African American boys. The boy is father to the man. It is my opinion that we ignore the needs of African American boys in early childhood, the time when the foundation for later achievement is laid. By the time alarming problems arise, in adolescence, prospects are more difficult to reverse.

It is not as though African American boys are doing fine and then suddenly, as adolescents, get into trouble and begin a downhill descent. Ray McDermott (1987) maintains that failure is an achievement that the children and the teachers actively pursue each day in school. Academic failure is not an accident. Academic failure, incarceration, and unemployment are outcomes of public schooling for African American boys. I make this statement without fear of contradiction, because more African American males between the ages of eighteen and twenty-two are in prison today than enrolled in college (U.S. Bureau of Justice Statistics 2000; Schomburg Center 1999, 320). Failure to get and hold a steady job and dependence on public assistance are outcomes of public schooling for too many African American young adults.

I often supervise student teachers as a part of my work as a professor of education. When I enter an elementary school and proceed to the principal's office, a committee usually welcomes me to the school. My welcoming committee is the group of African American boys who have been referred to the principal's office for discipline. If there are no African American boys sitting in the principal's office when I enter a school, I can almost conclude that there are no African American boys in the school. Any teachers and administrators who take inventory will concur that most of their disciplinary referrals are African American males.

Furthermore, in observing preschool classrooms, I have noticed that the African American males receive more disciplinary statements: stop, don't, cease and desist! African American males receive more suspensions and more expulsions. They have the lowest grade point averages and the lowest scores on standardized tests. Twenty-three million Americans are functionally illiterate, and the largest proportion of these are African American males. Conley examines the odds of being expelled or suspended from school: "Simply comparing blacks and whites indicates that African Americans are 61 percent more likely to receive such a penalty. Women are less likely to have been expelled or suspended during their educational careers" (1999, 78).

Robert Staples (1985) reports that one-third of African American males in urban areas are addicted to drugs. African American males have three times the chance of being killed by the time they are twenty-one years old compared with African American females of the same age, and they are most likely to be killed by another African American male.

Unemployment for African American males between the ages of fifteen and thirty-five is 50 percent. That means that African American males are highly unlikely to receive developmental work experience or even to know another African American male who is working who can serve as a role model. One of the macabre jokes in the African American community is that African American males should not have to pay into the Social Security system because they do not live long enough to collect it. There is a high incidence of mortality around the age of fifty-eight. Theoretically, an African American male who lives to be sixty-five will live forever—actuaries cannot even compute a life expectancy for African American males who live that long.

It is my contention that concerted action is needed to break the cycle and improve the fortunes of African American males if upward mobility is going to be achieved in the long term for black children, families, and the African American community at large. This is not going to be achieved by making school a paramilitary camp, dressing the children in uniforms, and pushing incarceration down to lower grade levels. The answer to improving the future for African American children is to *connect them to academic achievement.*

Most African American children, particularly African American males, do not like school. Many drop out intellectually by the time they are in the fifth grade and make it legal at the age of sixteen. People who terminate their academic careers too early, or those who finish with poor records, are not able to obtain employment that is stable enough to support themselves or a family. Children who cannot conceptualize a future for themselves do not have the motivation to defer the gratification found in premature sexual activity or substance abuse.

Although the number of African American adults between the ages of twenty-four and thirty-four who have completed high school is near equal to that of white adults (Conley 1999, 10), the large number of African American students who drop out of inner-city high schools suggests that perhaps many are temporary dropouts who eventually obtain a diploma or GED (Herrnstein and Murray 1994, 151). However, the profile of the temporary dropout created by Richard Herrnstein and Charles Murray causes concern. They suggest that GED students are more like dropouts than high school graduates in the problems they experience in the labor market. "The brighter dropouts may go back to get a GED, but they continue to share in common with the permanent dropouts a lower-class social background that has not inculcated a work ethic that makes for success in the labor force. Thus, GEDs are more like normal graduates in their intelligence but more like other dropouts in their success in the labor force" (ibid.).

I was invited by Barbara Sizemore, dean of the College of Education of DePaul University, to give a lecture at a high school in Chicago. My workshop was conducted in the library, and as I was speaking, I noticed a poster with a huge picture of Earvin "Magic" Johnson admonishing the students to stay in school. Aside from the obvious contradiction that Magic Johnson himself did not stay in school, it was interesting to me that the poster did not say, "Stick with basketball!" Of course, we know that African American boys do not need much encouragement to stick with basketball, because basketball is intrinsically motivating to them. They play basketball because it is culturally salient and rewarding. The mere fact that we must bombard inner-city children with admonitions to stay in school is an acknowledgment that participation in school is not intrinsically motivating to them. Comparable posters are not found in schools of white upper-income children, in part, because the way in which schooling proceeds in those settings is intrinsically motivating. When we change the way schooling is done, when we make it culturally salient for African American children, we will not need sports figures to encourage them to stay in school.

Letting Go of the Mantras

To create a new model of schooling that fits the contemporary African American family, we as educators must let go of mantras we have been taught to receive, memorize, and repeat. These beliefs, treasured by educators, excuse us for the disparity in outcomes for African American children.

The first mantra we have to release is that there is something wrong with the children. When, as a college supervisor, I visit student teachers and engage teachers in dialogue about what I consider to be the low level of instruction that is offered to African American children, I often hear the justification that "a large number of our children receive free or reduced lunch." I am told that "this is the best we can do with the population we serve." I am informed that "most of our children come from single-parent households."

Courses and seminars designed to encourage sympathy and empathy in teachers have done nothing more than cause them to have low expectations for African American and lower-income children. Although I separate these two populations, teachers have a tendency to lump them together. I am reminded of a story I was told by a friend, who is a physician. Her son, who attends an integrated school in a wealthy Detroit suburb, once said in class that his mother is a doctor. The teacher looked at him and said, "No she's not!" The anguished child came home and said to his mother, "Mom, aren't you a doctor? My teacher said that you are not!" This form of racial profiling is not uncommon.

For four years I was involved in a research project in an entirely African American public school in Claiborne County, Mississippi, consulting with school officials on ways to improve the educational outcomes of its children. Claiborne County has the lowest per capita income of any county in the United States and the highest rate of birth to unwed teenage mothers. (Washington, D.C., has a conception rate that is equally high, but in Mississippi there are fewer abortions and therefore a higher number of live births.) The African American community is characterized by a large number of unemployed, poorly educated single women with large numbers of children. The men are invisible. The only evidence of the presence of men in the community is the fact that the women continue to get pregnant.

Gathering data for the study, I visited the residences of the poor families in the community. I found it hard to believe that there are people living like that in America. The housing was more like that I have seen in developing countries in Africa and the Caribbean. The people were living in shanties, shacks, and trailers.

The Twenty-First Century Education Project was funded by the white city fathers (representatives from the major corporation and bank in the community). In the days of the plantation and sharecropping systems, the southern white community benefited from high birth rates among blacks— as high as nineteen children in a single family—because the children could pick cotton. Now that cotton is picked by machines rather than manually, what was once a benefit to the capitalists has become a liability, because many single women with large numbers of children receive food stamps and welfare benefits. Members of the white power structure now understand that it is more profitable to nurture an African American middle-income group to whom they can sell goods and services than to maintain a large underclass on public assistance. They now see the value—and profit—in improving the educational outcomes for the black children in the community.

It is also important to note that when the public schools were legally desegregated in the 1970s, every white child was withdrawn from the public school system and enrolled in the private "Christian academy." The practice was legal, of course, because African American children who were able to pay the tuition could also enroll in that private school. Additionally, city taxes to support the public schools have been eliminated—probably so that white families can divert that income to pay private school tuition. Money from the nuclear power plant located in the community, by way of contributions to the county's general operating fund, is used to finance the public schools attended by African American children. Therefore, "the deal," so to speak, for the African American population is that they do not have to pay school or city taxes.

As a part of my work, I wanted to develop a profile of the children in the community who entered the public school system. Toward this end, I tested each child enrolled in Head Start, using the McCarthy Scales of Children's Abilities (McCarthy 1972), which provides a measure of children's overall cognitive skills. The children in Claiborne County's two Head Start programs scored at or significantly above the national average on all scales except the memory scale, on which they scored significantly below the national norm. (See chapter 5 for greater detail about the test and scores.)

Interestingly, even though this is a disadvantaged population, the children who were three years old, just entering Head Start, scored better than the five-year-olds who had participated in Head Start for two years—indicating that there is nothing wrong with the abilities of the children coming into Head Start. The same pattern holds for the achievement data at the elementary school level. In reading, particularly, the children fall below grade level at fifth grade, and from seventh to tenth grade they are performing two grades below grade level. It seems as though the longer the children stay in school, the more their performance deteriorates. These data support the assertion that African American children do not enter school disadvantaged, they leave school disadvantaged. There is nothing wrong with the children, but there is clearly something wrong with what happens to them in school.

The second mantra we have to release is that there is something wrong with the parents. My brother, Phale D. Hale Jr., has pointed out that, whereas white teachers need to deal with issues of racism in working with African American children, African American teachers need to deal with issues of classism. Classism is displayed in a variety of comments: "I expose my children to enrichment activities and 'they' do not." "They do not come to parent meetings, sign their children's progress reports, or come to parent conferences." "They do not provide school supplies for their children or check their children's homework."

Let me state at the outset that I am not disputing charges by educators that lower-income parents often do not attend parent meetings or parent conferences or sign pupil report cards. These comments are made to point out that if our efforts as educators hinge totally on the social and cultural level of the parents, then we will continue to receive the same outcomes. The children who enter school on public assistance will leave school and move onto public assistance. The children who enter school with parents who are incarcerated will leave school and move into the criminal justice system. The objective of upward mobility will be lost.

Passing the Buck

If we are going to change the outcomes for the masses of African American children, we will have to let go of these treasured mantras and focus upon what we can do to intervene in the lives of children rather than engaging in an orgy of blaming the parents for the educational shortcomings of their children.

The basic unit of the family is the interaction between the parent and the child. Educators do not have the power and resources to change the functioning of the family unit (although politicians can provide the resources to effect that change). However, we do have the power to have an impact on the functioning of the school, the basic unit of which is the interaction between the teacher and the child. Instead of passing the buck back to the family, educators need to focus on what we can do to improve our efforts between 8:15 and 3:15 Monday through Friday.

The Principal as Instructional Leader

There has been a great deal of finger-pointing between colleges of education and public school districts. Politicians, newspaper columnists, and educators assert that teacher training institutions are remiss in providing skills to teachers, and new waves of accreditation regulations spring forth on a regular basis. National tests for teachers are advocated.

It is my contention that existing programs in colleges of education give students the background they need to be good teachers. However, school principals need to meet teachers at the front door of the school daily and give them the support they need to produce those outcomes for children. I am not speaking of only first-year teachers, because mentoring programs are already in existence to give support to new teachers. I am talking about creating a culture within the school wherein every teacher is supervised and supported in delivering instruction in such a way that no child is left behind.

I am not talking about principals' just spending more time in the classrooms. I am not talking about identifying the poor teachers. I am not talking about having teachers submit lesson plans on which they indicate the pencil-and-paper tasks children will be assigned. I am talking about principals' providing *leadership*, not just supervision. Providing leadership means coordinating the collaborative efforts of teachers. The most useful device we have for creating collaborative, multidisciplinary teaching is the thematic unit. By opening the classroom doors and having teachers develop units together, the principal can stimulate artistic teaching. For example, the whole school can participate in a unit on the ocean. They can study marine plant and animal life and the art, music, and literature of the ocean. There will be field trips, guest speakers, films, and projects.

When the principal initiates cooperative curriculum planning, teachers will be stimulated by one another's ideas. The parents will be invited to make enrichment contributions. Performances will be planned. Exhibits and open houses will showcase the projects and accomplishments of the children. Every teacher in the school will be swept up into making hands-on learning active and engaging.

Textbooks will no longer be used as the primary tool. Textbooks will become resources for projects and reports. Reading the chapter and answering the questions at its end will become passé. When a unit is planned on Native Americans, the children will build a teepee in one classroom, learning geometric principles as indigenous peoples have, from the bottom up. They will cook Native American food in another, learning arithmetic through measurement and the basic principles of chemistry through observation. They will study Native American dances, religious expressions and beliefs, art, clothing styles, burial practices, politics, family forms, literature, and agriculture throughout the school. The practical applications of mathematics in making clothes and engaging in agriculture will be highlighted.

Once the focus has shifted to teaching the curriculum in an engaging, exciting manner, teaching to the test will no longer be necessary. The principal's leadership will make the difference between whether the children are delighted by the curriculum or drilled on the test.

CHAPTER 4

Down the Up Escalator

The eyes of the owner fatten the horse.
— SPANISH PROVERB

After years of serving professionally as a consultant to families and school districts studying the reasons for the academic achievement gap affecting African American children, I enrolled my son in a private school for gifted children. In this chapter I share some of my personal experiences as his parent. These episodes document the terrain of quicksand and landmines African American males must negotiate to find success in school. If my son, an African American male in an exclusive school, receives racialized treatment, how much worse is it for a boy in the inner city with no advocate to keep him from falling through the cracks?

In a personal conversation on the plight of black children, V. P. Franklin suggested to me that "if Michael Jordan's son walks into a grocery store in a poor section of the inner city, the clerk is going to follow him around and think he is stealing something. If Michael Jordan's son walks into a grocery store in an affluent suburb, the clerk is going to follow him around the store and think he is stealing something! Regardless of the setting, his treatment is racialized." Ellis Cose has stated that "the racial gap . . . can only be closed by recognizing it and by recognizing why it exists. That will not come to pass as long as we insist on dividing people into different camps and then swearing that differences don't count or that repeated blows to the soul shouldn't be taken seriously. For the truth is that the often hurtful and seemingly trivial encounters of daily existence are in the end what most of life is" (1999, 191–92).

The African American community has been frustrated in seeking quality education for our children in America. The schools give the skills and credentials necessary for success in this society. The labor market responds to the schools in providing employment. Employment is the key to income, housing, wealth, and political power. By confining African Americans to inferior schools, and thus inferior skills and credentials, white America maintains the oppression of African Americans, while the myth of freedom and opportunity for all enables them to blame us, the victims, for our status.

Cinque (the *Amistad* freedom fighter) knew what he was fighting against because he could see his chains. Thurgood Marshall knew what he was fighting against because he could see the one-room schoolhouses and the out-of-date books. Rev. Martin Luther King Jr. knew what he was fighting against because he could see the fire hoses and police dogs commandeered by police chief Bull Conner in Birmingham. Our struggle is different today because of the degree of sophistication with which discrimination is packaged. It is rationalized and justified in the Darwinian capitalistic ethos of "survival of the fittest" and in the Protestant ethic.

We thought freedom from segregated education was imminent after the *Brown v. Board of Education* decision in 1954. In 1971, we thought freedom from unequal education was imminent when the Supreme Court upheld the use of busing to overcome the effects of segregation in public schools (*North Carolina State Board of Education v. Swann* and *Swann v. Mecklenburg Board of Education*). Certainly we believed that a child who was certified as gifted at an early age, who never missed a day of school, whose parent or parents paid full tuition and took responsibility for his transportation to and from school, and whose classroom was led by two full-time teachers—certified professionals with master's degrees—for every eighteen children—surely, we thought, this child would receive a quality education.

The main building on the campus of this school is named for Rev. Martin Luther King Jr., and the whole community celebrates his birthday each year with a candlelight vigil. But when I spoke with my son's teacher and the director of the school about applying the principles King espoused in helping African American boys succeed in this school, the teacher admitted that the African American boys do not do very well there.

I am sharing these episodes in the spirit of Jean Piaget. He probably never would have received funding for his exploratory research on children's thinking if he had written a proposal for funding. I know, because I have had that same difficulty. However, like Piaget, I have had an opportunity to draw meaning from my own difficulties in negotiating the school for my son. Piaget had his own children, and I have my child. I have been able to experience firsthand what many parents have complained about to me.

I am not sharing these episodes to indict the school. At this writing, my son is enrolled at the school for his ninth year. I might add that his past three years—his fourth, fifth, and sixth grades—have been the best years we have had. He has blossomed and has met all my expectations for him at this level. However, he would not be experiencing this success if I had not fought hard to counteract what would have been a poor foundation in the primary grades.

I have no axe to grind. I have often been asked why I did not withdraw him and change schools. My response is that when other parents have called me in distress about similar problems with their children's schooling, they reported having changed schools three or four times but still having failed to find the perfect place. I do not believe a perfect place is out there. I feel that parents should select a school whose philosophy they embrace and then work out the problems. I stayed at this school because I was able to work with the teachers and the director to sort through and resolve the problems.

However, I am sharing these episodes here to highlight the degree of skill and insight I had to bring as a parent to advocating for my child. Most of the debate about poor achievement outcomes for African American males centers upon single-parent households. I believe that we should bring to the table a discussion of the extent to which some teachers do not meet parents halfway and of the specialized skills required of me to counteract what I call "educational psychobabble."

This is a good place to explain the epigraph for this chapter: "The eyes of the owner fatten the horse." As a mother, I have been appalled by the extent to which members of the helping professions have functioned in an adversarial or competitive mode with me in raising my child, when we should really have been functioning in a partnership. I have been made keenly aware that I am the "owner" of my child, and that he will develop and flourish (become fattened) only if I take responsibility for his development (by keeping my eyes on him); it is us against the world. This is not the way it should be. This is not the way it was when I was growing up. We, as members of the helping professions, need to create the Beloved Community in which children are helped and supported, not attacked and tracked.

This chapter is written as a red alert. I have spoken with numerous African American women at book signings and lectures who have lamented allowing school districts to retain their sons in first or second grades. They have made comments such as, "We lost Willie in the first grade!" These experiences are rarely written about.

I am also mindful that white parents face challenges in negotiating the schools. However, black parents must endure the additional burden of racialized treatment. Furthermore, 85 percent of African American mothers of school-aged children are single. Thus, the black mother is apt to have less time to intervene for her child than a white mother, who is more likely to enjoy the security of a household supported by a white male. White mothers of children in integrated schools are also more likely to have entrée to the cultural networks of the school that enable them to bond with school personnel who provide insider information that is crucial to achieving success for their children.

Throughout the experiences of parenting my son through early childhood, I have been mindful of the ethnographic work of Ray McDermott (1987), who describes the effects of classroom politics on children's self-esteem and on their educational outcomes. Much of my earlier scholarship was an analysis of the literature on the early-childhood education of African American children. As I sat in parent conferences or engaged in telephone conversations about my son's behavior, I was amazed to hear my son's teachers repeating what I had written about.

My son, Keith, is now in the seventh grade. He is working at grade level academically. The scores on his Iowa Test of Basic Skills place him one to three years above grade level. He is taking eighth grade mathematics—a year above grade level. His behavior and citizenship skills are excellent. I still embrace the concept of the school and its philosophy. However, I am alarmed by the large gap between what I was told when I enrolled him and the reality that unfolded as he moved through each stage and we dealt with individual teachers.

On the pages that follow, I am going to share with you some important episodes that highlight the need for teachers to be more adept at applying principles of child development, more insightful in solving behavioral problems, and more sensitive to the nuances of cultural differences in classroom settings. As I stated earlier, extraordinary skills were called for on my part as a parent. I once commented to a teacher that I did not feel that I was a part of a "partnership." I did not feel that they were helping me with my son. I felt that they were flailing about and complaining and throwing his problems back on me. I told his teacher that I had to figure out what was going on with him—and them—and get him on the right path, because, unlike them, I had no one to give him back to.

As I have mentioned, the teacher-student ratio at my son's school is one-to-nine—not the one to thirty-four found in many overcrowded urban public schools. In addition, in language arts and math classes, two teachers work with groups of nine pupils. The other nine children in the class are rotated through enrichment classes and free-choice selections. At three years old, the children begin to choose enrichment classes. By the time they turn seven (usually, in the second grade), these classes of forty-five minutes each day are expanded to ten-week courses that encompass literature, art, music, computers, science, and physical education—including African textiles, Shakespeare, African literature, Holocaust literature, golf, keyboarding, anatomy, physics, chemistry, simple machines, and hip-hop dancing.

The children take French from the age of five through the twelfth grade. Through the French exchange program, sixth-grade children host a French child and travel to France as guests in that child's home. In the seventh grade, some of the children begin Spanish and continue both languages through the twelfth grade.

The concept of the school, in my opinion, cannot be beat. That is why the reality I encountered was so distressing.

Episode One: Tracking

During Keith's first year in Stage II (kindergarten) the focus was on his behavior. I had purposely enrolled him in the school for Stage I (the preschool program) the year before kindergarten because I did not want teachers and administrators to be able to say that he was starting off behind the other children. I took him through all of the IQ screenings and tests from age three to five so they could not tell me he was unqualified for the gifted program. The psychologist who evaluated him told me that his IQ was 131 (cutoff for "giftedness" is generally 125).

At the end of the prekindergarten year, when Keith was four years old, his teachers suggested that I seek counseling for him because of some minor misbehavior. From my consultations with school districts and African American parents I was familiar with the complaint that African American boys were rambunctious and aggressive. I began to get the same complaints about my son.

He was placed in Peggy and Mariah's room because it was felt that they could provide the structure he needed to get his behavior in line. One of my frustrations was that I did not have an opportunity to observe at home the things they were talking about. Many children today are being raised as "only children," and their parents have little opportunity to teach social skills and the give-and-take of friendship, as my parents did when I was raised in a family with four children.

By the second semester of the year (February) I began to get a barrage of notes and telephone calls complaining about Keith's behavior. These complaints rose to a fever pitch when he began to have conflict with Mary, a white female in the class, and he hit her. Unable to understand what was happening in the classroom, I tried to access my mental health insurance benefits and persuade a counseling social worker to observe the class and give an opinion. That effort was my introduction to managed psychological services in a health maintenance organization (HMO), and I discovered that they are no more effective than managed health services in an HMO. A plan may offer twenty mental health sessions a year, but in order to get them a member must be homicidal, suicidal, or a convicted member of the militia! Keith's teachers offered no meaningful analysis and no meaningful solutions—just notes and phone calls of complaint. I was ever mindful that my son and I were not a part of "the club" at this school, and I never knew at what point we would be asked to leave. In desperation, I visited his classroom myself and spent two days observing him, his classmates, and his teachers. I include here the actual memorandum I wrote his teachers. When I wrote it, I kept in mind Ray McDermott's (1987) framework for evaluating the politics of the classroom.

Memorandum
To: Peggy and Mariah
From: Janice Hale
Re: Ecological factors (grouping) that may be affecting Keith's behavior
Date: March 2, 1994

I thought that I would commit some of my thoughts to paper after spending a delightful day observing your classroom yesterday. You are both wonderful teachers and kind, sensitive persons. I also am impressed with the children in my son's class. They are delightful. I love the school and what you are doing for children.

There were two purposes for my observation. You had mentioned that Keith and Mary are again having conflicts, and the French teacher, Marcia, had called and expressed concern about Keith's behavior in her class. In the past, I have gotten reports about his misbehavior in his enrichment classes.

As I observed the class, I was impressed with the instruction and the interactions between the teachers and the children and between the children and their peers. I would love to watch you teach all day every day!

The only aspect of the class ecology that I feel is significant to Keith's difficulties is the grouping of the children for their academic work. The more I reflect on what I saw, the more importance I feel it has in understanding Keith's behavior.

His group, the Starlites, has eight children. There are five girls (one of whom is an African American female) and three boys (the only African American is Keith, my son). The other group, the Colorful Rainbows, has ten children. There are six white males and four white females.

I was first struck by how out of place Keith appears to be in his group. There is a female overtone that stands out by virtue of the gender imbalance. Also, Mitchell seems to fit in because he exudes less machismo than Keith. Drew appears to be the only one in the group that Keith can "bounce off of." However, upon closer examination and discussion with you, I understand that he and Drew have personality conflicts. Keith and Mary seem to have personality conflicts, as well. The other girls, Margaret, Donna, and the tall girl, are very frilly, with a "Barbie doll" persona. [During this observation, I did not consider Mitchell to be a person who seemed to fit with Keith because he was slight of build, blue eyed, and blond. However, I have

to admit that he and Keith became best friends in this grouping and remained best friends for several years.]

Consequently, Keith spends the most important part of his day in a group
with two children he has personality conflicts with. I am sure that this is a
source of anxiety he cannot verbalize. Second, when he encounters his enrichment teachers with the children in that group, they probably perceive
that he is not synchronized with that group. There is a female overtone, and
Keith stands out as not fitting into that group. He is male, tall, dark skinned,
and idiosyncratic.

On the other hand, in the Colorful Rainbows (most of whom are in their
second year—first-graders), there is a corpus of boys who look more culturally compatible with Keith. When an enrichment teacher encounters that
group, she is going to get geared up differently, because "here come the
boys." She is going to tolerate more male behavior. If Keith were in a group
like that, he would fit in to a greater extent.

Being assigned to the Starlites group, I believe, has other effects on
Keith's social comfort in the classroom. The boys that he is most attracted
to socially are in the other group. They have an opportunity to bond with
one another, which can carry over into their playground play and other encounters when they are not grouped. He, then, has to break into that group
and find a place for himself socially. He has not bonded with the children
in the Starlites, and his bonding with the boys he could bond with is inter-
rupted by being assigned out of the group where the majority of the boys are.

I asked him how he likes his group, the Starlites. He said that he wants
to be in the Colorful Rainbows—they have more people. He said that you
moved Ken out of his group to the Colorful Rainbows. He also reported that
Bonnie cried when she was told that Ken was moving.

This led me to reflect upon another deeper issue that stems from the
school's practice of ability grouping. I am not passionately opposed to ability
grouping per se when all other things are equal. It can serve as an instructional convenience and result in better time management, which benefits
all of the children. However, the way in which it is practiced here seems to
be to promote the white males into the higher ability group slowly but
surely. Six out of eight white males are in the higher ability group. Left in
the lower ability group are the two African American children (one male
and one female) and the majority of the girls in the class.

It seems to me that we are trying to construct a classroom ecology wherein all of the children can proceed at their own pace while the self-esteem and social and emotional health of all of the children are protected. One of the attractive features of the philosophy of this school is that each classroom contains two age groups and that the instruction is highly individualized so that the children can proceed at their own pace. The instruction I observed is individualized, so I do not see a need for grouping around ability level only, to the exclusion of social and emotional considerations.

In other words, if the children were reading out of basal readers and everyone had to be on the same page, ability grouping might be key to getting the class work done. However, with whole-language instruction, in which children are writing in journals and teachers have a ratio of one-to-four or one-to-five for language arts and mathematics, I do not see where grouping around ability is that essential, especially if it affects the self-esteem of half of the class.

When we spoke briefly after school and I commented that it seemed that the white males are being promoted into the higher group, you replied that several of them are phenomenally skilled. I commented that they always are! They have the best skills; get the best grades; score the best on standardized tests; get the best jobs; make the most money and rule the world! The issue for me is how a classroom environment can be crafted in such a way that all the children can achieve their potential, even those who are not "phenomenally skilled"!

This designation as "phenomenally skilled" must be based upon their performance in the subjects you teach—language arts and mathematics. Surely you do not mean to suggest that Keith cannot do physical education with these boys (he is the tallest child in the class) or art or music! My suspicion is that you, as the homeroom teachers, are grouping them together on language arts and mathematics as an instructional convenience to you. However, in education we give lip service to the notion that we should consider the "whole child." Considering the whole child means addressing the social and affective needs of each child as well as seeing the classroom as a community in which attention is given to meeting everyone's needs.

The head of the school mentioned at the community meeting that you (the faculty and staff) are always seeking to determine whether you "practice what you preach." I admire that introspection, and that is the spirit in which I am making these comments.

My suggestion is that the groups need to be reconstituted. They should be balanced so that every child has someone in that group that he or she can feel comfortable with. In my opinion, Keith does not have a comfort zone with the people in his group. The black male child is most at risk for feeling uncomfortable in the classroom. Long term, you might rethink the practice of spreading the black males out over all of the classrooms instead of placing them together. It is interesting to me that when I pick Keith up from his after-school program, he is generally sitting on a sofa with Anthony and Gary, the other black boys. [I later recanted that suggestion when my son was placed in a classroom with three other black boys: the teacher suffered burnout and retired at the end of that year. I do not feel that that teacher was prepared to deal constructively with the behavior patterns of black boys. I later suggested that one black boy be placed in each classroom. The boys could still have contact on the playground, in the cafeteria, and in elective classes. This practice significantly reduced the number of notes and telephone calls about discipline that we mothers had to endure.]

However, in the short term, I feel that the groups should be balanced with males and females and that personality should be considered. Specifically, I feel that you should at least separate Keith and Mary. I also would consider separating Keith and Drew. Keith should have an opportunity to bond with the boys his size and with those with whom he feels compatible.

Last year, when he was four years old, Keith and Dimetri were best friends. In January, Dimetri was moved out of the Stage I classroom to Stage II. Keith's behavior went downhill after that, and I was asked to take him to counseling at the end of that semester. I am not suggesting that there was a cause and effect relationship there, because I have looked at a number of factors. However, I do not know in hindsight what effect that had on him and who else there was for him in that classroom.

In sum, it may appear to you and some parents to be laudable on the surface to push children ahead on the basis of their ability. But consideration should also be given to the effect of policies on everyone in the classroom. You often speak of the classroom as a "community." So, it seems that everyone in the community is affected when the constitution of the class is changed.

Again, the appeal, theoretically, of a school for gifted children is that most parents do not want their children skipped ahead so that their social and emotional needs suffer. Parents want a classroom wherein the children can be educated with their age-mates — their social and emotional peers, while there is flexibility and individualization in meeting their intellectual needs.

This practice of moving children out of the classroom, moving children out of the group, and clustering the white males together does not seem to be compatible with the philosophy that was presented to me. Furthermore, with all of the screening and testing that was required for children to enter this school and with the fact that the children stay with one teacher for two years, you should know enough about the children to make reasonable placements without all of this shuffling of children to new classrooms and groups.

In terms of the personality conflicts, I also have raised the question of whether the children who are moving into the higher ability group have the "mainstream" personalities. Children who have "mainstream" personalities bond more easily with the teachers, and it is easier for teachers to recognize and extend their intellectual abilities. Children who are more idiosyncratic would then tend to cluster in the lower ability group and clash with one another. Changing the criteria for grouping (introducing cultural, social, and behavioral factors) would give those children with idiosyncratic personalities more opportunity to interact with those with mainstream personalities and create more emotional balance throughout the classroom.

I have committed this to writing so that we can discuss these ideas. I am coming back on Thursday, March 3, to observe Keith in the afternoon. May I have an appointment with you and Mariah when school has ended at 3:30 to discuss this together?

Again, thank you for bringing your concerns about Keith's behavior to my attention and joining me in a partnership to get him started on the road to a successful life.

Despite the balanced tone I tried to adopt in approaching Keith's teachers, I was very upset about what I saw in that classroom. When I shared the memo with my mother, she said, "It is my duty as your mother to tell you that it was a brilliant memo, but do not harbor hope that those people are going to let you change that school." To my surprise, they did. Not only did they meet with me several times, they changed the way the groups were constituted, as I had suggested, and reviewed the changes with me.

They thanked me for putting my comments in writing, which gave them an opportunity to review my memo for two weeks, discuss it, and retain a record of my opinion. Peggy commented that often when a parent is talking, she is thinking of what she is going to say next and does not fully grasp the point the parent is trying to make. She also noted that when she has a parent-teacher conference at the end of a busy day, she sometimes later forgets what was said. My memorandum preserved the information and gave them a chance to consider it intact.

Peggy also said that it was helpful to get feedback on her grouping from the outside. She stated that as the teacher she gets "caught in the picture frame," doing things as she has always done them and missing the stimulus from the outside to do something different.

The groups were reconstituted, and Keith was separated from Mary and Drew, the children he was having friction with, and placed with Jim, one of the boys in the other group whom he liked.

Mariah had commented to me that even though Keith, Mary, and Drew had friction, they always played together. I observed that Mary sat next to Keith in every room in which they were together, including the after-school program. I went so far as to ask Keith whether she sat next to him or whether he sat next to her. He reported that she sat next to him.

I pointed out to the teachers the power of their grouping assignments. Even though they had conflict, Mary and Drew still gravitated to Keith because they knew one another best and were designated by the teachers as being in the same group. When they changed the grouping, Keith found more comfort in the classroom, and the behavior problems stopped. No more critical notes, no more complaining phone calls.

I was alarmed that I, as the parent, had to lead the way to solving this problem. His teachers were accommodating and made the changes I suggested, but my suggestions did not seem to be in line with their usual way of solving classroom problems. When Peggy commented, "You are so thoughtful about him!" I looked at her in disbelief: "I am all he has!" I replied. Given my profession, I was keenly aware of the consequences of daily misunderstandings, conflicts, misdiagnoses, and prescriptions that do not add up to successful interactions in school for any child but particularly for an African American male child.

This episode has implications for teacher training. The concept of multicultural education is often limited to exotic foods and costumes. The need, revealed here, is for teachers to be sensitized to what McDermott calls the "politics of everyday life" (1987, 179). They need training in identifying the social context for misbehavior.

Episode Two: Whole-Language Reading Instruction

When I visited Stage II classrooms (kindergarten and first grade) as a prospective parent, it was explained to me that the children in this school were reading at the sixth-grade level. Everything that was needed to teach reading was available, my guide explained—literature, basal readers, journals—and the reading program was individualized to meet the needs of the children. This gave me a great deal of confidence because I felt that learning to read was my son's most important challenge at this stage.

I had no complaints with instruction until October of first grade, when I went to the parent conference. Keith's teachers showed me pictures of him on the monkey bars on the playground and complimented him on his physical prowess. At the end of the oohs and aahs, I asked when they were going to teach Keith to *read*.

My son's teachers said that they had been going over the sounds of the alphabet for the past year but that he did not yet seem ready to put the sounds together. Astonished, I reviewed with them all that I had been told about the language arts program: the two-to-nine teacher-student ratio, the journals, basal readers, and literature, the focus on the individual child.

I also noted that my siblings and I, while attending the de facto segregated schools of Columbus, Ohio, had all learned to read in the first grade. Each of us had graduated from college, and my mother had not had to teach us how to read.

"Why," I asked, "is my child not learning to read when so much progress has been made beyond the basal readers that served my generation so well?" I reminded them of the grand-theft tuition I was paying; that my son had been certified and qualified as gifted and had not missed one day in school since the age of four. How is it, I asked, that they cannot teach him to read?

I went home in a daze. I talked to my sister, who has a master's degree but is not an educator. She said, "Oh, Janice, everyone is getting Hooked on Phonics!" She told me about her foster son, who has cerebral palsy. Earlier in the school year, she said, his teacher had already signed the paper assigning him to the slow track, an educational purgatory from which he would never escape. My sister had ordered Hooked on Phonics and worked with him and his twin brother, who is normal but had not yet learned to read, either. When they were both reading, thanks to my sister's efforts, their teachers exclaimed that it was a "miracle." She felt that the teachers had not wanted to put the time and effort into teaching them.

Buoyed (or crushed) by her analysis, I added the cost of the Hooked on Phonics materials to the tuition I was already paying and began to work with my son for fifteen minutes a day. I found that the teachers had been correct—he did not know the sounds of the letters of the alphabet; but he learned them in two weeks of my working with him. Once he knew the sounds for *a* and *t,* it was relatively simple for him to put them together to form the word *at.* He then could add a *c* onto that and read *cat.* Within six weeks, he was able to read simple words.

When I returned to meet with his teachers, they, too, called his progress a miracle. This incident was the beginning of my distrust of the school and its teachers. I began polling the other parents of children in this classroom and discovered that the only children in this first-grade class who could read were the ones who had been taught at home by their parents.

I requested a meeting with the director of the school and my son's teachers so that we could discuss this issue in some depth. To the dismay of the director, my son's teacher stated that it would not bother her if my son did not read until he was ten years old. I told her that I did not know about white parents, but black parents don't play that!

I talked with them about the self-esteem issues that could ensue for a nonreading child whose classmates were able to read. I explained to them that my child did not have to be the smartest child in the class, but he certainly was smart enough to do the work that the other children were doing. I was not going to stand by and let him fall through the cracks. I told them that I did not teach him how to read before he entered first grade because I expected that they would do so. Furthermore, I am not a reading specialist, and I thought they were.

Before purchasing the Hooked on Phonics materials, I had spoken with a whole-language specialist at a local university. I did not fully understand the concept of whole language and wanted her to recommend one of her students who could tutor my son. Our conversation was a real eye-opener for me. Drawing diagrams on the chalkboard, she explained that phonics is included in the mix in whole-language instruction, not taught as a separate subject. She also said that whether a child responded to whole-language instruction is also determined by the degree of literacy in the home—the implication being that perhaps the degree of literacy in our home was suspect. The specialist became agitated and angry when I explained that whole language, or what they were calling whole language, was not working for my child.

When I spoke with an African American woman who taught phonics in the same department, she pointed out that the phonics people and the whole-language people do not talk to each other because the issue is so emotional. She also informed me that many African American parents had withdrawn their children from my son's school because the children were not reading by the third grade. One of her friends who had withdrawn her nonreading son from that school had placed him in a public school with a good phonics program, and he had begun reading immediately. Unfortunately, he had languished as a nonreader until the fourth grade.

As I continued to talk with people, I began to see that reading problems were not limited to my son, his teachers, and his school. It was shaping up to be a conflict between these two camps of reading instruction.

I related this story later in a lecture I gave in Teaneck, New Jersey. The reading specialist for the local school district, a white woman, approached me after the lecture. She said that she wished she could take me to a meeting she was having the next day. She concurred wholeheartedly that something was wrong in the mix in the new whole-language movement. In her experience it was affecting African American boys in the first grade. She found that they were not being given a good background in phonics. They were being lost in the literature-based curriculum, which did not contain vocabulary words to study and a controlled vocabulary lesson. The boys were upset, as were their parents, and their self-esteem was being damaged. When the children were referred to her, in the second grade, for reading remediation, she simply gave them a good dose of phonics instruction and was able to move them on to the third grade as on-grade-level readers. The question she raised was why the first-grade teachers had not given them some phonics instruction in the first place.

As I pursued this subject further in discussions with practicing teachers, one gave me the article, "The Hole in Whole Language" (Vail 1989). The article basically affirms everything that whole-language advocates argue but with the caveat that in first grade children need to be given clear phonics instruction so that they can learn the structure of the language. As my sister put it, "Whole language is fine, but someone has got to teach you how to *read!*" I asked that my son's teachers use controlled-vocabulary basal readers with him during the remaining months of the school year to create the "hook" he needed to begin reading.

My son's teachers all seemed to enjoy teaching the children who already knew how to read. The much-touted ability of five- and six-year-old children to read at the sixth-grade level occurred not because of the superior instruction offered at the school but, apparently, from the efforts of the parents. Thus, the benefit of attending this school emanated not from the superior educational experiences offered but rather from the children with whom students had the privilege of being educated. However, a parent who thinks that the instruction is the attraction might easily be fooled when any failures are deflected away from the teaching staff and projected onto the children.

My son's third-grade teacher later told me that the second- and third-grade teachers were complaining that the first-grade teachers were sending them a pack of nonreading children. She commented that one-third of the children in her classroom could not read (because of my aggressiveness, my son was not one of them). She also mentioned that the director of admissions had met with the teachers to explore ways to rectify the problem; the admissions officers had been working hard to recruit new students, but the reading problem was causing parents to withdraw their children.

The other interesting thing about the reading issue is that the outcome was determined by which teacher a child got. I talked to African American parents who did not know what in the world I was talking about. Their children happened to have been assigned to teachers who used basal readers and systematically taught their students to read. My son happened to get a teacher who believed that someone else should teach him to read.

None of this information, of course, is explained in the parent handbook or is covered at the parent meetings—it is not available formally. Parents must find their way through a maze as they try to build relationships with the teachers and the school.

Episode Three: Ritalin

My son's school experience in the second grade was a living nightmare. Stage III (second and third grades) represented a big leap in independence for the children at this school. The children became adept at maintaining individual schedules and walking all over the campus, as if they were college students. The experiences demanded by the parents and planned by the school were about a year ahead of what public school children are expected to master.

That fact is not bad in itself if teachers plan instruction so that the children can meet those goals. However, the teachers at my son's school did not patiently help individual children master those behaviors one step at a time. They seemed to be impatient and critical of my son's maturity.

Attending parent-teacher conferences felt like going to war. I took Advil on the way to the school and Tylenol on the way home. Although each conference was scheduled to last thirty minutes, the teachers usually had three hours' worth of issues to discuss. Never was I warned of the issues at hand. I always felt sucker-punched by their approach: they would rattle off a dozen different issues, all of which sounded serious, but would leave no time to address any of them. The teachers never had any suggestions for solving the problems they presented. They never placed any of the issues in the context of his age or the time of year, nor did they suggest that any other child might be facing the same challenge.

They looked at me as if my son and I were rocking their world; I found myself wondering if they were guessing how high they would have to increase the tuition before we could no longer afford it. When I remarked to his second-grade teacher how little we were getting for the amount of tuition I was paying, she replied, "I would be very happy to help you out! I would be very happy to help you find another school where you can realize a better return on the dollar amount you are paying!"

One of the issues she raised was that my son took too long to walk from a class in one building to his homeroom. "How long does he have?" I asked her. "He does not have a watch. If it takes him too long to walk with Anthony [another black boy], why don't you have him walk with a child who arrives within the desired time frame?" The assistant teacher had mercy on me and commented that, as this was the beginning of the year, a number of the other children were facing similar challenges in adjusting to the routine.

The teachers gave the children personal inventories before the parent-teacher conference. I began to hate the inventories because of the way Keith's teacher used them. The children were asked to assess their own abilities, interests, and attitudes on a scale of one to five. Most of my son's responses were threes. The teacher would flash the inventory before me so fast that I could barely read it. She would then hold it in her hands and point to the threes as evidence of each disorder she had diagnosed.

In one conference I had a serious discussion with his lead teacher and assistant teacher about my son's learning style in mathematics. His teacher complained that whenever his math group worked each problem in turn, or when the teacher sat with him as he worked problems one at a time, my son could complete his work in a timely fashion. But if he were given, say, twenty minutes to complete several problems independently, he would ask that the directions be repeated or would somehow just fall behind.

I diagnosed that as an issue of learning style. When I asked what they might recommend to move him from his present pattern to the preferred pattern of more independence, I was greeted with blank stares, as if they thought all they needed to do was register their complaint with me; it was my problem, as the parent, to solve the problem. As experienced teachers, I felt, they should have had the capacity at least to make recommendations so that we could move my son forward.

The only diagnosis my son's teacher could offer was that he might have attention deficit disorder and that he might need to take Ritalin. I later realized that he was insecure in math because he was competing with children who were being tutored by their parents or professionally. My child was trying to fight it out by competing on his own. The teachers all knew that this was going on, but until the "red book" incident, which I discuss later in this chapter, no one informed me. Judging by my conversations with the teacher who "broke the silence," they did not even see the unfairness of concealing this information.

When my son misbehaved, his teachers were the first to talk about the classroom being a "community" and the damaging effect his crimes had on the other children. However, they were curiously silent about the atmosphere of a covert "club," in which we were not included, and the effect it had on my son. My understanding of McDermott's "achieved failure" analysis is that often when the "politics of everyday life" in a classroom are not in a child's favor, behavioral problems can result (1987, 179).

We were decidedly not members of the club. Teachers in private schools receive low salaries in comparison with public school teachers. However, one of the perks is that they receive tuition breaks for their own children to attend the school. At my son's school, teachers receive a 50 percent reduction in tuition.

On the one hand, I believe that the quality of instruction is elevated when the children of faculty are enrolled in a school. On the other hand, this practice also creates the atmosphere of a club, whose members are the children of teachers and classroom staff and families who enroll two, three, or four children. The families all know one another, and the teachers know some families very well. Those parents know things I do not know, things that are not covered in the parent handbook and in parent meetings, that are important to his success in school. They have an underground network of information unavailable to "outsiders"; and it is harder still for an African American parent to penetrate that network. A child moving through the school as the second, third, or fourth child in his or her family to attend the school is not pounced upon for every infraction, judged pathological, in the way infractions are treated by an African American male child who is from a single-parent household with a mother who is not a member of the club.

In my view, the reasons an African American family enrolls its children in private school are quite different from those of a typical white family. Many white families enroll their children in "exclusive" private schools to control their social networks, so that their children will associate only with their "own kind"; others choose the private schools their friends' children attend. Far from finding a social environment populated by their children's friends, and the children of their own friends, African American parents who enroll their children in private schools (and thus, usually, predominantly white schools) often must go to extensive lengths to stay connected with the African American community—enrolling their children in organizations like Jack and Jill (a middle-class African American children's organization), the Boy Scouts, and church activities. It is my contention that white parents are more charitable about the school's academic short-comings for a number of reasons. First, the social aspects of being a member of the network have considerable value to them. Second, they are used to having to "supplement" their children's education. Finally, they see a quality education as just one component of their children's future success; among the other factors are the family's ability to finance higher education and membership in social networks that can assure entry to elite schools and lucrative future employment. African American families, on the other hand, do not have the luxury of focusing on the social "privileges" of private schools: because the money for tuition generally comes harder to us, we tend to be more exacting in what we expect for the money, and because so many of the doors to success are still closed, if not locked, to our children, academic goals are the overriding reasons we choose private education.

My son's second-grade teacher regularly recommended that I take him to one of her friends, who is a psychiatrist, so that he could be evaluated for attention deficit disorder and be given a prescription for Ritalin. Here was every complaint I had heard from African American mothers, coming at me in Technicolor! I told her that if I took him to a psychiatrist, it would be an African American male, not her best friend, who would simply prescribe what the teacher herself recommended. I also questioned whether she knew that it was against the law for a teacher to prescribe Ritalin, as was her practice every time we met.

Episode Four: Delayed Entry to Kindergarten

When my son was three years old, we went to an interview at another prominent private school in this community, hoping to enroll him in the preschool class for four-year-olds the following fall. I will call this school Private School One because it was my first choice. Our experience there was what caused me to choose his present school over that one. I will call his present school Private School Two.

The testing portion of the interview was conducted in an early-childhood classroom filled with toys and objects to play with and a classroom full of children. When I picked up my son, I was told that he was definitely a smart little boy. He had correctly solved twenty-four of the twenty-six items on a language concepts test. However, he refused to participate in the other tests because he wanted to play with the toys and play with the other children.

The director explained to me that they wanted only children who do what the teacher tells them to do. My son would not comply with the teacher's requests to their satisfaction. She said that they draw a circle of behaviors and abilities and accept only those children who fall within the circle.

As I pointed out in my earlier book, *Black Children* (Hale 1986), young children who can inhibit movement score better on standardized tests. Because African American boys tend to have more difficulty inhibiting movement during testing, the question could be raised as to whether the test is really measuring intelligence or merely the ability of the child to sit still. My experience in testing with my son at Private School One made me wonder whether it was his intelligence that was being tested or, rather, his willingness to resist the temptation to play with appealing toys, and the other children who were playing with these toys, in a new setting. The school's director further explained that my son seemed to be immature—which should not have been unexpected for a summer child. He was born in the middle of August. A great deal of data in the literature suggests that children born in the summer have more problems academically in the primary grades because they are younger than the other children. The cutoff point for children entering kindergarten is usually a September birthday. This problem is most pronounced for boys, and probably more so among African American boys.

The director suggested that I enroll my son in a class a year below his age level (a practice referred to as "delayed school entry"). The thinking is that he would then be the oldest child in his class and bring more maturity to the academic and behavioral goals he is presented with as he moves through school.

I was horrified. Being an early-childhood educator, I had carefully weighed every action and decision that affected him since conception, and I was now being told that he was not qualified for prekindergarten. Also, my son's father is six feet eight inches tall, and both of my brothers are six feet five inches tall. I knew at birth that my son would not be a small person, that in fact he would probably be the tallest person in his class among his age-mates. I did not want to subject him to being in a class with children a year younger than he, to make it worse.

His day-care provider had taught in the school I ultimately chose, Private School Two. (As a newcomer in the community, I had never heard of this school.) When I confided to her my outrage with Private School One, she suggested that I try this school for gifted children. I was delighted when they conducted his testing in a small office with no distracting toys or children and in the presence of only the examiner. I was delighted when no mention was made of "delaying his entry" to kindergarten by enrolling him in junior kindergarten. However, this issue of delayed entry to kindergarten was to resurface in the second grade.

Keith's second-grade teacher, Monica, recited a litany of complaints that seemed to hinge on his maturity level and the demands Stage III was making on the children to function with a high level of independence and maturity. As I talked with other parents, I began to realize that instead of being grouped with seven- and eight-year-olds, as it appeared on the surface in this combined second- and third-grade class, my son was actually grouped with seven-, eight-, and nine-year-olds. So many of the children's entry to kindergarten had been delayed, as Private School One had recommended to me, that a child like my son, who was the correct age for his grade, was placed at a great disadvantage.

The teachers did not take into consideration certain factors—his being a summer child, a black male, and a year or two younger than his classmates—in evaluating Keith's behavior. All I got was irritation and disgust. No effort was made to understand the context of his behavior. Another factor that I had to bring to the attention of my son's teachers was the fact that he was so tall. It is easy to forget that even though he is one of the tallest children in the class, he is actually the youngest! His height, as thus his presumed maturity, would intensify any irritation over his perceived immaturity.

Peggy Gaskill (1993), reviewing these issues in an article of the *Beacon*, the newsletter of the Michigan Association for the Education of Young Children, points out that kindergarten used to function as a child's first formal experience of school. Twenty years ago, activities and experiences were presented in a playful manner that matched the children's curiosity and interests. However, with the advent of day-care and preschool programs, kindergarten has taken on a more academic focus.

Because of the more-academic demands in kindergarten and first grade, schools have begun raising the entrance age for kindergarten and delaying a child's entry into kindergarten for a year. However, as a result, first-grade teachers have gradually changed their academic expectations for children entering their classrooms. Kindergarten is no longer a part-time, play-oriented introduction to school, it is a preparation for the more formal instruction of first grade.

Gaskill observes that because so many children struggle with the curriculum and escalating standards, the entrance age has been raised to keep the younger and less well prepared children out of kindergarten. It has become popular wisdom that the child who is the oldest in the class will be the most successful. However, what Sue Bredekamp and Lorrie Shepard (1989) call the "youngness effect" is produced for the youngest children in the class, who are at a slight disadvantage academically. They have found, however, that the effects of age on achievement overall are small and disappear by the third grade.

Based upon the way my son is blossoming in the seventh grade, I would agree that there is no long-term disadvantage over time. However, at a school such as the one he attends, where a great deal of independence is expected at a young age and where teachers are ever eager to play psychologists at work, boys, and particularly African American boys, are at great risk of being placed on the remedial track.

These misdiagnoses and examples of educational malpractice in the early years contribute to what McDermott calls the child's "institutional biography" (1987, 198). A child who is placed at Table Number Three, or with the Colorful Rainbows, the "Blue group," or any other designation of ability, in kindergarten usually will carry that designation throughout his or her academic career. There is little movement from Table Three to Table One.

David Elkind (1987) has observed that when parents delay school entry to ensure that their children are older than their classmates, they contribute to the problem of pushing the rigorous academic curriculum down into lower grades. The practice may increase the likelihood that a young child will do better because he or she is the oldest child in the kindergarten, but because this is not an option for parents who cannot afford to delay kindergarten entry, it further divides the educational opportunities of the haves and the have-nots in our society.

This can be a hidden critical issue for African American children who enter integrated upper-middle-class school settings. There is no clear indication that the ages of the children in a classroom span three years rather than two. The teachers at my son's school did not tell me. They simply trumpeted to me all the ways he seemed less mature than his classmates and left it to me to uncover what he was up against. Every time I left a parent conference in which I had successfully defended him, I wondered what other parents do who do not have my specialized background in education.

Gaskill (1993) notes that there are drawbacks over time to delaying school entry. Children who are old for their grade are entirely aware of being older (Shepard and Smith 1986), and some of the resulting problems do not surface for years (Peck, McCaig, and Sapp 1988). The children who are older tend, eventually, to be more mature than their classmates and become easily bored. In general, the literature suggests the possibility of too little challenge, which may lead to lower motivation to do what the other children are doing as well as behavior problems.

Gaskill also covers the research on various types of extra-year programs, known as prekindergarten, developmental kindergarten, begindergarten, transition rooms, readiness rooms, or pre-first-grade classrooms, that have been created for children who are viewed as too immature to benefit from school or as at risk for academic failure. The children selected for these programs are often males from low-income households. Gaskill finds that they are often able learners but become labeled as "slow," a designation that gets passed along from teacher to teacher and may stay with the students for their entire academic careers.

The research done on these programs does not support their effectiveness (Shepard and Smith 1986). Children who are enrolled in these transitional programs do about as well in first grade as other children who were enrolled in kindergarten at a young age.

My experience with my son, who did not "fit within the circle," is that these children need to be taught by someone who cares about the soul of the child. Someone, either his parent, a relative, or a caring teacher, must give that child the support he or she needs to catch up and acquire whatever skill is being imparted. As long as that child is passed along to the "special education" teacher or some other person who may be running flash cards but is not passionate about the child's success, as I was for my son, the child will fall through the cracks. This is the meaning behind efforts to increase the numbers of African American teachers who are teaching African American children. One part of that agenda is to increase the numbers of teachers who care about the souls of the children.

Episode Five: The Spelling Group

My son's third-grade teacher gave the children a pretest on their spelling words each Monday. They were to study intensely the ones they had missed, and the final test, the one that counted, was given on the following Friday.

October had been a busy month for me, and it seemed that my son was missing the same words on Friday that he had missed on Monday. Then, out of the blue, he brought home a test on which he had spelled all of the words correctly. I was so surprised that I praised him lavishly. He was silent. After a pause he said, "Something bad happened, Mommy. The teacher moved me back into the group with the first years"—that is, to the group of children who were a year below his grade level.

I was amazed, and angry, that the teacher would move him below grade level without consulting me. I asked him what exactly they did in the class between Monday and Friday to study the missed words, but he could not think of anything. Fortunately, the fall parent-teacher conference was two days away. I felt that I could restrain myself until then.

When I entered the room for the conference, the teachers began by exclaiming about Keith's artwork, and they showed me a picture of our house that he had drawn. (This reminded me of a first-grade conference in which the teachers who were not teaching him to read noted how well he could chin himself on the monkey bars. My apologies to Howard Gardner: language arts and mathematics are a priority for me, too.)

I waited throughout the conference until the teacher raised the subject of spelling. She had felt that Keith could benefit from a review of the rules of spelling, so she had moved him to the group with the first years. I recounted my conversation with my son exactly as it is written above. When I asked her what they were doing in the classroom to teach the children the spelling words, she replied that she *intended* to have them write each word in a sentence—in other words, *they had not gotten to that lesson yet!* I could barely contain my frustration: she had moved my son to a lower-ability spelling group because he could not perform a skill that she had not yet taught him?

Lowering my voice, I stated evenly that I do not ever want him in a group in the language arts or mathematics that is below his grade level. I stated further that if she ever felt the need to reassign Keith, she should consider his difficulty in performing at grade level as a red alert and contact me. "That means that you are to call me on the red phone, with the red light on it, wherever I am in the world!" I repeated that though I do not demand that my child be the smartest child in the class, he is certainly capable of doing whatever other children his age are doing, and he is certainly capable of functioning at grade level.

I asked her to move him back to the group with his age-mates the next day, which she did. I understood this episode to mean that it would be my job to teach him spelling. The next hurdle was obtaining the spelling list after the Monday pretest. Sometimes it was in his backpack, and sometimes it was not. I finally called his teacher and asked her why I was having such a difficult time obtaining the spelling list each week. She said that it was Keith's job to remember to put the spelling list in his backpack and that he sometimes forgot. She did not intervene because she was teaching him "responsibility."

I reminded her that every notice she cared about—field trip permission slips, collections of money, and snack schedules—were placed, without fail, in the backpack. She did not depend upon Keith's sense of responsibility to make sure those notes were delivered. I suggested that she create another way of teaching him responsibility and personally assure me that I would receive the spelling list each week.

Once I made sure that he reviewed the spelling words before Friday, Keith got 100 percent on his spelling test each week. He has an excellent memory. The point I am making in relating this episode is that because he was not learning the spelling words by osmosis, the teacher placed him below grade level, which was damaging to his self-esteem and could have contributed to his shutting down from embarrassment. This episode prompted me to comment to his teacher that *my son can learn whatever he is taught*. If he does not know it, it is because no one has taught it to him. His capabilities are not in question. He does not need counseling or medication. The only question is whether I am going to teach him or the teacher is going to teach him. Of course, because I was paying tuition and she was being paid, I was of the opinion that she should teach him. Please keep in mind that the teacher-student ratio in this classroom is one full-time teacher for every nine children.

My fear around this incident was that as early as October the teacher can quietly move my child into a group in which he is working below grade level. By January, she can administer an inventory that documents beyond a shadow of a doubt that he is doing work on the second-grade level, though he is in the third grade. By April, the school officials will be sending me to a group of professionals holding clipboards while they explain to me that my son needs to be retained. I felt that I was engaged in a constant game of *hide-and-seek* to protect him from low expectations.

Episode Six: The Red Book

One evening in the middle of October, as I was preparing dinner, Keith, who was eight years old at the time, took his red math book out of his backpack and announced that he had asked his teacher if he could work on math at home. He stated (with some anxiety) that the "first years" in his class (he is a "second year") are skipping the red book and moving on to the blue book.

I was not pleased that he seemed to be upset, but I was pleased that he was motivated to work in the red book. I recalled that his teacher had given me the red book at the beginning of the summer, and, at her instruction, he and I had worked together up to the section on fractions. But it had been difficult to get him to stop play and work with me, because he did not understand why he had to do it. So I was at least pleased that working in the red book now had meaning for him. I was puzzled, however, to discover that he was still working on fractions, where he and I had stopped at the beginning of the school year.

He sat at his desk and got to work, but he called for me to help because he did not know how to do fractions. I was upset: when we had encountered multiplication during the summer, I had had to introduce it to him. I asked his teacher in the fall why she was sending a workbook home with no accompanying teaching aids when he had not yet been *taught* multiplication. I felt that this was unfair to me.

I had sought refuge earlier in the local toy store, where I had purchased a workbook with illustrations that helped me teach him multiplication. I recognized that I was again in the same situation with fractions. Wishing to capitalize on this "teachable moment," I ran upstairs and retrieved the workbook. I came back down and showed Keith the two pages that introduced fractions and illustrated the concept. I explained that if he worked the problems on the two pages in this workbook, he could grasp the concept and then work the problems in the red book.

When he understood what I was saying, he looked at me in disbelief and exclaimed, "Mommy, I am trying to finish the red book. I don't want to do two other pages in this book!" He promptly fell on the floor crying. He said that he was dumb and stupid, that he cannot do math, and that everyone in the class is smarter than he is. As I looked at him and listened to this, I counted up how much I was paying in tuition for this.

It took me until the next evening to contact his teacher by telephone. I explained the situation to her and asked why she had not reviewed the progression through the books when we had met for parent-teacher conferences the week before. I wanted to know why Keith seemed to be panicked because the other children were moving beyond him. It seemed to me that the schedule for completing each book should have been discussed in the parent-teacher conference. I wanted to know whether he was supposed to be in a certain book at some point in his academic career. She said that they were expected to be in the yellow book by the next fall (the beginning of fourth grade). This meant that he had to finish the red, blue, and green books in less than a year. I felt that this should be achieved in an orderly fashion and that he should not come home in panic.

I asked why Keith was expected to pace himself in competition with his classmates. I observed that in our five years with the school, the teachers had not seemed to have any goals for my child. I seem always to be probing whether he is on grade level. And now, he had to take over pacing himself.

I commented further that either the teachers are committing crimes of omission or the parents are doing something that does not meet the eye. Finally, she told me the truth, and the information she shared with me became one of the inspirations for titling this section "Breaking the Silence." Keith's classmate, Sophocles, had skipped the red book, she explained, because he was the third child in his family to be in her classroom. His mother had at home the orange book, the red book, the blue book, the green book, the yellow book, and the purple book. They probably had a math assembly line at home!

Margaret had also skipped the red book, Keith's teacher continued, because at her mother's request the book had been sent home each evening since the beginning of the school year, and Margaret and her mother had completed five to ten pages a night at home. Max had skipped class instruction in the red book because his mother had completed the book with him during the summer. (The teacher had told us to work only up to the section on fractions, because she would be covering that in class.) Sophocles, Margaret, and Max were all in a grade below my son.

As I continued to talk with the teacher in disbelief, she admitted that at least half of the children in my son's class were being formally tutored either by their parents or privately. I was outraged. She said to me, "But Janice, what can I do?" I replied, "What can you do? You are the teacher. I am trusting you to be fair. I am trusting you with my son's self-concept."

This school has the most progressive philosophy of any school in the state of Michigan. It prides itself on an agenda of "diversity." It has a surface ethos akin to that of open education, the hippies, flower children, Quaker Friends schools, and the like. The teachers and staff often give lip service to the rhetoric about each classroom being a community and about the need to consider how each child in this community is affected by the actions of others.

I felt that their concept of community was betrayed by this practice of unacknowledged tutoring. If, as I am told, every child in the school is gifted, why is all of this underground tutoring necessary? Of course, I wonder who the testing is for. My son has reported that some of his classmates did not have to be tested for entry. All of the children of the teachers attend the school with a tuition rebate. Have they all met the standard my son had to meet? I have heard of families in which, because one child had met the standard, a younger child who had not was nevertheless admitted—on a "trial" basis. I told the director that the longer we stay in this school for gifted children the less I believe in the concept of giftedness.

This episode reminded me of a family story. My father's first pastorate was a church in LaGrange, Georgia, in the early 1940s. At the time, because of World War II, meat was rationed. However, the African American community was hit doubly hard because butchers would sell meat to white people but not to African Americans. So my father grew chickens in his yard and sold them to people in his community. He had the fattest chickens in the county. His secret was that he kept the light on in his chicken coop all night long, so that the chickens would keep eating all through the night.

After this conversation with my son's teacher, I began to reflect upon African American children I know who attended schools like this one who had to withdraw because of ulcers and other nervous disorders. I began to wonder whether it was this "feeding of the chickens" twenty-four hours a day by white parents, while everyone else was asleep, that caused unsuspecting African American children to burn out.

I explained to Keith's teacher that there is no child alive that I would want to see in such misery as my son had experienced, exclaiming that he was dumb and unable to learn math. I have no goal for him that is worth the destruction of another child's concept of self. I feel that it is possible for instruction and achievement to proceed in such a way that every child in the classroom can master the basic skills and emerge with his self-concept intact.

As we talked, I thought back to a heated exchange I had had with my son's second-grade teacher the previous spring at the parent-teacher conference. She had criticized him for not being independent enough in math. The implication was that the other children were "independent"; in fact, they did not need to be taught by her because they were being tutored at home or by professionals. My child had to fight it out by himself because I believed the official philosophy of the school and thought that the school would take responsibility for teaching him and would treat him fairly. If this charade were to be internalized as a fair learning environment, he would have nowhere to go but self-blame and low self-esteem. It would not take long for him to stop trying.

The frightening part of this episode is that his teacher was genuinely distressed over it. She knew that this sounded wrong but seemed to be genuinely puzzled about how it could really be wrong and what her role in it was. I suspect that this has been going on for so long, and teachers trying to respond to the wishes of each parent tend to lose their perspective on fairness to every child in the classroom.

Episode Seven: The Reading Group

Two months after the spelling group incident and the red book incident came the reading group incident. By now, my son was beginning to catch on. I did not even have to observe his classroom anymore because he was keenly aware of the politics of the classroom. He has always told me that he wants to start out low and move up in terms of academic rigor. He does not want to have the pressure of working above his ability level. However, he is also keenly aware of being placed below his ability level.

He complained in December that he and another child who was a second-year (third-grade) student had been placed in a reading group with children who were primarily first-years (second-graders). The other children, according to his report, could not decode the words; but the teacher would not allow him to correct them, and he was bored by having to sit and listen to them stumble.

I wrote a memo to his teacher, asking her to explain to me why he was in a group with mostly first-year children. I had been told the previous year that he could read anything he was given, so I could not see why he was placed in a group that was below his grade level. I asked her to itemize the skills he was lacking so that we could work on those skills and achieve his placement in the group of his age-mates by January. I was sure that she would agree that a child should be encouraged to change groups and not stick with the designation he was given at the beginning of the year.

I received a phone call from the teacher, who agreed to move Keith and Donald, the other second-year child, up to the group with their age-mates. She stated that they were now ready to move but that Keith had not been ready at the beginning of the year. I would have felt better if the idea to move him to the higher group had come from her. I would also have felt better if she had explained why he was in the lower ability group and had outlined for me the skills he needed to improve. The fact that the impetus had to come from Keith gave me the feeling that she was tracking him and was not nurturing his self-esteem and motivating him to achieve.

Everything I had complained about in the first, second, and third grades came to a screeching halt in the fourth grade. Perhaps it was the three hours I spent reviewing my complaints with the director. Perhaps I happened to get an excellent teacher for the fourth and fifth grades. Perhaps the school's instruction improves in the upper elementary grades. Perhaps my son has matured and is easier to communicate with. One of my friends suggested that everything got better because they do not want to be negatively portrayed in this book.

As I was writing this chapter, an issue of *Newsweek* came in the mail with a cover story, "How to Build a Better Boy: The Crisis Points in Child Development and What Parents Can Do" (Kantrowitz and Kalb 1998). The article notes that boys' crisis points are different from those of girls, identifying particular stages in the emotional and social development of boys where things can go wrong. The primary grades are highlighted—the same stages at which I had faced the greatest challenges with my son. In twenty-five years of teaching child development, this was the first acknowledgement by white scholars that I have seen that white males have difficulty negotiating teachers in early-childhood settings. I analyze this matter in *Black Children* (Hale 1986), in my discussion of the female orientation in classrooms, but I had not seen the issue addressed in mainstream developmental psychology.

The focal point of the article was, of course, young white males. One sentence was devoted to African American boys, a comment about growing up in single-parent households. Deeper issues related to African American males have been raised in my work and also in the work of Jawanza Kunjufu (1984, 1985, 1986).

One of the things that the article did not say is that even though white males face challenges in early-childhood classrooms, they are generally protected by their mothers, who serve as room mothers, field-trip drivers, and volunteers in the school. The children's mothers are thus able to oversee the placement of their children directly (not indirectly by memo, as I, a single working mother, had had to do). They can make friends with the teachers and become a part of "the club."

The recent spate of violent incidents affecting white young adolescent boys in Jonesboro (Arkansas), Paducah (Kentucky), Pearl (Mississippi), and, most notably, Littleton (Colorado) has stimulated interest in the development of white boys. This confirms my contention that if the statistics for white boys ever approached the pattern of outcomes for African American boys described in chapter 3, that would be the day the earth stood still: we would see a rash of White House conferences, task forces, and blue-ribbon panels designed to get white males back on track.

The article mentions a slew of books with titles like *Real Boys: Rescuing Our Sons from the Myths of Boyhood* and *Raising Cain: Protecting the Emotional Life of Boys* that were released that year. As someone once said, "When white America has the flu, African America has pneumonia." This article reports on research projects that are being conducted to obtain information about the development of white males with a view to maintaining their mental health and dominance. There is a need for the generation and support of research projects that intervene in the failure of African American boys, as well—a failure rate that is immensely more catastrophic.

Episode Eight: The Science Test

My son, Keith, was enrolled in physics in the fall of his fourth-grade year. When I enrolled him in the school, I was told by the admission counselor that all science instruction was hands-on: no textbooks were used. The children were engaged in experiments and projects. That sounded like a dream come true. However, the assumptions of the school about "parent involvement" turned this dream into a nightmare.

My son handled his physics class all fall, but he began to express anxiety as the day of the physics test approached. In place of textbooks, the teacher handed out xeroxed sheets that the children were to work on as they listened to his lectures and completed experiments, but Keith had lost everything. He had no textbook, and I had never studied physics in school.

I called his homeroom teacher, who copied another child's notes and sent them home with Keith. The notes were neither numbered nor dated, however, so I had no idea whether they were complete. He also attended a study session conducted by the teacher and obtained a study guide. I called his babysitter, David, into play. David, a high school junior who had studied physics, was hereby promoted from babysitter to tutor.

David worked with Keith on the day before the test. Incidentally, this was an open-folder test. The children could refer to their notes during the test, but to complete the test within the allotted time, they had to be familiar with their notes for them to be useful. The questions were not rote but integrative, so the children needed to understand the material, as well. Keith failed the test, with a score of 58. However, the purpose of the test was to help the children learn how to organize the material and develop test-taking skills. A test with a low score must be retaken. I, as always, was working to preserve my son's self-concept. I did not want him to become devastated by failure and internalize a negative evaluation of his abilities.

Consequently, I was pleased that the teacher sent the first test home for Keith to study in preparation for the retake. The children are required to take the test until they obtain a satisfactory score. (This is a good thing.) David reported that Keith had missed several test items because he did not understand the test terminology: he did not know how to interpret phrases such as "all of the above" and "none of the above" or understand that there could be more than one correct answer in a multiple-choice question. There were other test-taking skills that were needed to perform well. Because most of the items were not recall questions but, rather, were questions requiring interpretation and analysis, he had to become familiar with the teacher's logic. Also, although he had seen experiments performed in class, he had to be able to recall the experiments by name to answer the questions.

David also discovered that some of the questions on the test were not reflected in the notes Keith had or in the study guide. This made me wonder whether we had all of the notes that had been given.

Armed with the test, David tutored Keith again for the retake of the test. This time Keith scored an 85—a B+! Phew! On to chemistry.

I had never taken chemistry, either, but I was beginning to understand what was required of me as a parent, and so I decided to get on top of it this time. I first purchased a folder that had metal fasteners in addition to pockets. I asked Keith to notify me whenever he had chemistry and to bring to me the notes that were passed out in class so that we could punch holes in them and fasten them into the folder.

On his first day of class, he announced that the teacher had passed out two pages of notes and that he had (already!) lost one. I called his teacher, who found the sheet in the lost and found, and we were launched on our precarious walk through chemistry.

During that semester, I had occasion to speak with another parent of a child in the school. I was sharing my science war stories with her. Her son is a grade ahead of Keith. She told me what to look forward to the next year, in anatomy: In the fifth grade, notes are no longer distributed. The children are required to take their own notes on demonstrations and experiments. Just as I realized that my son had lost his notes before the test day, she had realized that her son had taken no notes in the class, and so she had gone to the class and taken notes for him! I pondered whether my son now had to compete *directly* with the mothers of his classmates.

In that same conversation, I mentioned that my son's two best friends had each scored 92 on the physics test Keith had initially failed. I mentioned that each of them had a brother who was two grades ahead of them in school. She guessed that they both had old copies of the tests at home.

In disbelief, I called the science teacher. I repeated our conversation and my frustration. He denied that a mother had come to the class to take notes, but he admitted that one had come and videotaped the classes! I asked whether he thought it fair to have some children relying on their own note taking and competing with others who can review videotapes. He said that that child had a learning disability. In the school for gifted children? I wondered.

We discussed fairness. I recommended that if he allows any children to keep old tests in the family, then everyone should be provided with old tests to review. Having access to previous tests is valuable at this age because they assist the child in following the reasoning of the teacher. As I stated above, most of his questions are integration and application questions, which is good, but it requires that the child get on the teacher's wavelength. I also asked the teacher to number the notes he distributes to the children so that I can know whether my son has all of them. I was grateful that he complied with my wish.

To his credit, Keith's teacher sent home at least three practice tests after my conversation with him. He also numbered the notes, which other parents found helpful, as well. Another parent called me when she discovered that her son was missing notes to obtain a copy of my son's notes.

In the fifth-grade anatomy course, the children were given a "questionnaire" in class before taking the test on cells, which helped acclimate them to the material that would be on the test, and Keith was able to prepare for this test without David's assistance. It kicked in! He got it. He received an 83 on the cells test, on his own, and a 91 on his anatomy test.

My point in relaying this episode is to highlight the high degree of skill I, as a parent, had to bring to decoding my child's failure and constructing success for him. The teacher is doing what he has always done. This definition of parent involvement requires a parent with an extraordinary level of skill. I shudder to think about the specialists we would have had to consult to solve my son's "learning disabilities," his "inability to focus," and variations along those lines if I had not been able to provide that structure and assistance.

Episode Nine: The Science Paper

The children in the fifth-grade anatomy course were assigned a paper on a system of the body. My son's team was asked to study and report on the respiratory system, and he was assigned the research on the lungs. I was surprised to receive a packet of information—addressed to me!—describing how to write the paper.

I first wrote a paper of this type when I was in the tenth grade. If the school decides that it is developmentally appropriate for children to receive assignments such as these, then it seems to me that it is the responsibility of the teachers in his school to teach them, step by step, how to complete the assignment.

Keith was also taking a class on study skills. I asked his homeroom teacher why the study-skills teacher could not take the children through the steps of writing a paper to complement instruction given in the anatomy class. I can understand that the science teacher is teaching anatomy and that teaching his pupils how to write a paper detracts from the time he has to teach his subject. However, I feel the same way when I must teach my undergraduate and graduate students how to write papers, a skill that they should have been taught earlier in their academic careers. I review writing and research skills from scratch in each course I teach so that all students have an equal opportunity, regardless of their backgrounds, to do well on my assignments.

I decided, without protest, to teach Keith how to write the paper because at least here, at last, was an assignment I knew how to do. I did not have to buy new materials or hire a tutor. I also knew that the need to write papers would be a constant in his schooling, and I felt that I could teach him properly so that he could function independently throughout his academic career.

My criticism here is that the teacher should be the equalizer in the classroom. All children should be taught by the teacher so that their fortunes are not totally determined by the skills of their parents. Educators seem not to recognize the injustice of sending projects home that the children cannot complete alone. They seem not to question the fact that they are really grading the parents' efforts, not the work of the children. They seem not to acknowledge the hardship placed on some children, whose parents are unavailable to give them the extraordinary assistance the projects require.

In the sixth grade, my son was again assigned a research paper, with no instruction from the teacher. Again, I helped him write it. This time, I called the director of the middle school and asked him at what point in the school's curriculum the children are offered instruction in how to write a paper. He responded that these skills are taught in the ninth grade. I recounted our experience with Keith's science paper and the fact that he had had a similar experience in his social studies class. I suggested that if the school is not *teaching* the children to write papers until the ninth grade, the teachers should not *assign* them to write papers until that time.

I have had conversations on this issue with my undergraduate and graduate students, who report that they were not formally taught to write papers as they moved through school. The teachers who gave these assignments assumed that someone else had taught them how to write papers. A white friend of mine has acknowledged that white parents endure doing the jobs of the teachers because they are afraid to challenge the schools or not to participate because of their fear that their children will fall into the underclass.

The hypocrisy is galling to me. This school offers scholarships to poor African American children from Detroit in the name of giving them a better chance. However, it is, in fact, no chance at all if the children must have parents who can homeschool them as required for their survival in this system. The parent of a scholarship student from Detroit is not positioned to do the detective work I have described in this chapter. If this school is truly committed to "diversity," as its spokespersons claim to it be, then school faculty and administration need to go beyond raising scholarship money for poor minority children and create a learning environment that is fair. To achieve this, they will have to face the issues I am raising in this chapter.

It is also galling to me that no one tells the truth when the achievement of African American children is compared with that of affluent white children. Although all studies find that the strongest indicator of achievement of children is the socioeconomic status of the parents, or "parental influence," they never translate that into the responsibilities the schools pass on to the parents for those children to achieve success. Therefore, we have no clue as to what we need to do to close the gap between the achievement of white and African American children.

My conclusion here is that we need a different model for educating children who are outside of the middle-class mainstream. We need a different model of "parental involvement" in communities where the family is not strong. Educators in inner-city schools, of course, would argue that they do not expect the same level of participation from parents in schools with children who are disadvantaged. However, the quality of the instruction thereby suffers. Instruction is dumbed down, and both expectations and outcomes suffer.

I argue that schools have to find a way to create an instructional accountability infrastructure, independent of the parents, that delivers the same quality of instruction found in the suburbs and in private schools. The schools need to assume that responsibility themselves and network with religious, fraternal, and civic organizations for help.

We do not need more tests to determine whether the children have acquired the skills they need before moving to the next grade level. What we need are supervisory strategies for principals to provide instructional leadership and give teachers the support they need in working with children whose parents are not highly skilled in supervising the teachers of their children.

PART 2

Creating the Village

CHAPTER 5

Twenty–First–Century Education Project

Report and Recommendations

The SAT [Scholastic Aptitude Test] and tests like it were put into effect not to fix the problems of American education, but to bypass them. They were supposed to find a few gifted students, even if they went to bad schools, send them to universities on scholarship, and leave the majority alone. Today young Americans are penalized much more severely if their schools are bad than they were back when ETS [the Educational Testing Service] was created.

—Nicholas Lemann

I n the winter of 1992, the county board of supervisors and the board of education launched an ambitious plan for economic development in Claiborne County, Mississippi, which includes the city of Port Gibson. They acknowledged that long-term growth could not proceed without a strong public school system that prepares the future citizens of the county to enter the workforce. With that in mind, they turned their attention to creating a partnership between the public and private sectors to strengthen the public schools.

The initiative was called the Twenty-First-Century Education Project.

James E. Miller, county administrator and planner, on behalf of the board of supervisors, contracted with me to conduct a study of the community and make recommendations aimed at improving the educational outcomes for children educated in the public schools. The study of this community was my first opportunity to think about how to apply my ideas on school reform in a real-life setting. The analysis of this community and the recommendations I made are shared in this chapter.

Long-Term Community Development Issues

My first recommendation was that elevation of the achievement of the children in the public schools of Claiborne County had to be approached in terms of long-term strategies embraced by the entire community in addition to short-term strategies that could bring immediate results. Success would not be achieved in the long run from drilling children, teaching to the test, using computer programs distributed by test manufacturers to inflate achievement scores, and improving test-taking skills as a primary focus.

I identified overarching issues that were essential as the backdrop for academic achievement. The overall intellectual climate in the community needed to be elevated, and the support systems provided for the children needed to be strengthened. Some of these issues may have seemed to be tangential to academic achievement, but in fact they were central.

Teen Pregnancy

James Miller, in a personal conversation, reported that 90 percent of children in the Claiborne County school system are living in female-headed households. The majority of these women are on public assistance. Many are illiterate, many are frustrated, and many are being mistreated by the men in their lives.

While I was conducting this study, Miller told me of a ten-year-old child in his district who was pregnant. I was also told that a nurse from Jackson, Mississippi, who periodically speaks to classes of fourteen-year-old boys and girls had reported that several of the girls have babies by that time. Miller stated that most of the younger girls—as young as thirteen—are being impregnated by older men in the community, who range from twenty-three to thirty-six years of age. Teenage pregnancy is by and large not occurring because of sexual activity between age-mates but, rather, because adult men are preying on young girls. Miller states further that Mississippi has the lowest legal age of consent for girls in the nation (the age below which statutory rape is charged) because the legislature of white males has been unwilling to create a law that would render white males vulnerable for prosecution on account of sexual activity with African American girls under their control during the time of slavery and sharecropping.

I suggested that intervention strategies be devised to eliminate teen pregnancy. I am not prescribing a solution here, because it is important that the solution is compatible with the values of the community regarding abstinence, family planning, and pregnancy termination. However, it is imperative that the community recognize the importance of taking action and develop and implement an intervention. Miller reports that any child can request and be given contraceptives at no cost without the necessity of parental consent. However, nothing is being done to let the children know of this availability.

There is no abortion clinic in Port Gibson. Abortion seems not to be the choice for girls in this community, which is probably why the county's rate of out-of-wedlock teenage pregnancy is the highest in the nation. Adoption appears to be rejected by the pregnant girls' mothers, so most of the children are raised in multigenerational single-female-headed households. The result is a large number of live births and a preponderance of teenaged mothers' keeping their babies.

This important issue must be addressed in the long term if the community is serious about improving the academic achievement of the children in Claiborne County. It is also a sensitive issue. For individuals to achieve upward mobility requires them to choose a path that is different from the familiar path taken by those they love. In *Unbank the Fire*, I make the point that critically evaluating the cultural patterns of significant others in one's life is a stressful psychological process; as one teen, who was admonished about avoiding pregnancy so young, responded, "Are you saying that what my mother and grandmother did was wrong?" (Hale 1994, 114).

Recreation and Cultural Enrichment

The absence of adequate recreational and enrichment activities for the children in the community is related to teen pregnancy. The education of children should not be focused solely on the schools. Growing children also need recreational outlets to broaden their experiences. One part in the process of teens' learning to delay the gratification found in premature sexual activity and substance abuse is the formation of a positive self-concept, high self-esteem, and the ability to conceptualize a future for themselves. This energy to construct their futures derives, in part, from involvement in activities that provide them with opportunities to identify and develop their talents and interests.

The churches and civic organizations need to join hands with the schools in raising the overall level of cultural experiences for children in this community. Recreational outlets are needed that children can access in the summer and after school, such as debate teams, drama guilds, literary societies, art classes, and sports programs. The community should sponsor academic competitions (such as the NAACP's ACT-SO) and cotillions, debutante balls, or "beautillions" (for boys).

Coming-out parties of this sort give the message that girls are presented to society as candidates for marriage at the age of eighteen and that there are citizenship criteria for being a part of the cotillion (such as good grades, no out-of-wedlock pregnancies, community service, and raising funds for charity). The activities presently offered in the community seem to be provided by middle-class families and organizations for their own children. There is a need to extend the outreach of these offerings so that children who are most in need of them are included. Here again, we see that middle-class families, even in the most poverty-stricken communities, understand the enrichment that is necessary for the optimal development of their children. What is lacking is a level of consciousness that enables the community to work together to extend these experiences to all children.

Mentorship

A related issue is the importance of providing mentors for boys and girls who can create ongoing personal relationships with them. The school should be at the center of these mentorship programs, although they can be initiated by churches and fraternal organizations. The principal and teachers should know who the mentors are so they can become a part of the network of concerned adults who can be activated as needed on behalf of the child. I have discussed the need for mentorship for African American boys in *Unbank the Fire* (Hale 1994, 193–94). In the Claiborne County community, there is a great need to provide mentors for African American girls, as well, to penetrate the cultural patterns that result in such an alarming rate of teen pregnancy.

Participation of Churches

A striking feature of the landscape in Port Gibson is the proliferation of churches; there is a church on virtually every corner. Residents of this community should take a long-term view of the consequences of perpetuating the practice of churches' splitting into smaller and smaller congregations. One result is that the community is frequently called upon to support numerous church-building programs and other financial initiatives. However, more important, only one of the churches is able to support a full-time pastor. Most of the pastors are ministering to three or four churches, often across state lines.

Church pastors have served a pivotal role in the African American community throughout American history. The leadership they historically have provided in advancing the interests of the African American community and creating cultural programs for children has greatly enriched the community. When the church congregations become increasingly smaller, their ability to support pastors deteriorates, and the pastors must minister to a large number of churches or work other jobs to support themselves. This drains the community of invaluable leadership.

During my study of this community, I found it difficult to involve the members of the clergy in meetings. Some of the pastors either did not live in the community because of pastorates in other locations or states or were burdened with full-time jobs. One church in the community split and called upon the pastor to pastor both sides of the split! As a Baptist, I understand that the right to separate and create a new church is worth fighting for, but I feel that it is important for activists to understand the effect of this expression of conflict on the development of the greater community.

Meetings were held with teen mothers and those considered to be at risk for becoming teen mothers. When asked about the kinds of activities offered in their churches, only two answers were given: choir and usher board. Church activities for children and teens are clearly designed to enhance the Sunday morning worship services rather than to nurture the children in these congregations. Perhaps community leaders can explore the feasibility of church mergers, or at least interchurch cooperation, in providing enrichment activities for children.

Housing

The lack of affordable housing near available jobs is a formidable barrier to independence for women who are on public assistance. In Hermanville and other parts of the county, residents live in dilapidated trailers and shanties. Many women spoke of the difficulty of getting off public assistance when they do not have access to housing near available jobs and there is no transportation that enables them to get to work from where they live.

Long Bus Rides to School

Schoolchildren in Claiborne County have to take long bus rides to school each day. Some children ride two hours each way from their rural homes to the Port Gibson school; the buses are so crowded that some children must stand for the entire ride. I noted that the bus rides could be shortened if more buses were made available. It was not so much the distance that was the problem as the number of stops the buses had to make to pick up or drop off all the passengers. I further recommended that the bus schedules be reorganized so that no child had to ride the bus for more than thirty minutes each way; the starting time of school could be staggered to achieve this, or new buses could be purchased. Children cannot be expected to perform optimally in school when they have to endure four hours of bus travel daily.

Transportation to School Meetings

Parents reported encountering transportation constraints in attending meetings of the parent-teacher association and conferences with teachers. I recommended that options be explored for providing transportation to such meetings or for holding meetings at the county supervisor's office, which was closer to most parents' homes.

Educational Recommendations

The recommendations in this report were intended to improve the overall educational experiences for the children of Claiborne County. Philosophically, the proposal was designed to move away from the "skill and drill" teaching method and toward the preparation of thematic units and hands-on instruction that would tap multicultural modalities and stimulate creativity and higher-order thinking skills.

The proposal suggested that instruction be oriented toward enrichment rather than remediation. The foundation of this idea is that children who receive an enriching educational experience are motivated to learn, and the growth in knowledge that results is reflected in stronger performance on assessment measures.

An additional feature of this model is the creation of teacher- and child-friendly educational environments that are less institutional and more homelike.

Instructional Coordinator

I also recommended that an instructional coordinator be appointed to serve as the liaison between the Claiborne County school system and the consultant during this process of educational intervention. This recommendation was made because there was no one at the time fulfilling the function of what would be an associate superintendent of curriculum and instruction in a larger school district.

The instructional coordinator would be responsible for working with the teachers in the classrooms to implement instructional change. He or she would work with the consultant and the principal in designing in-service training and then follow through with the teachers in the classroom to implement the strategies identified. Too often teachers attend workshops but upon returning to their classrooms find it difficult to translate the information into change for their students. The instructional coordinator would regularly meet with teachers, provide assistance, and conduct evaluations so that the schedule is followed and instruction is monitored.

It was further recommended that the principal and the instructional coordinator accompany the consultant on a tour of exemplary schools in southeast Michigan, which might serve as a shared vision of the direction of the change—a picture being worth a thousand words. In a larger city, this purpose could be achieved by pairing a low-achieving school with a high-achieving school in a sister-school relationship, allowing teachers to visit one another's classrooms and share instructional strategies.

Change the Utilization of Instructional Aides

To their credit, the school board funded an instructional aide for every elementary classroom. The aides all have baccalaureate degrees. However, they were being used as teacher's aides, not instructional aides. Their responsibilities included cutting out pumpkins, preparing audio and visual aids, and grading xeroxed work sheets, but they were not directly teaching the children.

Small-Group Rather Than Whole-Class Teaching

I recommended that instruction move away from whole-class teaching to individualized teaching of smaller groups. The instructional aides who were present were a tremendous resource, but they could have been used more effectively. It should not be possible upon entering a classroom to tell who is the teacher and who is the aide merely by what they are doing with the children. Both teacher and aide should be engaged in working with the children in small groups or individually.

Playground

I observed a glaring need for a state-of-the-art playground for the elementary school as well as space indoors for physical education and dance. Such facilities could also be used by the greater community for recreation. The model proposed in this report emphasizes that all developmental modalities of the child be supported and that African American children need to move, play, and release energy to be able to focus on their academic tasks.

Profile of Performance of Children in the Claiborne County Schools

As a preliminary step in preparing this report, Donald Reeves, the director of testing for the Claiborne County schools, compiled the necessary data to provide a picture of student outcomes for the district. In addition to providing standardized test scores by grade and gender, Reeves' report addressed a number of questions:

1. Is there a high school proficiency examination?
2. What is the dropout rate?
3. What is the gender profile of grade point averages?
4. What is the student-code violation rate?
5. What is the student daily attendance rate by grade?
6. What is the nonpromotion rate by grade and gender?
7. What is the college enrollment rate?
8. What is the college completion rate?
9. What marketable skills do students possess upon graduation?

Head Start Linkages

This community enjoys considerable funding for Head Start, with the children located in two centers. I felt that it was important to get a picture of the cognitive ability patterns of the children as they entered the school system. In this way, when an intervention was designed, we could be precise about pinpointing the age at which to begin.

The cognitive skills of each child enrolled in Head Start were tested, using the McCarthy Scales of Children's Abilities (McCarthy 1972). The test is an individually administered test of general cognitive abilities that can be used with children from two-and-a-half to eight years of age; administration time for children under the age of five is approximately forty-five to fifty minutes. The test consists of eighteen individual subtests, which form six scales: verbal, perceptual, quantitative, memory, and motor scales and an overall general cognitive index made up of the verbal, perceptual, and quantitative performance scales. The general cognitive index should be evaluated with the knowledge that the national average for these tests is 100. The national average for each of the subtests is 50.

The general cognitive index for the children in both of the Claiborne County Head Start programs was significantly higher than the national average—112.58 for the children at the Pattison Head Start center and 103.63 for the children at the Claiborne Head Start center. On the memory scale they scored significantly below the national norm, and their performance on the perceptual performance scale was normal. On all other scales the scores of the Claiborne County children were significantly higher than the national averages. Given the socioeconomic conditions of the children in this community, this is exceptional performance.

A review of the mean performance of the children by age reveals that despite the relative economic disadvantage of this population, the children scoring best are the youngest children in Head Start; the older children who have attended Head Start the longest have lower scores. It would be interesting to conduct a longitudinal study to determine whether there is a decline in the performance of individual children over time. It is clear from these data that the children enter Head Start ready to learn and that there is nothing wrong with their ability patterns.

One important component in the design of an effective intervention is a continuous system of education, from the cradle through college. I recommended that the in-service training include Head Start teachers and any other teachers of preschool children in the community for whom funding is available. Equally important is the effort to provide a preschool experience for every child in the community. This can be achieved at subsidized half-day nursery schools and at home, by mothers of preschoolers, who can learn educational activities to engage in with their children through home visits by instructors and in parent-child centers.

The Pattern of Achievement in Elementary School

The pattern identified in the Head Start testing holds for the achievement data on the elementary school level. The children were at grade level in reading in the first and second grades, but by the third grade they were two grades below grade level, as measured by the Stanford Achievement Test, and they remained so through the tenth grade, where they scored at the eighth-grade level.

The children scored somewhat better in mathematics: they performed at grade level from the first through fourth grades, but they fell one grade below grade level at the fifth and sixth grades of various years of the testing and remained so in the seventh and eighth grades. They returned to grade level in the ninth grade and fell below grade level again in the tenth grade. It seems as though the longer the children stayed in school, the more their performance deteriorated. These data support the assertion that African American children do not enter school disadvantaged, they *leave* school disadvantaged (Hale 1994, 156).

School Dropout Rate

For each year of the three-year period that was reported, the school dropout rate was between 3 and 5 percent. This was very low, given the low level of achievement of the children in the community, probably because of the controls implicit in a small town such as this. The town is so small that it would be difficult for a child to fall between the cracks by frequently "ditching" school or by dropping out entirely. In addition, the occupational opportunities are so limited that students who left school before graduating would have to leave town to seek employment, which would presume the existence of a family network in another city and permission to do so. The county has no fast-food outlets for employment and few career opportunities.

Many of the children are permitted to fall between the cracks within the school, however, such that they are basically marking time in terms of achievement. Certain controls keep them in school, although this is not universally the case. I was asked to provide consulting services in a small town in Georgia that is experiencing a dropout rate of 80 percent among its African American boys. In Port Gibson, in comparison, a total of seventy-three students dropped out of school in the three-year period, of whom fifty-three were males and twenty females.

Analysis of Grade Averages

The Claiborne County school system grades on a four-point scale in the first to twelfth grades. Kindergartners receive simple grades to indicate their progress: S for satisfactory and U for unsatisfactory. Beginning in the first grade the children receive letter grades A through F. Here we see the pattern identified at the beginning of this book: the children who are most at risk receive the harshest form of evaluation. Children in the elementary grades, and particularly in primary school, should not receive report cards that look like college transcripts. Reports to parents in elite private schools do not crush first-graders with Fs. It is imperative to create a system of evaluation for at-risk children that is loving, supportive, and formative.

An analysis of the grade point averages of this student population shows that female averages are higher than those of males. Also, the number of students receiving at least a 3.00—a B average—who are female exceeds the number of males.

Of the top twenty-five students in the 1993 twelfth-grade graduating class, five were males and twenty females. The grade point averages seem to be highest in the third grade, where the females average 3.17 (B). The grade point averages are lowest in the seventh grade, with even the females recording an average of 1.60 (D+). In the first and second grades, the grade point average for males is 2.60 (C+); by seventh grade, it has also slipped to D+.

Nonpromotion Rate by Grade and Gender

Students in the Claiborne County school system are "retained," or not promoted, for one of two reasons: either the student has not passed the number of courses or specific subjects required for promotion or the student has accumulated twenty-five or more unexcused absences. The majority of the students being retained, in all grades, are males. The data also show that more students are retained at seventh grade than at any other time in their school careers.

Seventh-Grade Retention

The focal point of this study was the elementary school and Head Start, or preschool, levels. However, I included a recommendation on a matter that was of concern to many parents. Forty-two of the 205 seventh-graders included in this study (20 percent) failed to be promoted to the eighth grade. The overwhelming majority of those retained were boys. Close inspection revealed that departmentalization—the practice under which students move from one classroom to another for instruction from teachers focusing on a single subject of study—begins in the seventh grade. The explanation was offered that self-contained classrooms are more costly and teachers can teach more students under departmentalization. Therefore, as a fiscal measure departmentalization was instituted at that grade. Plans were under way to push departmentalization down to the sixth grade the following year, for the same reason.

While considering this issue, I reflected upon the fact that the eighth grade was the most difficult year I had experienced in school. In junior high school, we had self-contained classrooms in the seventh grade. In the eighth grade, we moved into departmentalization.

I was an honor student, but my first year under departmentalization was nevertheless a traumatic experience for me. In the seventh grade, our homeroom teacher knew how much homework we had been assigned in the subjects she taught and regulated the amount when special projects were due. When we moved into departmentalization, I felt overwhelmed when three or four teachers gave us homework and projects, entirely unaware of the amount or difficulty of assignments given by other teachers. Although I found this frightening and difficult, my response as a secure middle-class child was to rise to the occasion. I made the superior honor roll that year—all As. An at-risk African American boy might meet departmentalization with the opposite response—to cave in.

I discussed this issue with an adult African American man I met in Massillon, Ohio, while on a speaking engagement. As a child he had fared well in the sixth grade. His academic achievements were such that he was selected to participate in a minority-to-majority transfer program, in which he left his predominantly African American school and attended a predominantly white school. Facing not only cultural differences to be negotiated but also encountering departmentalization for the first time, he completely fell apart academically. His parents were uneducated and could not interpret what was happening to him. He was too young to understand it himself, of course, and he became another casualty of the educational system. These well-intentioned efforts to improve his educational fortunes had resulted in catastrophe.

In this setting, I recommended that self-contained classrooms be reinstituted through the seventh grade and that departmentalization begin gradually in the eighth grade in preparation for high school. African American children have a particularly strong affective orientation (see Hale 1994, 215–18), and if they are to achieve they need a great deal of warm, nurturant support from their teachers.

Departmentalization can create a crisis for children, particularly those who are marginal students. They must learn to handle assignments from several different teachers who do not know how much homework the others have given. They need to learn to handle this situation before they reach high school, but later is better than sooner, and slowly is better than abruptly.

College Enrollment Rate

Compared with the days in the 1930s when my father had to leave Mississippi to obtain higher education (Hale 1994, 68–79), the students in the Claiborne County schools have three possibilities for postsecondary education near their community. Alcorn State University is just fifteen miles from Port Gibson, Hinds Community College is thirty miles away, and Jackson State University is fifty-five miles away.

For the period reported, 50 percent of the graduating senior class enrolled in some kind of postsecondary education. Of these, 60 percent attended Hinds Community College, 28 percent attended Alcorn State University, and the others chose Jackson State University, Southern University in Baton Rouge, or the University of Southern Mississippi.

These rates of college enrollment do not, however, reflect rates of college graduation. For one exemplary year, the total number of students in the high school graduating class was 112. Seventy-nine applications for further study or training were filed. Of these, 60 students entered college—

25 males and 35 females. Only 13 actually completed degrees, and only three of these thirteen were males.

Student Marketable Skills after Graduation

Before 1992, the Claiborne County public schools operated under a one-curriculum system designed to prepare students to attend four-year colleges and obtain baccalaureate degrees. There was no preparation to enter the workforce for those students who would not attend college. The high school taught basic vocational education courses, such as typing, industrial arts, shop, and home economics, but those courses offered little in the way of preparation for jobs or careers. Essentially, the students had no marketable skills after graduation.

In October of 1992, the Claiborne County Vocational-Technical Complex opened for the purpose of providing vocational and technical skills to students and adults. Six courses of study were offered:

1. *Intensive business training:* This program provides training in the area of microcomputers, special electronic typewriters, transcribing equipment, and record keeping. The students are able to apply their training in a simulated office.

2. *Child-care occupations:* This is a two-year program that provides training as a paraprofessional in early-childhood education.

3. *Industrial maintenance:* This program is designed to prepare students for employment as maintenance personnel for various types of industries. The program provides shop and classroom learning experiences in the areas of construction, electricity, instrumentation, plumbing, air conditioning, welding, fabrication, and custodial services.

4. *Allied health and related technology:* This program introduces the student to the health careers field, the basic health sciences, and basic skills in laboratory and clinical settings.

5. *Building trades:* This program provides students with the knowledge and skills needed to work in construction technology.

6. *Diversified technology:* This is an academically rigorous course of study comprising forty instructional modules for students planning technical careers. Twenty of the modules are studied in the twelfth grade.

The admission requirements for the vocational-technical high school program are the following: (1) eleventh- or twelfth-grade classification; (2) a recommendation by the counselor or a teacher; (3) a grade point average of 2.00 or higher; and (4) completion of algebra 1 and basic biology.

Once prepared, my report was presented to the Claiborne County Board of Supervisors, the Board of Education, the funders, and the community at large. The politics of actually beginning the work on the proposed model proved insurmountable. The superintendent had not been hired by the board of education but was, rather, a public official, and he was fervently opposed to this initiative by the County Board of Supervisors. A fragile coalition had been created to allow the study to be conducted, but the politics could not be sustained for long enough to enable the recommendations to be implemented.

These recommendations are included here to illustrate the exigencies of creating educational change in this type of community and to preserve the analysis, which might be of value in settings in which similar issues need to be considered. Although the model could not be implemented in the Claiborne County schools, I gained many insights from studying the community, which were then incorporated into my model.

Comments about implementation of the model at this point would be mere speculation. The issues surrounding implementation will be determined once the program has been piloted. I am negotiating with school districts and funding agencies to initiate this project. The model, described in detail in the next chapter, has been reviewed by educators across the country, and there is consensus that it has all the elements necessary for success.

CHAPTER 6

A Model for Culturally Appropriate Pedagogy

> *Leave no child behind.*
> —Marian Wright Edelman

The quality of education that most African American children receive today is far below that of most white American children. Representative Augustus Hawkins (D-California) succinctly states the essential question of the modern "American dilemma" as it relates to the education of African Americans in asking, "What do you do with a former slave when you no longer need his labor?" (quoted in Kozol 1991, 188). Our children are being educated in schools that deliver the girls to public assistance and the boys to unemployment and incarceration.

In my opinion, there is a wide gap between what our children are doing in school every day and what an American adult will be called upon to do in the twenty-first century to achieve economic solvency and financial independence. Jonathan Kozol notes the qualitative differences in outcome between inner-city schools and the schools of the suburban middle class:

> The children in one set of schools are educated to be governors; children in the other set of schools are trained for being governed. The former are given the imaginative range to mobilize ideas for economic growth; the latter are provided with the discipline to do the narrow tasks the first group will prescribe.

Societies cannot all be generals, no soldiers. But by our schooling patterns, we assure that soldier's children are more likely to be soldiers and that the off-spring of the generals will have at least the option to be generals. (1991, 176)

In this book, I offer a model solution that places the school at the center of the effort to achieve upward mobility for inner-city African American children. The school is the appropriate focal point because everyone is required to attend school. Everyone does not have a functional family, nor does everyone attend church; but everyone is required to attend school.

In her book *For the Children*, Madeline Cartwright reports that as a principal in an inner-city elementary school in Philadelphia, she had instructed her teachers with the following admonition: "We might not know what kind of life our youngsters had before they stepped into our school; we might not know what happened to them last night or what's going to happen to them tonight. But we *do* know what's happening to them *here* . . . and every effort will be made by every one of us to make the hours between eight and four a time when our children can be children" (Cartwright and D'Orso 1993, 144).

The model I present here has three components. The foundational component is classroom instruction; the other two components, cultural enrichment and the instructional accountability infrastructure, support instruction in the classroom (see figure 6.1). The guiding principles of the model are as follows:

1. Future success requires that children be connected to academic achievement
2. It takes a whole village to raise a child
3. Children learn what they are taught
4. School is interesting
5. Learning is fun

Classroom Instruction

The first guiding principle of the model presented here is that improvement of the quality of the future for African American children requires that they somehow become connected to academic achievement. Figure 6.2 presents

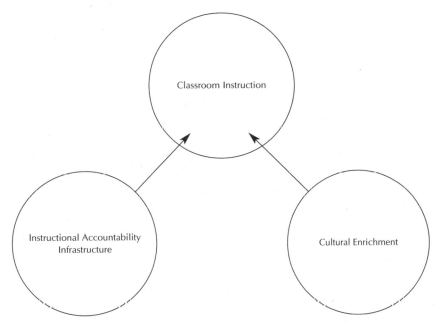

Figure 6.1   A Model of Culturally Appropriate Pedagogy

a diagram of the instructional component of this model. Most African American children, particularly African American males, do not like school. Many drop out intellectually by the time they are in the fifth grade and make it legal at sixteen years of age. People who do not finish high school and those who finish with poor records are not able to obtain jobs through which they can support themselves or their families. Children who cannot conceptualize a future for themselves do not have the motivation to defer the gratification found in premature sexual activity or substance abuse.

There are three generally recognized purposes for educating children: (1) imparting skills, such as the ability to read, write, spell, and calculate; (2) creating information growth—a cadre of knowledge about the world that most educated people know; and (3) providing children with the opportunity to develop talents and interests that can lead to fulfilling leisure time pursuits, the identification of careers, and an opportunity to make a creative contribution to the world. It is the perspective of this model that the way in which these purposes are achieved (educational strategies) is just as im-

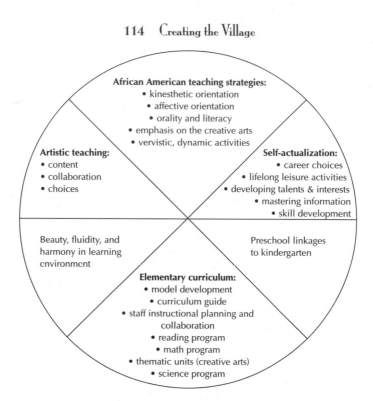

Figure 6.2   Classroom Instruction

portant as what is taught (educational content). A process of education must be crafted that motivates African American children to regard academic activities as interesting and fun. They must be guided on a journey to a lifelong love of learning.

Ralph Ellison, author of *Invisible Man*, has captured the African American craving throughout their sojourn in America for a culturally appropriate pedagogy: "If you can show me how I can cling to that which is real to me, while teaching me a way into the larger society, then I will not only drop my defenses and my hostility, but I will sing your praises and I will help to make the desert bear fruit" (1986, 75). I describe here seminal ideas for the foundation of a new model that can create an educational process for African American children that is capable of building the bridges they need to enter the twenty-first century as independent, contributing members of our society.

Theoretical Background

For the past thirty years, desegregation has been the focal point for educational reform designed to benefit African American children—despite the fact that in most urban areas with a large African American population, there has been a declining pool of white children to integrate with African American children. Other efforts at improving the academic achievement of African American children have involved remediation programs at the middle school and high school levels, with varying degrees of success. The critical issue now being raised by African American scholars is how we can create schools that educate African American children effectively wherever they are found. Central to this examination is the question of whether we can bring about an improvement in educational outcomes for African American children without recognizing their unique culture.

As researchers study the problem, they have begun to formulate theories that explain the disparity in academic achievement between African American children and white children. One theory posits a kind of "soulfulness" that characterizes African American life. African American children are exposed to a high degree of stimulation from the creative arts. They are surrounded by stimuli from the visual arts, such as posters, paintings, and graffiti; the audio arts, in the form of phonograph, radio, and tape recordings; the video arts, such as television and films; and the fashion arts, in forms such as creative hairstyles, hats, scarves, and a general orientation toward adornment of the body, an orientation that grows out of the African heritage.

The performance styles that permeate the African American community are further evidence of this affinity for the creative arts. African American children learn from an early age the significance of perfecting performer roles. This expressiveness is seen in the behavior of African American preachers, athletes, singers, and dancers and is cultivated in individuals throughout the African American community.

The scholarship reviewed in my earlier work, *Black Children: Their Roots, Culture, and Learning Styles* (Hale 1986), applies the findings of scholars in the fields of history, anthropology, psychology, linguistics, philosophy, art, and religion to the enterprise of devising educational strategies that complement African American culture and may result in educational gains for African American children. Aspects of this African American culture have been described by scholars who emphasize its roots in traditional West African culture (Perry and Delpit 1998; Hilliard 1997, 1995; Asante 1988; Gay and Baber 1987; Jones 1983; Levine 1977; Smitherman 1977; Akbar 1976; Mintz and Price 1976; Banks 1976; Dixon 1976; Gutman 1976; Wilson 1972; Young 1970). Analysis of their descriptions suggests at least nine interrelated dimensions of African American culture (outlined by Boykin [1986, 61]):

1. *spirituality*, an approach that views life as essentially vitalistic rather than mechanistic, with the conviction that nonmaterial forces influence people's everyday lives

2. *harmony*, the notion that one's fate is interrelated with other elements in the scheme of things, such that humankind and nature are harmonically conjoined

3. *movement*, an emphasis on the interweaving of rhythm, percussiveness, music, and dance as central to psychological health

4. *verve*, a propensity for relatively high levels of stimulation and for action that is energetic and lively

5. *affect*, an emphasis on emotions and feelings together with a special sensitivity to emotional cues and a tendency to be emotionally expressive

6. *communalism*, a commitment to social connectedness, which includes an awareness that social bonds and responsibilities transcend individual privileges

7. *expressive individualism*, the cultivation of a distinctive personality and a proclivity for spontaneous and genuine personal expression

8. *oral tradition*, a preference for oral and auditory modes of communication in which both speaking and listening are treated as performances and in which oral virtuosity—the ability to use alliterative, metaphorically colorful, graphic forms of spoken language—is emphasized and cultivated

9. *social time perspective*, an orientation toward time as passing through a social space rather than a material one, in which time is seen as recurring, personal, and phenomenological

Wade Boykin (1978) suggests that the average African American home environment provides an abundance of stimulation, intensity, and variation. A relatively high noise level exists, with television playing a significant portion of the time along with constant stereophonic music. Usually, large numbers of people occupy a living space, and a variety of activities are taking place.

This condition has been analyzed by some social scientists as "over-stimulation" creating "conceptual deafness" (Marans and Lourie 1967; Goldman and Sanders 1969; Wachs, Uzgiris, and Hunt 1971). However, Boykin believes this stimulating African American home environment produces a high degree of psychological and behavioral "verve" in African American children. Exposure to more constant high and variable stimulation, he argues, has led to a chronic activation level. Therefore, African American children have an increased behavioral vibrancy and an increased psychological affinity for stimulus change and intensity.

This means that African American children participate in a culture that is highly dynamic. They thrive in a setting that uses multimedia and multimodal teaching strategies. They also favor instruction that is variable, energetic, vigorous, and captivating.

It has been pointed out by a number of scholars that schools are rather unstimulating and monotonous places to be (Silberman 1970; Holt 1964). Boykin suggests that such factors as investigatory exploration, behavioral change, novelty, and variability have not been incorporated into the classroom. Boykin and colleagues have identified two groups of cultural themes and the classroom dynamics informed by these themes. The "Afro-cultural" themes are movement (which relates to the premium placed on the interwoven mosaic of expressiveness, dance, percussiveness, and rhythm), verve (a receptiveness toward relatively high levels of physical or sensate stimulation), and communalism (a sensitivity to the fundamental interdependence of people). Mainstream cultural themes are individualism (which refers to a person's disposition toward fundamental autonomy, independence, individual recognition, and solitude), competition (an individual's focus on doing better than others and the notion that for one participant to succeed, others must fail in some fashion), and bureaucratic orientation (strict adherence to structured rules and regulations, with a policy against deviation from sanctioned procedures) (Ellison et al. 2000, 4).

The Afro-cultural themes are African in origin and have been maintained and transmitted across generations in communities and families of

African descent throughout the world. He suggests that they will find some level of expression in the lives of many African American children. The mainstream cultural themes are principally of European and North American origin and are likely to be present in the major institutions of mainstream American society. "Both sets of themes may likely find expression in the lives of African American children," Boykin notes. "But given the central place of Afro-cultural themes in many African American communities and family activities, they have special developmental potency for many African American children, particularly those of low-income background who are more likely to be more distanced from mainstream values and practices" (Boykin 1994, 5).

African American Teaching Strategies

African American children are generally more kinesthetic than white children and have a higher level of motor activity (Hale 1986, 75–95). There is also medical evidence that African American males have a higher testosterone level than white males (Loscocco 1994). African American children, particularly the boys, should not be required to sit for long periods of time without an opportunity to expend energy. Learning activities should be designed that enable the children to move as they learn. Quiet activities should be alternated with active learning.

Teachers should be trained to be patient with the rambunctious and outgoing nature of African American males. Conceptualizing these behavioral styles as normal will correct present tendencies to define the behavior of African American males as pathological, needing medication and special education placement for emotional and psychological disorders (Hale 1986).

African American families exhibit a strong affective orientation in child rearing (Ellison et al. 2000). Most African American households contain a large number of people, and children are accustomed to having their learning mediated by people. African American children therefore learn best when their learning is oriented toward people rather than toward objects. They will respond best when taught in small groups with a great deal of nurturing interaction between the teacher and the child and between each child and his or her peers. Therefore, whole-class instruction groups and reading groups should be as small as possible (Hale 1986).

The large class sizes and high teacher-student ratios found in most urban school districts are major barriers to the achievement of African American children. The National Association for the Education of Young Children makes the following recommendations:

1. for four- to five-year-olds, a ratio of two adults to no more than twenty children

2. for six-, seven-, and eight-year-olds, a ratio of no more than twenty-five children for each two adults, one of whom may be a paraprofessional, and no more than eighteen children to one professional teacher

3. the grouping of children spanning two or three chronological ages, with individualized movement in separate subject matter areas

A key feature of the model presented is the use of parents and community volunteers to work with children with special needs, to reduce whole-class teaching, and to increase the ability of the teachers to work with children in small groups. The role of "relief" teachers (which is a misnomer — they should be called instructional aides) can be restructured so that they spend more time in direct instruction of children instead of the more mundane activities that engage much of their time, such as cutting out pumpkins, grading work sheets, and assisting the office clerical staff. Churches in the community can be approached to "adopt a school" and provide classroom volunteers who can give instructional support to the teacher. The churches should also be tapped to provide mentorship programs for the African American males in the school

African American culture has a strong orientation toward oral communication, whereas the dominant culture is oriented toward literacy. Early-childhood and elementary education settings should understand the strengths in orality that African American children bring to school so that teachers can connect those strengths with the literacy experiences that the schools define as intelligence (Hale 1986).

Instructional strategies should be selected in the key curricular areas that are compatible with the latest research on the learning styles of African American children (Ellison et al. 2000; Boykin and Miller 1997; Hale 1994; Hale 1986). For example, whole-language instruction in reading and writing holds a great deal of promise as a strategy that taps higher-order think ing skills as well as providing the flexibility to use literature that is culturally salient to African American children. However, it is important that this approach be teamed with a strong phonics program in the first grade.

Mathematics instruction should utilize manipulatives rather than textbooks and xeroxed sheets. Similarly, science instruction should focus on hands-on learning, emphasizing experiments, projects, and inventiveness.

Given the immersion in the creative arts that most African American children experience in their home environments (Hale 1986), infusion of the creative arts into instruction would increase the interest in activities and stimulate motivation to achieve. Waldorf education offers a good model of teacher training in which each classroom teacher masters figure drawing, clay modeling, painting, graphics, and chalkboard drawing with colored chalk, bringing the arts into all subject matter areas. Waldorf educa-

Historical Background of the Waldorf School Movement

The first Waldorf school was founded in Germany by Eli Molt, a businessman who owned the Waldorf-Astoria cigarette factory, for the children of his factory workers. Concerned about the social fragmentation and economic collapse that occurred in Europe after World War I, Molt engaged Rudolf Steiner, an Austrian philosopher, to create the approach for the school.

Steiner's educational philosophy was based on the premise that, to avoid the possibility of another global conflict, a new educational path had to be created to transform the cultural and social life of the people. This new education would devote equal attention to developing clarity of thought, sensitivity of feeling, and strength of will in the growing child. The first school was opened in 1919. The faculty was given total responsibility for administering the school and complete freedom to develop educational policies and methods.

Waldorf schools flourished and grew throughout Europe and North America until World War II, when Hitler closed all of the Waldorf schools in Germany. Many others throughout Europe were closed during the war, but after 1945 the Waldorf school movement began to grow and spread to several more continents. The international Waldorf school movement now consists of six hundred schools on seven continents.

The Waldorf Approach

Waldorf education stresses the essential dignity and individuality of the growing child. When the teaching methods of Rudolf Steiner are used, the process of education

tion also has created eurythmy, a dance-exercise modality through which the more academic aspects of the curriculum, such as language and mathematics, are taught.

Philosophical Background

Educators commonly affirm that learning environments for young children should be child centered and as homelike as possible. However, because so much scholarship has given pathological overtones to the African American home, this principle is often not applied to programs designed for African American children.

For example, as Wade Boykin has repeatedly noted, African American culture is highly dynamic (Boykin 1978, 1994; Boykin and Miller 1997; El-

becomes an art. Part of the artistry lies in the use of a curriculum that is adapted to the phases of the child's physical, psychological, intellectual, and spiritual development from kindergarten through high school. A culturally rich humanities program is combined with experientially taught sciences, foreign-language instruction, and extensive artistic experiences. Subjects are introduced and developed in a sequence that addresses the developing consciousness of the child.

During the eight years of elementary education, the children in a Waldorf school class are led by the same class teacher. The class teacher introduces them to the wonders of nature in the early grades, and the later study of science builds on this foundation. Complementing this study of the outer world is the study of the inner world—history, the story of humanity through the ages. This method of teaching from what we might call the two great books—the book of nature and the book of humankind, or civilization—fully engages, nourishes, and stimulates the unfolding of consciousness in the young child. Other teachers contribute to this process. Instruction in music, eurythmy, handwork, and foreign languages begin in the younger years, and subjects such as gymnastics, woodworking, and gardening are later added to the curriculum. In high school, teachers who specialize in the sciences and the humanities provide the students with an opportunity to integrate their academic experiences into their personal development.

I am grateful to Rene Querido, of the Detroit Waldorf School, for the information on the history and methodology of the Waldorf school movement.

lison et al. 2000). A large amount of the stimulus in the environment of African American children is variable, colorful, and rich. As pointed out above, this makes it more difficult for them to thrive under classroom instruction that is monotonous, repetitious, and static.

A model of classroom instruction for African American children should diminish the use of xeroxed work sheets, workbooks, textbooks, and a skill-and-drill orientation. Emphasis should be placed instead on hands-on activities, projects, interrelated learning experiences, field trips, speakers, and classroom visitors. The intent is to create a learning environment that complements the culture of the African American community and stimulates higher-order thinking and creativity among African American children.

When children are engaged in skill-and-drill activities throughout their educational career, they become skill-and-drill people. The model of education that guides the traditional urban schools in which most African American children are found originated in early-twentieth-century America (Comer 1988, 1997). At the height of the Industrial Revolution, there was a need for a large population of unskilled workers to occupy blue-collar positions in factories.

But times have changed. In the future, there will be little employment opportunity for poorly educated people. It is possible now to identify the characteristics that will be required for economic viability in the twenty-first century. Future jobs will require people who can think, who have imagination and can solve problems, who are creative, innovative, and have vision, who are self-starters, who can work independently or cooperatively. For many African American children being educated in urban and rural schools, the connection between the skills needed to be economically viable in the future, to function independently as adults, and to make a creative contribution to the society, on the one hand, and the abilities being developed as a part of the learning process on a daily basis in school, on the other, has been lost.

Church organizations and groups, such as the Nation of Islam, have made some well-intentioned efforts to improve educational outcomes for African American children, and, because the teachers have sincerely cared for the children and taught them conscientiously, these efforts have had some success. However, often those models were characterized by uniformed children in assigned seats, doing skill-and-drill seatwork even at young ages and receiving instruction geared to tests (instead of geared to a quality curriculum), with a rigid militaristic orientation. Those children eventually made gains when they were compared with their counterparts in traditional schools. Because there were few alternative models of instruction specifically for African American children, over time this highly structured, rigid form of education was considered "the way" to produce certain educational outcomes for African American children.

In contrast, the model I present here embraces the work of Alfie Kohn (1993). Kohn proposes that intrinsic motivation is developed in learners by giving attention to the notion of what I call artistic teaching, in which children are motivated by the interesting manner in which content is presented, are given opportunities to explore ideas and content in meaningful collaboration with their teachers and peers, and are presented with choices in the curriculum.

This model is designed in such a way that the children receive a multidisciplinary exposure to the curriculum, enabling them to develop their interests and talents in the process of mastering information and skills. The identification of talents and interests is the first step toward building careers that lead to lifelong personal satisfaction and self-actualization.

The time has come for educators to think about the kinds of people we are trying to produce through the educational process. For example, many school districts use the slogan, "Every child can learn." That sounds like a beautiful, inspirational sentiment on first reading. However, it is a passive goal. It suggests that every child can learn if someone decides to teach him or her. When "Every child can learn" is considered next to "Leave no child behind," it seems condescending and one-dimensional.

More attention needs to be given to the kinds of African American children we are trying to produce. We must ask whether we are interested in educating our African American children to have a creative impact on our society or whether, instead, we intend for them to iron other people's clothes and serve only as consumers and a reserve labor force.

Peter Jennings (1993), in an ABC documentary on the "revolution" in American education, observed that "education is how a society hands out its life chances. How it gives people options. Philosophers sometimes say the best definition of freedom is a good range of options. A new revolution in learning would give many more Americans real freedom." The time has come to clarify the values we want to permeate the educational process. Most Americans would probably agree that the schools should produce citizens who are responsible and honorable. The words of W. E. B. Du Bois, written in 1906, still ring true today:

> When we call for education, we mean real education. We believe in work. We ourselves are workers, but work is not necessarily education. Education is the development of power and ideal. We want our children trained as intelligent human beings should be, and we will fight for all time against any proposal to educate black boys and girls simply as servants and underlings, or simply for the use of other people. They have a right to know, to think, to aspire. (1968, 251)

Development of the Elementary Curriculum

A curriculum guide is an essential document that enables teachers to crystallize an approach to learning; it provides a statement of the content of instruction. Such a document can also serve as a spiritual focus that gives the school an identity and a vision. The guide should include a statement of the school's vision and program objectives as well as the following information:

—*Philosophical and theoretical framework:* This will present those constructs that guide teachers' decisions regarding what is taught and how it is taught. Philosophical ideals address what we believe we "should" do for children; theoretical issues refer to what we conclude is true about how children learn.

—A *statement of goals for children in the various curricular areas and at different stages in their development:* The language that describes these is fairly abstract ("aesthetic appreciation," "fluency of written expression," "mathematical problem solving," for example).

—A *description of what the school considers to be necessary knowledge and skills:* For each curricular area and at various grades, the language that describes these expectations is more concrete and detailed. These are the objectives we hope the children will attain ("recognizing beginning and ending sounds," "letter formation," "writing in paragraph form," and "computing multiplication algorithms involving two and three digits" are a few examples).

—*Evaluation strategies*: The guide should describe how the teachers monitor child learning during instruction and how they provide feedback to the children (*Roeper City and Country School Curriculum Guide* 1993).

Public schools do not generally provide such a guide, though private schools commonly do. The work teachers do in creating such a guide involves them in clarifying their objectives. Too often public schools consider themselves to be teaching whatever their textbook series teaches in each subject matter area. This alternative mission of the school is enhanced when a unifying vision is committed to paper.

Daily opening exercises, such as those practiced in Waldorf schools, should be created for the children at each grade level. These activities include poems, songs, and physical activities that enhance concentration and focus the children's minds and bodies spiritually, ideologically, and physically for the work of the day.

Teachers of preschool children should be involved in curriculum planning along with grade school teachers. One component of successful adjustment for children is to create continuity between the preschool and grade school curriculum and instruction. A curriculum guide should be used for the preschool program in the elementary school that clearly states the philosophy, goals, objectives, and evaluation strategies, such as the preschool curriculum, "Visions for Children," described in *Unbank the Fire* (Hale 1994, 169–88).

A companion piece to the creation of the culturally appropriate pedagogy is the identification of elementary reading, science and mathematics programs that will achieve the optimal outcomes for African American children.

Reading Program

Whole language is a program of instruction in which the teacher stimulates literacy through literature that is read aloud to the children instead of using basal readers with controlled vocabulary. Whole-language instruction also offers the attraction of providing involvement with rich, colorful literature that is intrinsically motivating and interesting to children. On the other hand, there is strong evidence that children benefit from the solid structure of linguistic knowledge that stems from a good background in phonics, although a heavy reliance on phonics to the exclusion of the higher-level thinking skills associated with reading often penalizes African American children in the intermediate grades.

Therefore, this model involves teachers in considering the merits of both approaches and in creating a fine-tuned instructional balance that meets the individual needs of the children. Cultural salience is particularly important for African American male children. It is critical to expose them to written material that is stimulating and interesting to them. This can be a bridge that leads them to reading literature that is more Eurocentric — the absorption of which is rewarded on standardized tests.

This is a good place to interject a tenth episode, which I experienced with my son in the third grade. During a parent-teacher conference, Keith's teacher told me that he does not like to read. When the children were instructed to select a book for their monthly book report, Keith was always the last one to select a book. On occasion, two weeks of the month would have passed before he had selected a book. When the class took field trips to the library, he most often came back empty-handed, while some of his classmates would have selected ten books.

As usual, this information was imparted to me with a blank stare, dumped in my lap with an expression that said, "Don't pass Go, don't collect 200 dollars, go straight to jail!" No suggestions were forthcoming, and the information was issued, as always, as an indictment.

My response was, "If he says that he does not like to read, it is because of what you have over here for him to read!" Here is a child who was read to every day of his life. I purchased books for him before he was born, books with only one word on each page. Now, at eight years old, he does not like to read?

His teachers were very innovative in assigning monthly categories for book reports. I took him to the bookstore and spent an hour helping him select his book. (The books in the library were old and were less appealing.) It was always possible to fit his interests into the category. For example, for the category "women at work," we selected Oprah Winfrey; for the category "a child in an exotic setting," we selected an adventure story about an

African girl. I also selected books for him by Walter Dean Myers, who writes stories for preadolescent boys about basketball and inner-city adventures. It was during this episode that I discovered that boys in general are reluctant readers at this age. By providing him with culturally salient reading material, I was able to connect my son to the joy of reading.

Later, I also encouraged him to sign up for enrichment classes that were offered in Shakespeare's plays and the legends of King Arthur. When he walked into the class on Shakespeare, the enrichment teacher exclaimed, "Keith, what are you doing here!" He was the only boy in the class; the other children were white girls.

One of my friends, Caroline Jackson, who majored in English literature at Yale University, told me that she could ensure any student good scores on the Scholastic Aptitude Test (SAT) and Graduate Record Examination by sequestering the student in her apartment for a year and requiring him or her to read one Victorian novel every week. This would enable the absorption of the Anglo Saxon vocabulary and culture that would assure a good score on the test. Although cultural salience is critical to connecting "reluctant" readers to reading, it is also important to move them along to Anglo-Saxon literature eventually.

Teachers should explore the merits of involving children in everything whole-language proponents recommend from birth to kindergarten: "big books," conversation, coziness, and verbal reasoning. Included would be dictated stories, handwriting, alphabet recognition, and identification of beginning sounds of words. From kindergarten through third grade, regular, daily multisensory training, such as phonetic sounds and word decoding, would be added to the playful literary offerings, making them equal partners in teaching.

Leaving nothing to chance, a third wave of effort is suggested for children who are not able to read when they enter school, to complement the activity of the teachers in the classroom. That third wave would be tutoring by a family member, an older student in the school, a college student, or a member of the community, using an individualized program such as Hooked on Phonics. The rationale for this component is presented later, in the discussion of the instructional accountability infrastructure. Also discussed in that section is the institution of a monitoring system in which no child is left reading below grade level. This monitoring program, instituted by the school and the community, will provide the support that middle-class parents routinely provide for their children. It is my firm conviction that the vast majority of our educational problems would be solved if schools would commit themselves to making sure that, beginning in the first grade, every child is reading at grade level.

John H. McWhorter, an African American professor at the University of California, Berkeley, argues in his book *Losing the Race* (2000) that most black students do not work as hard as white or Asian students. He suggests that it is because the culture they come from fails to give as high a priority to academic achievement and partly because many of their peers regard academic striving as "acting white." This perspective stands in contrast with the thesis of this book. My point is that the schools are not connecting African American children to academic achievement.

African American children work very hard in certain arenas, such as sports and entertainment, for which there is intrinsic motivation. In most cases, the instruction in schools is not culturally salient for African American children, and opportunities are overlooked for which culturally salient content and modes of instruction can be used to motivate them to embrace academic tasks. Episode ten is an illustration: my son would have been dismissed as a nonreader if I had not stepped in to show his teacher that, given books that stimulated his interest, he would readily embrace reading.

Mathematics Program

The mathematics program must involve the children in hands-on active involvement with materials rather than relying on textbooks and paper-and-pencil activities. Mathematics activities should also be integrated in all possible aspects of the children's day—record keeping, measuring, estimating, weighing, and so forth.

It is also recommended that teachers visit mathematics magnet schools that are equipped with mathematics labs and explore the value of setting up such a center in their school. There should also be a monitoring and tutoring component for each classroom in mathematics, possibly using an individual program such as Hooked on Math, taught by a family member, an older student, or a member of the community. This monitoring system in mathematics will operate to insure that no child is left behind, performing below grade level, in mathematics.

Science Program

The science program, too, should emphasize hands-on instruction and minimize the use of textbooks, except as resources. The scientific method should be emphasized, including observation, measurement (including estimation), inference, and experiment design. An important focus should be on creativity and inventiveness.

Justifiably, a large proportion of time in elementary school classrooms is spent on the acquisition of reading and mathematics skills. However, curriculum planning should go beyond what in many cases is mere skill-and-drill learning in those areas. A useful vehicle for broadening instruction to provide comprehensive education for children is the creation of thematic units that extend over a two-week period. The units should be developed by the teachers jointly under the leadership of the principal or the instructional coordinator. Thematic units should be created by elementary school teachers in the areas of social studies and science, which will incorporate the arts and multicultural modalities for instruction. Units developed in the social studies will include subject matter related to African American culture.

The format for the units should be designed in such a way that the instruction incorporates multicultural modalities that nurture multiple intelligences, as suggested by the work of Howard Gardner (1983, 1999). Gardner suggests that Western social scientists have a narrow conception of intelligence. Most intelligence tests assess an individual's abilities only in the areas of linguistic and logical-mathematical intelligence.

Gardner identifies five more varieties of intelligence. Spatial intelligence has at its core the ability to find one's way around in an environment, to form mental images, and to transform mental images into physical ones; this intelligence can be expressed in visual art. Musical intelligence is expressed in the ability to perceive and create pitch and rhythmic patterns. Bodily-kinesthetic intelligence is revealed in gifted fine-motor movement, as seen in a surgeon, or gifted gross-motor movement, as seen in a dancer or an athlete. Interpersonal intelligence involves understanding others — how they feel, what motivates them, how they interact; this realm of intelligence is expressed in social skills. Intrapersonal intelligence refers to an individual's ability to be acquainted with himself or herself, to have a well developed sense of identity.

Gardner urges consideration of the range of human faculties in any assessment of intelligence and in efforts to develop human potential. These seven forms of intelligence are equally important, Gardner believes, and even if they do not exhaust all possible forms of knowing, they at least offer us a more comprehensive picture of intelligence than we have previously had.

Gardner addresses the fact that the SAT and IQ test scores reward children who are able to give quick responses to short-answer questions. In the short run, these tests can predict the children who will do well in school. (I submit, though, that they do not predict as accurately those who will not do well.) However, he maintains, the tests do not have good predictive value for what happens beyond school because there is only a modest correlation between scores on IQ tests and success in the professions.

The thematic units would be designed so that opportunities for learning would incorporate the five neglected intelligences outlined by Gardner: spatial intelligence, through the visual arts; musical intelligence, through composition and interpretation; bodily intelligence, through athletics and dance; interpersonal intelligence, through attention to social skills; and intrapersonal intelligence, through attention to the formation of each child's personal identity. The units will serve as a vehicle for increasing students' vocabulary and level of information and knowledge about the world, broadening the practice of reading and mathematics skills into a truly well-rounded educational experience, and providing them with an opportunity to identify talents and interests they can develop and extend into meaningful work. Someone said that you should love the work you do so much that you would do it for free, but you do it so well that people pay you to do it.

Infusion of African and African American Culture into the Units

The thematic units can be utilized as a vehicle for infusing cultural salience into the curriculum. In-service training should be designed to familiarize teachers with the multidisciplinary basics of African American culture. This broad framework will enable teachers to incorporate the folklore, artistic artifacts, proverbs, literature, music, and history of Africans of the diaspora whenever possible. Thematic units also provide the vehicle for infusing the curriculum with the culture of any other ethnic groups represented in the classroom; they are an excellent multicultural vehicle.

Evaluation will be enhanced by employing portfolio assessments in which a child's work is collected and progress and growth are measured over time. The bell-curve grading system should be eliminated, particularly in elementary school, and the emphasis should be on mastery of criterion-referenced material and growth of skills and abilities.

A central element of the Waldorf methodology is "bookwork," in which the children create their own workbooks, recording the work they do in units not only graphically but also artistically. Their illustrated books constitute a record of their work in each subject area and at every grade level.

Beauty and Harmony in the Learning Environment

Many classrooms in inner-city settings in which African American children are educated are overly institutional and often stark in decor. An important activity for teachers of this model will be to arrange the classrooms so that the environment is aesthetically pleasing to the children.

Unbank the Fire includes photographs of elementary school classrooms that present an alternative to desks and chairs lined up in a row facing the blackboard. These classrooms look like living rooms, furnished with sofas, easy chairs, and rocking chairs. There are rugs on the floor, and the children work at small tables in groups of four to six instead of at individual desks (Hale 1994, 210–12).

Classrooms at the Detroit Waldorf School have nature tables, which serve as a spiritual focal point of the classroom. Framed paintings, including nature scenes and the children's art, give the rooms a peaceful harmonious tone.

Instructional Accountability Infrastructure

The second component of the model of culturally appropriate pedagogy presented here is an accountability system that maintains instructional standards within the school at the classroom level, where education is delivered (see figure 6.3). Misguided attempts have been made to influence educational outcomes by wielding bigger and more intimidating baseball bats at school systems, including publishing test scores, placing school systems on probation, firing superintendents, reconstituting schools, creating diplomas of attendance for people who do not qualify for a high school

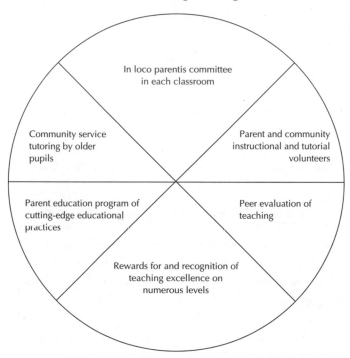

Figure 6.3   Instructional Accountability Infrastructure

diploma, creating ever more intimidating tests for rising juniors (new eleventh-graders) to penalize the children who have not been taught enough to pass the tests, and creating charter schools to bypass entire school districts.

It is the perspective of this model that a supervisory system that incorporates evaluation, training, and rewards needs to be instituted at the building level so that excellent instruction is delivered to all children. This infrastructure functions on its own in schools attended by children whose families are connected to the "culture of power" (Delpit 1988, 1995). The very fact that those families can exercise choice in selection by removing their children and placing them in private schools, or that they already have, causes schools to maintain practices that are competitive. In inner-city schools, the children receive whatever the professionals deem appropriate to provide for them.

With the siphoning off of the creative teachers and administrators who are drawn to innovative programs, I do not believe that charter schools and school vouchers will cause inner-city schools to improve under competition. School vouchers are essentially a tuition relief for those parents who can afford private schools. Parents who cannot afford private schools will not be able to provide the necessary supplement to the vouchers nor the transportation to schools that are far from home.

This component is designed to incorporate practices into the school that provide teachers with instructional support. These practices include recruiting other adults who can assist them in working with children in small groups and individually; instituting peer evaluation of teaching so that good teaching practices become a part of the culture of the school through peer reinforcement rather than in response to directives from above; rewarding teachers for excellent outcomes for children on numerous levels, including the intellectual growth of individual children under their care; involving parents in in-service training and observation of schools in which cutting-edge practices are employed; encouraging older children in the school to donate time to work with younger children; and identifying a church that will adopt the school and provide community volunteers for tutoring, male mentoring, prevention of teen pregnancy, and enrichment activities.

Theoretical Underpinnings

Educators constantly decry the fact that parents of lower-income children tend to be uninvolved in the schools; many do not attend parent conferences or even review their children's progress reports. This situation is often described by exasperated teachers who feel that too much is expected of them when they lack the support from parents that is customary in school districts serving white middle-class children. The past thirty years have seen major upheavals in child-rearing practices and parental education among white middle-class families that need to be understood if those who are involved in educating lower-income and African American children are to understand what they are up against.

Almost twenty years ago, a cover story in *Newsweek*, titled "Bringing Up Superbaby," analyzed the forces that have influenced white middle-class parents (Langway et al. 1983). The creation of the Head Start program in the 1960s brought to the public an awareness of how much young children desire stimulation and want to learn. This interest in how to get lower-income African American children on the right track early grew out of the protests (also called riots) in urban areas. White middle-class families began to realize that the preschool experience was important for advantaged children, as well, and early-childhood education as we know it was born.

However, they took this interest in early-childhood education a step further, and thus the "superbaby" phenomenon was born. Affluent families began to play music to babies in utero and to use flash cards to teach infants to read. Baby gymnasiums were created to work off baby fat, and elite preschools were opened, with admission requirements of letters of reference and intelligence test scores for two-year-olds.

There began to be a shift in the amount of time and energy affluent parents spent providing enrichment activities for their children. These parents left nothing to chance. They did not depend upon the schools to teach their children to read and calculate. The children came to school reading, having been taught by their mothers. This commitment to education was expressed in the affluent public suburban school systems by parents who formed parent councils and volunteered to provide the programs they desired. Those who could afford private education created schools for gifted children to provide the enrichment they desired. Many of these families have turned to homeschooling, however, because it allows them control over their children's education, which they primarily consider their own responsibility.

These parents have upped the ante in the past thirty years. Suburban public school systems and private schools cannot take all the credit for soaring standardized test scores based upon the activity of the professionals in the classrooms alone. These jobs are plum teaching positions because the teachers have to focus not so much on teaching the basic skills as on enhancing the learning of children who come to school already motivated and involved in the process of learning.

When the parents desire more than the professionals offer, a cadre of white, non-wage-earning mothers can enter the schools as volunteers to complement the offerings of the schools. It is they who create the Math Pentathlon, Odyssey of the Mind, publishing centers, and science fairs. Furthermore, the schools are pressured to be conversant with options such as homeschooling and the exodus to private schools because many of the families in affluent school districts choose these paths. A major exodus from the public schools would be a threat to public financial support of the schools and property values in those communities.

In inner-city communities, the families that are served by the public schools cannot as readily withdraw their children and enroll in private schools. The working poor lack the time (Toppo 2000) and often the skills for homeschooling. Therefore, the schools that serve inner-city children are not motivated to maintain the standards of the best schools in the community by fear of a mass exodus to those schools by their constituents.

It cannot be emphasized too strongly here the advantage white middle-class children enjoy when the family can be supported entirely or mostly by the earnings of the father alone (Conley 1999). This means that white middle-class mothers, who are usually well educated, are free from the need to earn salaries and can devote their talents and energy to raising and educating their children. Although mothers in middle-class African American families are often as well educated as white middle-class women, they usually contribute at least half of the income necessary to sustain their families. Because of the economic disparity between the incomes of African American males and white males, more pressure is placed on African American mothers to direct their energy toward producing income. African Americans and Hispanics have to work more hours (on average, nine hours more each week) to earn the same amount of money as white Americans (Toppo 2000).

Approximately 17 percent of white families are headed by a single female, compared with 65 percent of African American families (more telling yet, 85 percent of African American children in school live in female-headed households) (Schomburg Center 1999, 130). Whether they are married or not, African American mothers are not positioned to provide homeschooling and the extraordinary enrichment opportunities that are becoming routine for their white counterparts.

An instructional accountability infrastructure is needed for school systems that serve low-income African American and poor children. Instead of bemoaning the disparity in parental involvement in African American and lower-income school districts, educators should accept the realities: that the energies of middle-class African American mothers are greatly divided between demanding jobs and pressures to sustain their families and their communities; that the time of working poor African American mothers is limited by time-consuming modes of transportation and usually low-paying jobs that offer minimal benefits and no vacations or provisions for respite; that African American mothers on public assistance often were and are teen mothers with low levels of education, sometimes abuse substances, often are abused by men, and have a compendium of pressures and problems that keep them from conforming to traditional models of parent involvement (Billingsley 1992). The instructional accountability infrastructure would create an apparatus to ensure excellence within the school that emerges from an understanding of the existential situation of the parents.

Leadership

A central problem in educating inner-city children is the number of children who fall through the cracks and accumulate academic failure year after year. As a supervisor of student teachers in inner-city schools, I have mused about the question of who is supervising the teachers. The "Ozzie and Harriet" approach to schooling calls for the parents to supervise their child's teachers to obtain the desired services.

Parents who operate under a great deal of stress and who have not achieved a high level of education themselves often do not know how to prevent a child's failure. It seems to me that the answer in schools with a large "at-risk" population is for an infrastructure to be built from within, one in which that function is served by the professionals who are paid to maintain educational standards. At present, school reformers are asking the parents of poor children to turn into something they are not and function like white upper-income parents.

When there is no instructional accountability infrastructure in the schools, teachers have a great deal of discretion regarding whether a child will be allowed to fail and be retained at grade level or fail and be socially promoted. These problems become cumulative and almost impossible to rectify at higher grade levels.

A friend who teaches chemistry in an inner-city high school has observed that 25 percent of the children in her class cannot read the chemistry book, and so she has to design instruction for tenth-graders at a nonreading level.

She blames the parents for the fact that the attendance of children in her school drops off dramatically in the eighth grade; by ninth grade half of the students have dropped out permanently.

I asked her to go with me for a visit to the first grade in the elementary school that feeds her high school, to observe the children who, nine or ten years hence, will be her chemistry students. They want to learn. However, many of these children are not being taught to read at grade level. Teaching reading is hard work. Many children who are not taught to read by their parents before entering school fall through the cracks. Class sizes in the first through third grades should be reduced, in recognition of the challenges teachers face in helping children achieve grade-level performance.

School reformers generally focus on the credentialing and licensing of teachers and on the use of standardized tests to improve performance, but the solution will not be found along those lines. I have taught in colleges of education for twenty-six years. One look at the curriculum that teachers must master reveals that teachers in training are taking plenty of courses and are having plenty of field experiences. One look at the numbers of degrees and postgraduate courses of the teachers in most elementary schools is evidence enough that taking courses and obtaining credentials is not the answer.

The answer is found in supervision and instructional leadership within the school once teacher training has been completed. If there is any problem with training, that problem is found in the training of *principals* in urban school systems. Most principals were trained before the current movement to empower schools and decentralize authority came into vogue. Less supervisory support is coming from central offices, and more and more schools are being given their own budgets and encouraged to operate as self-contained units.

In a large school district in southeastern Michigan where the mayor was given control of the schools, a local university offered to provide training to principals in managing the business affairs of a school building, such as preparing budgets, overseeing repairs, and coordinating contractors. The university was silent, however, on the issue of preparing principals to provide instructional leadership and remedy the problems in the classroom that are at the heart of it all.

Very little course work in colleges of education is devoted to training principals to be *instructional leaders*. Consequently, following human nature, they will tend to do what they do well: discipline the children, make sure the buses are on time, supervise cafeteria noise and efficiency, conduct PTA meetings, and so forth. It is imperative that administration and supervision programs within colleges of education be redesigned to train principals to function in providing instructional leadership with minimal central-office support.

Where parents have the skills to supervise the teachers to the benefit of their individual children, things do not fall apart. However, in schools in which the parents have neither the inclination nor the skills to play that role, the principals can make the difference in whether children succeed, fail with retention, or fail with social promotion.

Politicians are coming up with bigger and better baseball bats with which to *penalize* the children because no one has taught them. In Michigan, a bill was passed this year to prevent children from moving to higher grade levels if they have not mastered the requisite skills. Most states have "rising junior" examinations, which determine whether the students will receive diplomas of high school completion or diplomas of attendance. These activities are engaged in because no one wants—or knows how—to penetrate the classroom.

When I speak with administrators of school districts, I hear unbelievable solutions—giving teachers vacations as prizes for stimulating student achievement, having principals write ever more complex educational plans (that sit on the shelf unimplemented) as solutions. I call this the carrot-and-stick approach, granting prizes to underachieving teachers and increasing standardized testing of children. School reform should not be approached from the outside, in the form of rewards to teachers for good performance and punishments to students if they are allowed to fall between the cracks. School reform should be centered within the classroom. The focus should not be solely on child outcomes but on the processes that produce those outcomes. Someone other than the child's parent has got to enter the classroom and work with teachers to give them the supervision and support they need on a regular basis to produce those outcomes.

The model I am proposing maintains that someone within the building must step up to serve the function of the instructional leader for the teachers. Ideally, that person should be the principal. However, an assistant principal, or a staff person who is designated as an instructional coordinator, could also fulfill the purpose. The instructional leader will work with teachers to plan units of instruction; observe teachers on a regular basis; and then meet with teachers, giving feedback on instruction and providing resources to improve on weaknesses.

It is important to emphasize the planning function of this instructional leader. The doors of the classrooms need to be opened, and teachers need to plan instructional experiences and strategies together with other teachers at the same grade level or along curriculum content areas. The principal (instructional leader) in this school will spend time observing in every classroom and comparable time conferencing with teachers on the basis of the observations. The principal will also be the building-level person who monitors the outcomes for the children, reviewing reports of the activities of the in loco parentis committee and the cultural enrichment committee to identify any children who are falling through the cracks.

The In Loco Parentis Committee

A key feature of this component, the in loco parentis committee, would monitor the children's progress and provide the support each child needs to perform at grade level. A committee would be created for each classroom, comprising a teacher who teaches the same grade, a volunteer from the community (drawn, perhaps, from the church that has adopted the school), and a parent representative who has a child in the classroom. This committee would meet with the teacher at regular intervals and evaluate each child who is not performing on grade level in reading or mathematics to determine whether the child needs private tutoring, counseling, or alternative instructional strategies (with no stigma attached), in the same way middle-class families intervene when their children are not progressing normally in school. The in loco parentis committee also keeps the principal apprised of the progress of children who are not performing at grade level.

In other words, the school will take responsibility for the children who traditionally fall through the cracks. This team of teachers and volunteers will evaluate the extent to which the family can provide intervention such as tutoring. The tutor could be a grandparent, an older sibling, an uncle,

aunt, or cousin. Anyone willing to tutor could be given the necessary training and support.

If it is determined that there is no family member who can be depended
upon, the committee can look within the school. Older children in the
school (or at a higher grade level outside the school but within the school
district) could be involved in a program of community service wherein they
allocate a percentage of their time weekly to enrich the school, tutoring
younger children in basic skills.

Other parents in the school could be involved in volunteer efforts to
tutor children who need one-on-one support. Their own children would

---

Definition and History of the Term *In Loco Parentis*

Parents have the ultimate legal authority for the education of their children. The
schools have authority over the children in loco parentis, that is, "in place of the parents." The concept of in loco parentis dates back to an old English law that gave
schoolmasters power over pupil behavior to whatever extent necessary to control
conduct within the school. According to Mary Lou Fuller and Glenn Olsen, "Parents
could never give up all authority over their child because of the 'natural relation of
parent and child . . . the tenderness which the parent feels for his offspring, an affec-
tion ever on the alert, and acting rather by instinct than reasoning' (*Lander v. Seaver*,
1859)" (1998, 210).

The school and the teachers act in loco parentis in relation to children while they
are in school, taking responsibility for their safety, welfare, and education. Although
parents are required to send their children to school, in compliance with state com-
pulsory attendance laws, they do not entirely abdicate their authority over the up-
bringing of their children. "The issue becomes one of finding the balance between
the school's right and responsibility[,] delegated to it by the state, to prepare children
to be knowledgeable, productive citizens of a democratic society and the parents'
right and responsibility[,] inherent because of their being parents, to guide the up-
bringing of their children" (ibid.). The legal issues between parents and schools are
based upon the tensions between certain rights and responsibilities that the state del-
egates to the schools.

I call the classroom committee the *in loco parentis committee* to recognize that it
may be necessary for teachers or committee members to intervene in response to a
child's failure when a parent fails to do so. Teachers must do what is necessary for the
success of a child, in some cases, in place of the parents.

benefit because more of the teacher's time could be directed toward enrichment rather than remedial activities in the classroom.

Volunteers in the community could be recruited from sororities, fraternities, or church and civic groups that are receptive toward adopting schools and providing support and service. Many organizations have an untapped willingness to adopt schools. However, the schools need to structure programs such as this so that their energies can be used more effectively.

One benefit of this component is that virtually no cash is required to implement these changes. What is involved is a restructuring and creative use of the resources that are readily available.

I want to see educators replace the slogans "Children learn what they live" and "Every child can learn" with two new slogans: "Leave no child behind" and "Children learn what they are taught." The first is the rallying cry of the Children's Defense Fund. The second is a phrase that came to my mind during the spelling-group episode described in chapter 4, in speaking with my son's teacher, who was trying to blame him because he did not know something. I exclaimed that I had worked with Keith on academic tasks and discovered that he could learn whatever he was taught. If he did not know something, it was because no one had taught him. His educational potential was not in question. The only issue we had to resolve was which of us was going to teach him. I also would like to see schools broadcast the proclamation, "We are family"! You can go ahead and play the recording by Sister Sledge!

At Yale University, instead of fraternities there are secret societies, the most prestigious of which is Scull and Bones. Former president George H. W. Bush is a member, as are other illustrious white males who have held leadership roles in America. The rumor is that members of Scull and Bones have the assurance that their lifetime incomes will never fall below a certain level. They are in "the Family."

The same thing can be said about upper-class families. Many of their children are given trust funds, and though the impetus is to raise children who are independent, contributing members of society, once they are in "the Family" they are all provided with safety nets. I am proposing that we create an academic safety net for every child in the school. Any child who enrolls in this school is "in the Family" and will not be left behind.

Cultural Enrichment

The creation of a model of cultural enrichment for the children to complement the instructional efforts of the school is the final component of this model (figure 6.4). This will be accomplished through the involvement of key segments of the community, such as parents, churches, and civic and business sectors, in engaging the children in extracurricular and cocurricular activities that promote upward mobility. The participants in the project will identify the resources in the school's community, such as the African American churches, the YMCA, and recreational programs, in an effort to harness the resources that already exist in the community.

There is active debate about which influence is more important, the instructional activity of the teacher at school or the contribution of the parent, in fostering school readiness. It is the position of this project that both of these influences are critical to the success of a child in school. An oft-

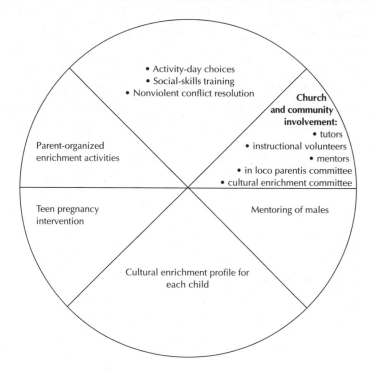

Figure 6.4　Cultural Enrichment

quoted African proverb says that it takes a whole village to raise a child. The cultural enrichment component is designed to bring that concept into form.

This component addresses the need for the child to become the canvas for the artistic work of the teacher. Inner-city children cannot be connected to the future if they participate in unsupervised street life at home and receive instruction in school that does not motivate them. It is important to provide enrichment activities for the children by providing those activities at school and also by orienting the parents to those opportunities that are available and to the importance of getting their children involved.

The arena of human activity that enables children to develop social and political skills, to identify talents and interests that can lead to satisfying leisure time activities and careers, and to find meaning in their daily lives does not come from the activities that children engage in in the classroom—at least not in the classrooms that serve inner-city African American children. These skills are developed through enriching activities outside the classroom. Therefore, it is essential that inner-city children be given an opportunity to participate in activities that enable them, in the words of Howard Thurman (1980), the African American theologian and mystic, to identify the genuine in themselves.

Male Mentoring

Through the cultural enrichment component of the project, all of the programs offered in the school and in the community will be identified. In some cases suggestions will be made so that the services are extended to create a more formal relationship with the school. For example, many African American churches are providing programs involving mentoring and rites of passage to African American boys between the ages of ten and eighteen.

A classroom teacher, a building principal, or a superintendent of a school district can ask for the name of the family's pastor of every mother who is raising a male child as a single parent. The educator can then host a social event to bring together the pastors represented in their classroom, building, or school district, asking each pastor to identify decent men in their churches who might serve as mentors to individual boys. The educator can then structure contacts between the boys and the mentors. The school would keep on file the names of the mentors and pastors of each boy, and, when particular boys need support in the case of disciplinary referrals or poor academic performance, the mentors and pastors could be included in conferences and in designing solutions.

Teen Pregnancy Intervention

Teen pregnancy among African Americans severely impairs the ability of families to fulfill their functions. Something must be done to reverse the trend of the intergenerational transmission of premature parenthood. A concerted community response to this problem is required. A significant intervention needs to be designed to make a long-term impact. This intervention should begin at the age of nine years old.

Cultural Enrichment Profile

A cultural enrichment profile for each child in the school will need to be created, recording the involvement of the child in cocurricular, extracurricular, church, and civic activities that foster the intellectual enrichment and social and political skills he or she will need to achieve upward mobility later in life. Many churches, schools, and communities pride themselves on the enrichment and character-building activities they offer for children. However, it is important to determine which children are taking advantage of those offerings. It may be that a small group of children are involved, but the majority are not. It is also important to determine the categories of participation. Are the children involved in athletic activities exclusively? Is there a balance between sports and participation in debate, literary societies, art classes, science enrichment, drama guilds, music, dance, and civic organizations?

On a speaking engagement to a city in Michigan some years ago, I spoke with a school administrator who reviewed the extracurricular and cocurricular activities of African American children. She discovered upon close examination that the participation of both boys and girls was overwhelmingly related to sports. Again, balance is important.

The human experiences that enable a child to make an impact on the world and a creative contribution to society do not occur exclusively in the classroom. Extracurricular and cultural activities play a large part in the identification and development of children's talents and interests that enhance their self-esteem and enable them to become high achievers.

Teachers will also utilize this profile in conferencing with parents. Parents will be apprised of activities that are available in the school and community, and they will be encouraged to involve their children in participation.

Parent-Organized Enrichment Activities

Linkages will be created among parents so that they can trade services with one another to provide affordable cultural activities for their children. One parent may be able to provide piano lessons in exchange for sewing lessons provided by another parent. An organization modeled after the African American social club, Jack and Jill, can be created within the school in which the parents plan cultural excursions within the metropolitan area to broaden the exposure of their children.

An organization of this type will teach parents how to identify cultural experiences in the community and will expand the focus of traditional parent organizations that serve as fundraisers. It will also help the families get to know one another and network as they work together to enrich their children's lives and experiences. These goals will be achieved by the establishment of a cultural enrichment committee in each classroom, composed of community volunteers (from the church and business community), teachers, and parents. The cultural enrichment committee will be supervised by the person in the building who serves the function of the instructional leader.

Choices

The concept of offering children choices, mentioned previously in the instructional model as a feature of artistic teaching, is also a part of the cultural enrichment component. Providing children with some choice strengthens their interest in creative and academic activities. Allowing them to choose which topics they will study in greater depth or the manner in which subjects will be explored strengthens intrinsic motivation and connects them to academic achievement.

One progressive private school in Michigan provides free-choice selections to children beginning at the age of three. By the time the children are seven years of age, the forty-five-minute free-choice time is extended to ten-week courses, with four sign-up periods a year. One public school in Michigan has free-choice periods every Friday morning. Another school I have visited creates an "activity day" beginning at 2:00 every Thursday. In each classroom, children select from an array of extracurricular and cocurricular activities. The teachers report that they have 100 percent attendance on Thursdays because the children treasure the activities. On one occasion, I was told, one boy who had been absent on that day showed up at 2:00 for the beginning of the free-choice activities!

Social Skills and Nonviolent Conflict Resolution

One of the results of the changing configuration of the American family at the beginning of the twenty-first century is that many are not fulfilling the functions of families in years gone by. This is particularly evident in the social skills children bring, or fail to bring, to school.

James Comer (1988, 1997; Comer et al. 1996; Comer et al. 1999) points out that a key element of academic achievement in schoolchildren is the ability to elicit a positive response from school personnel and peers. This requires a high level of social skill. Often the parents of inner-city children were unsuccessful in negotiating the schools themselves and therefore are unable to impart those skills to the children. Consequently, an important feature of the cultural enrichment component is the identification and development of a social-skills curriculum.

A companion effort will be the development of a curriculum for nonviolent conflict resolution. When children are educated in an environment in which they are respected as human beings capable of making choices and their developmental characteristics are honored, they will eventually respond by respecting other people and property in their environment. Too often, inner-city children are treated harshly, punished corporally, and denied an opportunity to express their feelings constructively. They then vent their frustrations on those closest to them and on their own environment. This model seeks to construct a different climate, one in which the children will be engaged in a dialogue that opens up a different way for them to be in the world.

Current Reform Proposals

The culturally appropriate pedagogy model of school reform suggests that three spheres of activity must be addressed to close the achievement gap as it is documented in this book (see figure 6.5).

1. The model of classroom instruction emphasizes cultural salience in teaching, curricular materials, and assignments. Academic rigor is implemented throughout elementary and middle school so that the students can master honors English and calculus in high school.

2. Through the creation of an instructional accountability infrastructure, the principal or a building-level instructional coordinator functions as an instructional leader, building an infrastructure within the school that assures mastery (moving toward excellence) of academic material for every child.

3. In terms of cultural enrichment, the school is conceptualized as the Family. The school takes the leadership in coordinating the parents and the larger community in planning cultural enrichment experiences for the children. The community is conceptualized as the Village. The school assures that all of the children within the school (the Family) receive the support that is normally provided in middle-class families.

These spheres of activity transcend the types of curricular materials that are used by teachers. They transcend the reading or math program that is employed. The concepts of the Family and the Village highlight spiritual and philosophical values that transform the culture of the school, taking it far beyond books and materials.

This book is not intended to be a review of current school reform proposals. For that, the reader is directed to *The Catalog of School Reform Models* prepared by the Northwest Regional Educational Laboratory with assistance from the Education Commission of the States. The first edition of the catalog includes an initial listing of forty-four models of school re-

Classroom Instruction

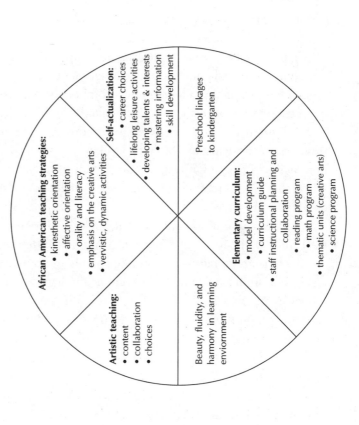

African American teaching strategies:
- kinesthetic orientation
- affective orientation
- orality and literacy
- emphasis on the creative arts
- vervistic, dynamic activities

Self-actualization:
- career choices
- lifelong leisure activities
- developing talents & interests
- mastering information
- skill development

Artistic teaching:
- content
- collaboration
- choices

Beauty, fluidity, and harmony in learning enviornment

Elementary curriculum:
- model development
- curriculum guide
- staff instructional planning and collaboration
- reading program
- math program
- thematic units (creative arts)
- science program

Preschool linkages to kindergarten

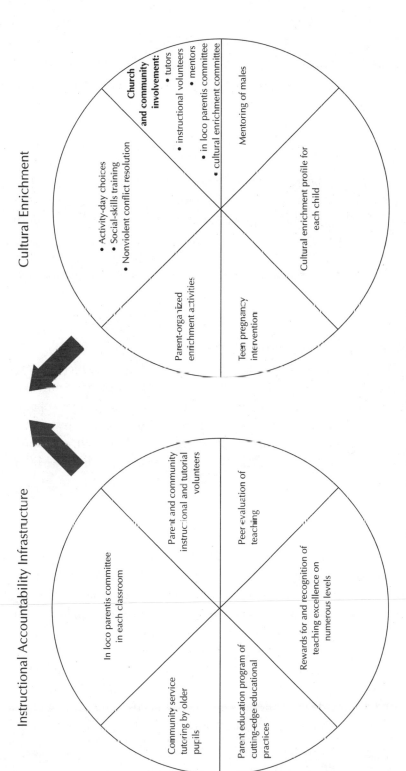

Instructional Accountability Infrastructure

Cultural Enrichment

Instructional Accountability Infrastructure circle:

- In loco parentis committee in each classroom
- Parent and community instructional and tutorial volunteers
- Peer evaluation of teaching
- Rewards for and recognition of teaching excellence on numerous levels
- Parent education program of cutting-edge educational practices
- Community service tutoring by older pupils

Cultural Enrichment circle:

- Activity-day choices
- Social-skills training
- Nonviolent conflict resolution

Church and community involvement:
- tutors
- instructional volunteers
- mentors
- in loco parentis committee
- cultural enrichment committee

- Mentoring of males
- Cultural enrichment profile for each child
- Teen pregnancy intervention
- Parent-organized enrichment activities

Figure 6.5 Culturally Appropriate Pedagogy

form in two categories: entire-school models and skill- and content-based models (reading, math, science, and the like). "After years of work to improve public education, student achievement is improving but still remains below acceptable levels. This is particularly true for populations who traditionally have been poorly served by our schools. For example, on the 1994 National Assessment of Educational Progress reading assessment, 29 percent of white fourth-graders scored below the 'basic' level in reading, but 69 percent of African American students and 64 percent of Hispanic students scored this poorly" (Northwest Regional Educational Laboratory 1998, 1).

The *Catalog* points out that it is difficult to provide definitive evaluation of educational reform models because consensus has yet to be established on the most appropriate instruments for measuring and comparing student achievement. They also judge it to be difficult and expensive to conduct long-term, systematic research across multiple sites using rigorous research designs that involve experimental and control groups (ibid.).

D. W. Miller provides an insight into why it is difficult to speak definitively about current reform proposals. Miller suggests that governmental funders and foundations do not spend enough on research, or they support the wrong kind. He maintains that educators and policy makers resist findings that challenge cherished beliefs about learning. "As a result, education reform is often shaped by political whim and pedagogic fashion" (Miller 1999, 17).

This chapter sets down some distinctive principles and practices that make for effective schooling for African American youth. I am not saying that traditional reforms currently under discussion, such as longer school days and summer school, cannot help some children. What I am saying is that practices such as summer school, extended school days, the elimination of recess, removing children from the classroom and placing them in special education, social promotion, retention, diplomas of attendance, exit exams, and other approaches based on failure and stigma are not central to school reform. Those practices just create repositories for failure.

Many examples of the kinds of activities that are appropriate and constitute true reform come to mind. The special education budget could be employed to include the children with special needs in the regular classroom, manned by the regular classroom teacher, the special education teacher, and an instructional aide all working together as a teaching team. It is appropriate to create peer tutoring and resource rooms in which older children serve as tutors of younger children to fulfill community service requirements. It is always appropriate to reduce class size and whole-class teaching within classrooms, to have children work in small groups, and to have tutors sit with children and assist them during the presentation of class material. It is also appropriate to institute mastery instruction and evaluation practices, wherein children would be allowed to correct and revise their own test papers and thereby raise their grades. Grading practices in middle and high school should be changed, so that students receive no credit for grades lower than C and classes would be repeated until mastery was achieved.

As Asa Hilliard writes on the back cover of *Unbank the Fire*, "Education is much larger than schools . . . and the success of children and teachers is a function not only of professional preparation but also of spiritual and human values." To achieve true school reform, we need a transformation in the spiritual and human values that undergird the education of African American children.

CHAPTER 7

The Role of the African American Church in Creating the Village

JUST BECAUSE
Just because I don't sing
Doesn't mean I ain't a singer.
Just because I don't shine
Doesn't mean I ain't a star.
Just because you don't see me
Doesn't mean I ain't there.

I am here
Growing quietly
Growing strong
Day by day
Striving on
Past my youth
Past my play
Looking on
Looking ahead
Waiting my turn.
 —JA J. JAHANNES

The African American church is a key institution in the crafting of the Village. It would be a wonderful development for every school to be adopted by a church. As the religious historian Albert Raboteau (1995) notes, the church has served both as a source of stability and as a vehicle for change in the African American community. The church has supported African Americans through large-scale social change associated with migration and urbanization. In the arena of civil rights, the churches not only reacted to social and political change, they were in the forefront of bringing it about. In addition to these external frontiers, over the past five decades the internal theological, liturgical, and institutional developments within African American churches have shaped contemporary African American religious life (ibid.; Franklin 1992).

In addition to what it does for its members, the black church has always served important functions for the African American community as a whole. "[The church] is in this respect both a preserver of the African-American heritage and an agent for reform. Indeed no successful movement for improving the conditions of life for the African-American people has been mounted without the support of the church" (Billingsley 1992, 350). It is a mistake, the sociologist Andrew Billingsley maintains, to think of the black church in America as being primarily a religious institution, as white churches are thought of, because community service has been an important element for the black religious institutions from the beginning. As Rev. Cecil Murray has remarked, "The coming-to-church-for-personal salvation days are over. Now we are looking not only for personal salvation but for social salvation" (quoted in Schneider 1992).

Billingsley notes that when Absalom Jones, Richard Allen, and others walked out of the white Methodist church in Philadelphia more than two hundred years ago, they did not form a new church. They formed the Free African Society, with forty-two members. The society fostered "socioeconomic cooperation in the form of savings, mutual aid, education to children, and charity to indigent, widowed, and orphaned members. Only three years later did Richard Allen form Mother Bethel, the first African-Methodist-Episcopal Church in America" (Billingsley 1992, 352).

Black churches are a major institutional presence in the black community. According to Benjamin Mays and Joseph Nicholson, the black church possesses a certain "genius of soul . . . that gives it life and vitality, that makes it stand out significantly above its buildings, creeds, rituals, and doctrines; something that makes it a unique institution" (1969, 278). Billingsley suggests that a key element in the genius of the church was complete

ownership and control by African American people. "It represented freedom, independence, and respect for leadership, as well as the opportunity
for self-esteem, self-development, leadership, and relaxation. Moreover, . . .
the black church was a community center and recreational center that encouraged education, business development, and democratic fellowship beyond its members" (1992, 354). The theologian C. Eric Lincoln has called
attention to the multiplicity of functions of the black church: "Beyond its
purely religious function, as critical as that function has been, the black
church in its historical role as lyceum, conservatory, forum, social service
center, political academy and financial institution has been and is for black
America the mother of our culture, the champion of our freedom, the hall-
mark of our civilization" (cited in Billingsley 1992, 354–55).

The African American church is the most important institution in the
African American community and is supported and controlled entirely by
African American people. African American churches were burned and
bombed during and after the modern civil rights movement because they
represented black power, independence, and self-determination. The
African American pastor, in the words of my father, Rev. Phale D. Hale Sr.,
"is the freest person in the African American community. He is the only
person who is free of economic sanctions from the white power structure,
because he is paid totally by African American people."

The African American church serves such a unique function in the
black community that some white politicians have recently sought to limit
their influence by threatening to withdraw their tax-exempt status if they
engage in political activity. This effort at intimidation is analogous to the
ban on African drumming during slavery because messages that could not
be interpreted or intercepted by the slave owners were being sent by means
of the drum.

The role of the African American preacher has been distinctive in
American society. The African American preacher serves as a prophet or
emissary, like Moses, who spoke to the pharaoh on behalf of his people.
African American preachers have tried to "call the Anglo preacher out,"
as Rev. Martin Luther King Jr. did in his "Letter from Birmingham Jail,"
addressed to the white American clergy (King 1964). "Where are you?" King
wanted to know.

As my father explained it to me during the height of the civil rights movement, "When the white preacher preaches against the inequalities found in American capitalism or the moral decadence of racism, his coattails are pulled by the plantation owners and industrialists who sit on his board of trustees and pay his salary. They quietly suggest that he restrict his sermons to 'Jesus and him crucified'!"

Some African Americans declare that they do not want to hear about politics at church. To them I say that the African American church still serves as the "talking drum" in the African American community. At church, as no place else, parishioners can hear announcements and discussions of issues and mobilizations that are critical to African American people.

It is more difficult to hear alternative voices in the media. Some newspaper publishers in the African American community are capitalists who identify with and belong to the party of the affluent political right, and so the editorial policies and politics of some African American newspapers do not render them a reliable source of information on certain issues. Additionally, one person may own African American newspapers in several major cities. This one person becomes a powerful, invisible molder of African American public opinion who can be influenced by forces outside of the African American community. The same can be said about some civil rights organizations that are sustained by donations from large and wealthy corporations that can influence their policies and programs. The African American church stands alone as an institution in the black community that is positioned to provide unfiltered information that, like former congresswoman Shirley Chisholm (1970), is "unbought and unbossed."

The African American church has a dual role in supporting the model of school reform that is outlined in this book. The first role of the church is a nonsectarian function. The church is being called upon in this model, first and foremost, to supply a cadre of volunteers to enter the schools, to serve on in loco parentis and cultural enrichment committees, to tutor children in the classroom, and to supply men and women who can mentor children and develop rites of passage programs. No religious dogma is called for, and thus there should be no cause for concern about issues of separation of church and state.

The second role for the African American church is to craft cutting-edge Christian education that will enrich the lives of the children who are in the Family (members of the church) and children who are in the Village

(African American children wherever they are found). In the appendix of this book, I draw upon my training in religious education to discuss the "Christian education" sponsored by African American churches that complements their outreach mission to the public schools. In this chapter I make some suggestions to teachers and administrators on how they can implement "character education" and introduce service and social-action projects into their schools to enable children and youth to become more altruistic and caring for others.

It is important that the black church conceptualize her mission as ministering to African American children wherever they are found. I shall never forget an incident that occurred at the church in Ohio that housed Visions for Children, an early-education program that I founded and ran. The members of the church evicted our program after firing the pastor. The board of trustees asked me how many children served by my program were members of their church. I looked at them in disbelief that they could even ask such a question. How could they conceptualize their Christian mission as sending aid to those in need in Africa but draw the line so close at home that the poor African American children right at their doorstep did not fit into their definition of Christian mission and ministry unless they were members of their church? Their response was a telegram, telling me to vacate in two days.

Fortunately, the perspective of that church is not typical of African American churches. Billingsley, in a random sampling of seventy-one black churches in the northeastern United States, discovered that most of the churches were actively involved in providing family-oriented community outreach programs; the average number of outreach programs operated by each church was four. His findings further reveal that "taken together[,] some 31 percent of these programs were aimed specifically at children and youth. Another 51 percent were of the more inclusive family support and assistance type; 8 percent were directed to adult and elderly individuals. Finally, 10 percent of these programs were more general community service and community development activities" (1992, 374).

A large proportion of these programs involve education and community efforts to assist schools. The challenge for public school educators is to move beyond being a mere recipient of overtures from churches; they must create a vision of how the church can be involved as a key player in creating the Village as it is outlined in this book. As I have discussed this idea with leaders of church organizations, they have always expressed a willingness to help public schools. However, when they approach the schools to adopt them, the schools do not give the churches anything meaningful to do. They assign them to lunchroom duty as monitors or some other such perfunctory tasks. The schools need to invite the churches to the table as collaborators in helping the school reach its goals. School district administrators and teachers must recognize the African American church as the major institution it is in the African American community. Every teacher and administrator should be on intimate terms with the pastors and parishioners in the churches that surround their school.

Let me state clearly that the discussion in this chapter is also an action plan for churches as they examine their concept of ministry to children and youth in the Family and in the Village. The model of school reform in this book requires the collaboration of churches ready to step up to the plate in supporting the development of the African American children in their community—including those who are not church members.

Character Education

In the view of Philip Vincent, an educator with an academic background in philosophy, religion, and psychology, the underlying cause of many problems in our schools, homes, and society at large is a lack of good character. "An individual with good character knows how to act toward others," he argues, and also knows "that individuals should be treated with respect and that one should act in a responsible, caring manner" (1996, 12).

Much of the difficulty "at-risk" children experience in school derives from a lack of social skills. They have not been properly socialized before entering school and have not received the "social cultivation" from their families that would enable them to interact with adults or their peers in such a way that they are perceived as having the potential for personal and academic achievement.

This is a key point made by James Comer (1988, 1997; Comer et al. 1996; Comer et al. 1999). In developing his school improvement program, Comer observes that although the parents of the children in the schools in which he worked wanted their children to succeed, they were often unable to provide them with the skills and experiences necessary to get them off to a good start. Even when the parents knew what was needed, they were often under such economic and social stress that they were unable to provide it. It is therefore incumbent upon other institutions, such as the schools and churches, to provide the children with the skills they need to deal effectively with the people and navigate the institutions they will encounter in the larger society.

As William Huitt (1998) notes, there is much agreement on the point that educators ought to help individuals to attain "the good life"; there is also a commonly held view that government—and hence, the public schools—should be neutral in defining what the good life is. The Association for Supervision and Curriculum Development (1996) recommends the development of consensus around a relatively small number of moral and character traits that can be the focus of a kindergarten-through-twelfth-grade educational program. These traits must be incorporated into a curriculum that enjoins young people to strive for excellence in the attainment of both character and competencies. Huitt outlines three major issues in the education of young people today:

1. *development of a vision for one's life,* which includes a definition of one's life mission and desired lifestyle
2. *development of one's character,* which deals with issues of direction and quality of life
3. *development of competence,* which generates income and drives lifestyle (1998, 1)

Moral education, Huitt observes, focuses upon values, which are essentially orientations or dispositions. Character is different from values in that it involves action or activation of knowledge and values. Values are the foundations for character; good character is defined in terms of one's actions.

Huitt (1997) also points out that in the industrial age, character development traditionally focused on values such as obedience to authority, work ethic, and working in groups under supervision. However, modern education must promote character based on values appropriate for the information age: truthfulness, honesty, integrity, individual responsibility, humility, wisdom, justice, steadfastness, and dependability.

Lawrence Kohlberg (1984) has built upon the cognitive theories of Jean Piaget (1962) to explain how moral thinking develops in children. The analysis view of values education assumes that moral and character decisions are made rationally. Therefore, the focus in values education has been on changing the moral thinking of children from egocentric to sociocentric. However, there is scant evidence to support the belief that changing moral thinking will automatically lead to a change in behavior. Huitt (1998) recommends that efforts to teach values or clarify values be combined with behavior-based learning strategies that enable students to put their thoughts and feelings into action in a variety of social circumstances or service-learning settings. This combination is most likely to have an impact on the two most important aspects of character not included in values education — volition and action.

Huitt notes that these components come into play in a rapidly changing context, and therefore we cannot teach our students a list of specific behaviors that will lead to success in all aspects of their lives. Some values are relative, and students must be taught to develop their own principles as they move through life. However, we also must acknowledge that there are some absolutes with respect to morality and character, which are recognized by members of specific communities, the major world religions, and philosophical orientations.

> We, therefore, have an obligation to teach [moral values] in the family, in our school setting, in our religious organizations, and to support this effort in our communities. . . . In sum, as parents, educators, affiliates of religious organizations, and community members, we have an obligation to provide young people with training appropriate to their age level that would assist them in holding to the absolutes that are common across the scriptures of the major religious traditions, while at the same time helping them clarify and defend their own acquired values. (Huitt 1998, 6)

There is a strong relationship between the call in this model of school reform for teaching social skills and nonviolent conflict resolution in the schools and the call for character education. Although religious traditions have offered guidelines to help individuals develop the traits associated with good character, character education can be taught in school without concern about conflicts between church and state. Character education should be taught with a view toward helping children understand the universal principles for building a healthy and productive life. A key to developing the moral strength of children and youth is to impart critical thinking and reasoning skills and to help them develop positive behavior habits.

We should be dedicated to the development of the intellect as it is related to the ability to think and reason and, therefore, to respond to moral concerns. As they grow intellectually, students should be challenged through the school curriculum to think and analyze ideas and propositions.

Children and students must also be provided with opportunities to practice positive personal traits such as respect, responsibility, and caring behavior toward others in their school and church environments. Community service on the part of all children, beginning in the fourth grade, enriches the school but also instills within the children the expectation that they will make a contribution to the world they live in. Encouraging children to tutor younger children helps them to learn at an early age that they have a responsibility to assist others. It is equally important for children to learn that they should assist younger children socially as well as academically. Older children should model proper behavior for younger children to see and follow.

In consultation with teachers who have asked for suggestions about controlling the rambunctious behavior of African American male children in primary school, I have recommended that a young African American male could be matched with an older African American male, who is assigned to that child as part of his community service. The mentor could sit with the younger boy during meeting time and assist him in finding his space and sitting still. He could be his partner in stressful situations, modeling appropriate behavior. A warm, nurturing relationship would hence develop for the younger child in place of the punishment, reprimands, and tension he might receive from his teacher.

I used this strategy in my home as a single parent when my son was six years old. I chose a male babysitter who was the son of a friend, whom I met through the African American children's social club, Jack and Jill. David Ellison, the person who served as my son's tutor, was thirteen years old at the time. I paid David to babysit, and in that capacity, he helped Keith master the fine points of video games. He taught him to ride his bicycle when the training wheels came off. He taught him to rollerblade and play basketball.

When I gave birthday parties for my son, David came over after the party and helped Keith put his gifts together and figure out how to make everything work. He visited us on Christmas Eve and served the same function. My son learned how to be "cool" from David. He walks like David and talks like David.

David enabled me to provide male modeling for my son separate from a personal relationship of mine with a man. Too often, single women press suitors into the father role before the men are ready. In other cases, a succession of "daddies" and "uncles" move through a child's life. By designating David as my son's "big brother," we created an ongoing relationship that has blossomed into a lifelong friendship. This same kind of pairing could be created in a school.

Philip Vincent has identified five important areas for the development of character education:

1. *The establishment of rules and procedures*: Rules and procedures promote a businesslike, productive environment. Students know what is expected of them and how to go about their work. In addition, when students know and understand the school's rules and procedures, an environment is established in which character traits such as taking responsibility, acting with respect, and practicing caring toward others can occur. It is also critical that the children and youth be involved in helping to formulate the rules by which they will be governed.

2. *Cooperative learning*: Students who work together during classes and meetings recognize peers as having something worthy to contribute. It is easier to accomplish tasks when a group learns how to work together. Far too often teachers have students working by themselves, sitting in rows or listening to the teacher talk. Yet this is not how the real world works. The success of many companies depends on the effectiveness of employees who meet and work as teams. The success of many school programs also hinges on how well students can work together. By working together we reach out and touch others and thereby become connected with some aspect of their lives.

3. *Teaching for thinking*: Thinking and reasoning skills play an im-

portant role in the development of character. The skills students learn should be developmentally appropriate, with each skill building on previously learned ones. Students can apply these skills using a wide variety of academic methods and strategies, including thinking maps. (See Vincent 1996, 104–8, for a detailed discussion of the use of thinking maps for teaching thinking skills.) Students, when they move toward the high school years, should make use of some ethical dilemmas, but this should not be their teacher's sole application of teaching for thinking. Thinking skills must be developed and applied in all aspects of the curriculum.

4. *Literature rich in meaning:* Exposure to great literature brings students to the joy that reading provides. We should be careful to insure that our students are reading material that is worth reading and provides strong examples of character.

5. *Service learning, both within and outside the school environment:* Students should be given the opportunity to practice caring behavior. For many students this is the beginning of assuming adult responsibilities and connecting with the world around them. Students who are involved in service learning develop a sense of responsibility for helping to provide for others' well-being. Even in neighborhoods that are unsafe outside the church or school grounds, students can practice service within the safety of their school or church building. Service outside the church, and perhaps outside an immediate community, can be encouraged for all students. This is especially critical for high school students as they are beginning to take their place as adults in our world. (Vincent 1996, 147–49)

Two books by Barbara A. Lewis, *The Kid's Guide to Social Action* (1991) and *The Kid's Guide to Service Projects* (1995), are excellent resources for creating service projects and social-action projects for children and youth.

Cultural Education

The impetus for the integration of schools during the 1950s and 1960s came from the leadership and membership of African American churches concerned about the quality of the education for African American children and youth. Today we have churches that provide after-school tutorials, gospel nightclubs, Saturday ethnic schools, church-sponsored schools, charter schools, and other cultural programs.

The Saturday ethnic school is a model developed in Los Angeles (see Adams 1972). This program, which operates from 9:30 A.M. to 1:00 P.M. each Saturday, teaches the history and culture of African Americans and seeks to build self-esteem and high aspirations in the children. Following the morning assembly, the children are organized into classes according to age, and the stories, history, and demonstrations are presented at the under-standing level of each class.

The ethnic school supplements the Judeo-Christian tradition with the African American tradition. Individual and group identity for African Americans can be achieved only by teaching both traditions. The school provides experiences for building a strong self-image, self-respect, and self-understanding. It teaches black love without teaching white hate. It is a learning experience that enriches the adult teacher as well as the student.

Eight Los Angeles churches came together and formed an organization they called EGO, which consisted of four key elements: (1) the board in-cludes the pastor, one layman, and one parent from each church; (2) the project director has overall responsibility for implementing design, train-ing staff, and providing curriculum materials; (3) the coordinator at each church is the administrator for that church's school; and (4) volunteer teachers are recruited from the churches and communities. Each church directs a house-to-house canvass of the communities involved, conducted by the volunteer teachers, who preregister youngsters, explain the program to the parents, and invite both parents and children to the opening session. Covering six blocks in all directions usually yields a large number of chil-dren. Parents are invited to participate as volunteers on all levels.

Parents of children who attend the Saturday ethnic school constitute the advisory committee, along with volunteers at each site. Representatives from each local advisory committee serve on a central governing board re-sponsible for policy and for the distribution of funds. The director also serves on the board.

Volunteers who staff the ethnic school are trained in workshops pre-ceding the opening of the school and continue in-service training through-out the year. The school is set up according to grade levels. Because of the lack of materials available, trained volunteers write and rewrite materials according to the reading level of the youngsters.

Many churches are also creating tutorial projects in recognition of the overcrowded conditions that exist in schools that educate African American children. Teachers frequently send children home with assignments that presuppose that parents have the time, the skills, and the inclination to help their children—expectations that are not always met in lower-income families—and these tutorial programs attempt to provide this help and guidance.

African American schoolchildren are often shuffled off to remedial classes when all they need is individual attention. Tutorial projects have been created by churches in the African American community in which adult parishioners, teachers, and high school and college students volunteer. Children can bring their homework and receive the help they need from the Village in mastering assignments.

Another example of church programs are the rites-of-passage programs for African American children and mentoring programs. The church of which I am a member, Hartford Memorial Baptist Church in Detroit, has an exciting rites-of-passage program for males and females. The male program, called the Kafo Academy, includes boys aged ten to thirteen. They participate in structured activities every Saturday morning from 8:30 to 12:30 during the academic year. Upon successful completion of the program, at the age of thirteen, the boys take a church-subsidized trip to West Africa for two weeks, where the rites-of-passage ceremonies are held. The program for the girls, the Kentake Academy, is similarly structured; the rites-of-passage ceremonies are performed in Egypt.

It is critical that churches persist in sponsoring programs such as these that expose African American children to their cultural heritage. Unfortunately, in many communities the church provides the only opportunity to teach our children about Africa. My second book, *Unbank the Fire* (Hale 1994, chap. 8), includes a detailed discussion of the blending of African traditional religious beliefs and Christianity.

The importance of understanding African retentions in African American religious traditions bears repeating. According to Lawrence Levine (1977), the retention of traditional African beliefs and practices was facilitated by the delay that occurred in the conversion of the African slaves to Christianity. For two hundred years there was considerable debate among whites as to whether to give their religion to their bondsmen. They were afraid that baptism would lead to freedom and that labor would be lost, given the prohibition within the Christian tradition against work on Sunday. They also feared that the slaves would develop notions of religious equality.

This vacillation on the part of the slaveholders allowed the slaves the time to accommodate their African religious beliefs and practices to the harsh economic and social system in which they found themselves, with its suppression of their freedom to worship in traditional ways (an example of which is the prohibition against using the drum). When conversion to Christianity did come, therefore, it was not at the expense of the slaves' folk beliefs.

In fact, African and European beliefs intersected at numerous points. "The African practices and beliefs which had the best chance of survival in the New World were those that had European analogues, as so many of the folk beliefs did" (Levine 1977, 60). The concept of faith is particularly germane, because there is an ineluctable relationship between magic, medicine, religion, and faith. Faith is particularly strong when a people feel a lack of control over their lives. The absence of power helped to perpetuate the slaves' sacred universe and to intensify their search for supernatural aid and solutions.

Bronislaw Malinowski observes that "we find magic wherever the elements of chance and accident, and the emotional play between hope and fear, have a wide and extensive range. We do not find magic wherever the pursuit is certain, reliable, and well under the control of rational methods and technological processes. Further, we find magic where the element of danger is conspicuous" (1954, 17). In Levine's view, the slaves' magical folk beliefs were a central and necessary part of existence. They stood beside their Christian beliefs and supplemented and fortified them. Both were sources of strength and release; both served to preserve their sanity. Christianity assured them that the present condition would eventually change and that retribution would come in this world and in the next. It also reinforced their feelings of dignity and self-worth. Their folk beliefs provided hope and a sense of group identification. They also provided the slaves sources of power and knowledge that were alternative to those existing in the master class.

Leonard Barrett (1974) maintains that African traditional religion was the motivating force of all African peoples, and it continued to be expressed by Africans in bondage. Africans conceive of the world not as a place in which to contemplate life but rather as an arena for activity. Their aim is to live strongly; they pray for long life, health, and prosperity and the strengthening of family, clan, and ethnic group, because they live through them. The ancestors are the guardians of posterity, and people are heavily dependent upon them for all aspects of life.

This point was poignantly made in the 1997 movie *Amistad*, directed by Steven Spielberg. *Amistad* is the story of a group of Africans who created a mutiny aboard a ship transporting them between some islands in Cuba. They were tricked by the navigator, whose life they spared, into traveling to Connecticut instead of back to Africa, as they had intended. A famous trial ensued over whether they should be set free, returned to Cuba, or prosecuted for murder. The appeals went all the way to the Supreme Court. John Quincy Adams, a former president of the United States, was drawn into the case as the defense attorney by abolitionists who fought for the liberation of Africans from slavery and the return of the *Amistad* Africans to their homeland.

Following is an excerpt from a discussion between Joseph Cinque, the leader of the *Amistad* rebellion, and John Quincy Adams, which was one of the most powerful scenes in the film:

JQA: Cinque, look, I am being honest with you. Anything less would be disrespectful. I am telling ya, I am preparing ya, I suppose, I am explaining to you that the test ahead of us is an exceptionally difficult one.

CINQUE: We won't be going in there alone.

JQA: Alone? Indeed not. No, we have right at our side, we have righteousness at our side. We have Mr. Baldwin, over there.

CINQUE: I meant my ancestors. I will call into the past—far back to the beginning of time and beg them to come and help me at the judgment. I will reach back and draw them into me and they must come, for at this moment I am the whole reason they have existed at all.

What a coherent belief system we have lost! What a coherent belief system we must recapture for our children! What an assignment for the African American church!

V. P. Franklin argues that the shared experience of slavery served as the foundation for the "cultural value system" handed down from the Africans to their American-born offspring. In his *Black Self-determination*, which is a history of the experiences that formed the African American culture, he uses "the testimony and narratives of enslaved and free African Americans from the end of the eighteenth century to the beginning of the twentieth, as well as African American folk songs, beliefs, and religious practices, in an attempt to provide a viable explanation of the meaning and significance of self-determination, freedom, resistance, and education in the lives and experiences of the masses of African Americans in this society" (1992, 4).

Teachers and parents can use folktales to illustrate the importance of faith and perseverance to African American children (see Hale 1994, 150–51). Such stories can teach these children that they can achieve power in the midst of a powerless community. The Br'er Rabbit stories star a rabbit trickster and invites comparison of the conflict between the rabbit and the fox with that between the slave and the slaveholder. Numerous other folktales feature the slave as trickster.

Teachers and parents should also make use of the body of literature that features black heroes, from the mythical John Henry to Jack Johnson and Joe Louis, who refused to accept the "place" reserved for African Americans. There is also a vast literature about the contributions to society of such African Americans as Jackie Robinson, Marian Anderson, Rev. Martin Luther King Jr., and W. E. B. Du Bois, all of whom suffered racial indignities but triumphed in the end. These stories transmit the message to African American children that the quicksand and landmines along the road to achievement for African Americans are obstacles that can be overcome.

These stories help African American children depersonalize oppression when they encounter it and enable them to place their personal difficulties into the context of the overall African American liberation struggle. I am reminded of a conversation I had with Rev. Otis Moss Jr., who was my pastor when I lived in Cleveland, Ohio, about the despair felt by African American students upon encountering racism in a university setting. He asked me to remind them of the racism Du Bois must have experienced at Harvard in 1896. He evoked the African American tradition in which I was raised, the faith that has brought us as a people this far along the way.

Proverbs teach African American children the folk wisdom and life skills drawn from the African culture. Teachers and parents should realize that these skills play an important part in the resilience African Americans have displayed against overwhelming oppression and should help preserve the foundation of this faith and perseverance.

The African American cultural tradition teaches African American children important lessons about the struggle implicit in human affairs. The tendency of many white Americans to distort human history and to paint a picture of never-ending American victories has robbed white children of legitimate lessons about overcoming adversity. The suicide rate among white males, the highest in the country, is an example of what happens when one has been raised in a culture that expects unending triumphs. When a young person encounters the defeats and frustrations that are a part of living without having a tradition of overcoming adversity, he or she is likely to personalize defeat.

In contrast with the suicide rate among white males, the suicide rate among African American females is the lowest in the country. African American culture has provided a religious tradition that emphasizes faith, perseverance, and resilience. African American females have embraced that religious tradition more than men, as measured by their church attendance, participation, and leadership, because they have had such overwhelming responsibility for the survival of the family and the community that they could not afford to find their relief in flight and substance abuse.

Teachers should expose children of other ethnic groups to the literature of the African American culture, so as to give them the benefit of stories that emphasize such resilience. It is also important, in addition to teaching African American children about the rich culture of ancient African civilizations, to educate them in the economic, political, and social struggles taking place in Africa. *Ebony* magazine conducts surveys of readers' reactions to each article it publishes; the editors have found that African American subscribers have little interest in current events in Africa, and the magazine has consequently reduced its coverage of African affairs in recent years (Alex Poinsett, former senior editor of *Ebony*, personal conversation).

African Americans are the most affluent and well educated of all Africans of the diaspora. It is critical that educational experiences are created that raise their consciousness of themselves as Africans so that they will take their rightful place of leadership among African peoples of the world. As the president and founder of TransAfrica, Randall Robinson, has said, "the waters that divide us are not as deep as the blood that unites us."

CHAPTER 8

Where Do We Go from Here?

A Call to Action

Those who profess to favor freedom,
and yet deprecate agitation,
Are men who want crops without
plowing the ground.
They want rain without thunder and
lightning.
They want the ocean without the
awful roar of its waters.
This struggle may be a moral one;
Or it may be a physical one;
Or it may be both moral and physical;
but it must be a struggle.
Power concedes nothing without a demand.
It never did, and it never will.
— FREDERICK DOUGLASS

The Supreme Court decision in *Brown v. Board of Education* was handed down in 1954. Almost fifty years later, despite the powerful impact of the ruling, "plus ça change, plus c'est la même chose" (the more things change, the more they remain the same). The African American masses are still being educated in separate and unequal schools. The most notable difference is that today, those African Americans who can purchase better educational opportunities for their children cannot be legally prevented from doing so. However, those students whose parents cannot afford to pay tuition for private school or to purchase homes in neighborhoods with good schools are still relegated to inferior schools. One of the reasons we, as a community, have not moved ahead is the powerful manner in which education speaks to the very fabric of the belief system of American society.

Most white Americans understand that education is the key to obtaining the skills for entry and success in mainstream society. Their status is determined by the work they do, the neighborhoods in which they live, and the schools their children attend. These status indicators are also doubly powerful because they dictate the social circles in which a person will move and with whom he or she will socialize. In other words, it determines the people who are in one's world.

Even those whites who are not flaming racists find themselves powerless to avoid becoming classists. In the name of protecting their property values, they seek housing in upscale, predominantly white neighborhoods. Claud Anderson asserts that white Americans have an 8 percent comfort rate with the presence of African Americans. That is, they become uncomfortable when the percentage of African Americans surrounding them exceeds 8 percent. This goes for neighborhoods, schools, and the overall population in America. Anderson outlines the various strategies that have historically been employed to maintain that rate and documents whites' frustration when the overall population of African Americans exceeds that rate. Whenever any entity in their environment tips above the 8 percent comfort rate, they either move or take steps to maintain that ratio (Anderson 1994, 169). African Americans are, in short, a pariah group in America.

An African American physician who lived in my subdivision built a new house in a more expensive subdivision about four miles away. The new house was burned while it was being built—twice. The first fire did about $100,000 worth of damage. He rebuilt. The second fire burned the nearly completed house to the ground.

Several African Americans live in that subdivision, which contains million-dollar houses. I have friends who live in that subdivision who cannot conceive of their neighbors doing such a thing. Their dismay and disbelief is exacerbated by the fact that they experienced no racism when they purchased their homes. The FBI, who investigated the incident, stated that these types of arsons are usually perpetrated against new houses, while they are being built, rather than against purchased houses because the owner, while overseeing construction, is highly visible: everyone can see who the purchaser is long before the house is occupied. When an existing house is purchased, the neighbors often do not know who the owners are until they move in.

My friends who live in this subdivision could not understand why their neighbors would do such a thing. I offered Claud Anderson's argument as an explanation. My friends had moved into the subdivision eight years before this incident, at a time when there were very few African Americans living there. I suggested that the influx of the new black home owners might have pushed their neighbors past their comfort zone: as more African Americans moved into the neighborhood, whites began to fear that their property values would decline.

These arsonists were not trying to kill the family, any more than the arsonists who set fire to basketball star Reggie Miller's $5 million home in Indiana were trying to kill his family. The houses were burned when the families were not there. Reggie Miller's family was not at home; the physician's family had not yet moved in. The arsonists were trying to send a message to the potential African American resident that the comfort zone had been exceeded and that they did not want any more African Americans in that subdivision. I think the African Americans who were potential home buyers got the message. I do not think that there will be a mad scramble to move into that neighborhood.

What Has Not Changed

The same message is conveyed in white flight from schools. In this era, no one is standing in schoolhouse doors, and national guardsmen are not needed to integrate the schools. The measures that are being taken are subtle but equally effective. In the name of "quality education," whites have been creating smaller and smaller political enclaves so that they can restrict and delineate economically homogeneous school districts. State legislatures have been maneuvering to create subtle structures for maintaining private school excellence within predominantly white suburban public school districts. Jonathan Kozol (1991) calls this using public money to create a private school system within the public schools.

Public funds have been identified for gifted and talented programs that primarily benefit white middle-class children so that in those unusual circumstances in which white children are educated in the same buildings with African American children, they can receive a separate, superior education. White children, based upon their ability to score higher on standardized tests, receive entrée to the program and an enrichment curriculum. Most African American students receive a remedial curriculum.

Although, in theory, magnet schools were designed to integrate the schools, there are bizarre instances in which they, too, are being maneuvered to disproportionately enrich white children and remediate African American children. While doing research on a project in Port Gibson, Mississippi (discussed in chapter 5), I visited a magnet school in southeastern Michigan because I was interested in obtaining information about their state-of-the-art science and mathematics laboratory. The director's explanation of the way the "local" advisory committee had structured the federal desegregation funds for this program startled me.

There were three elementary schools in this school district. It was decided that "integration" would occur between a predominantly African American school and a predominantly white school. To achieve this, the advisory committee set up the state-of-the-art magnet school in the African American school and bused a contingent of white children to that school. Once in the school, they—and only they—could make use of the science and mathematics laboratory. The African American children did not go to class with them and had no contact with them or with the science and mathematics laboratory. Essentially, the white children functioned as a school within a school.

Similarly, a contingent of African American children was bused to the predominantly white school. At that school, there was no state-of-the-art anything for them to access. The African American children were given remedial language classes. Even more startling, once the African American children had been "remediated," they were bused back to their original school, and another group was sent over. This, in the opinion of this Michigan advisory committee, is integration.

Movements are under way to provide vouchers and tax credits for families who are sending their children to private schools so that private schools can receive public money. All of these are blatant efforts to maintain the inequality that has relegated African Americans to inferior educational outcomes since our arrival on this continent.

White Americans have brought a high level of sophistication to bear upon creating education inequality that benefits their children to the detriment of African American children. As Christopher Jencks points out, "Despite the pious rhetoric about equality of opportunity, most parents want their children to have a more than equal chance of success—which means, inevitably, that they want others, not all others but some others, to have less than equal chances" (quoted in Kozol 1991, 199).

A major thrust of civil rights organizations before 1975 was to eliminate inferior schools to the benefit of the masses of African American people. After the *Brown* decision, the NAACP, the Southern Christian Leadership Conference, the National Urban League, and other civil rights organizations actively opposed the "massive resistance" campaigns against school integration. Civil rights leaders pursued court-ordered busing plans to remedy past discriminatory practices, and they pushed for the government to force employers to develop "affirmative-action plans" in their hiring programs. These activists were often thwarted in their attempts to bring about racial and educational change by the opposition of powerful and conservative judges and legislators. In the post-civil-rights era (1980s and 1990s), the strategies put forward by civil rights organizations have been unsuccessful in bringing about significant educational improvements for low-income African American children in urban areas.

The only frontier that has been open to the African American community is the opportunity for the African American middle class to use their economic resources to move to communities where they can access integrated, quality schools or to send their children to private schools. This strategy has been applied on a family-by-family basis. A strategy has not been devised that can successfully eliminate inferior schools to benefit the masses of poor and working-class African American children. This book outlines a remedy for this situation that should be embraced by the civil rights organizations.

Even schools of choice do not represent choice for everyone. Most African American children are still stuck in the worst public schools while the best teachers and the most motivated families access the exciting new models. Furthermore, the poor parents of children stuck in the inferior neighborhood schools are paying, through local taxes, for the children who flee to be bused to the schools of choice. A large school district in southeastern Michigan was paying $11 million a year to bus the more fortunate children to their school of choice. This tab was being paid by the families whose children were "going nowhere fast," as my father used to say.

Civil rights coalitions, politicians, and school board members are called upon to embrace the model in this book that can result in quality education for the masses of African American children. As this book recommends, issues of quality of instruction, cultural enrichment, and instructional accountability should be advocated by those who control education for African American children. If civil rights organizations, politicians, and school board members will support the implementation of this model, we can begin to close the achievement gap. To do so, we need to create a partnership between scholars and activists.

A greater outcry was heard from the black middle class when a black General Motors vice president was denied membership in an exclusive country club in Michigan than has been expressed over the fact that the majority of African American males exit the public schools for unemployment and prison rather than college. No agitation, no justice.

It seems that because we have been thwarted in finding a path to economic and educational equality, a certain phenomenon has emerged, evident in almost every issue of *Jet* magazine. The past five years have seen a proliferation of celebrations of milestones and commemorations of events that occurred in the civil rights movement: a banquet to commemorate the fortieth anniversary of the signing of this or that bill, the thirty-fifth anniversary of the march from here to there, the recognition of this or that figure from the civil rights movement. Much of this celebration is merely a walk down memory lane, back to the period in the 1950s and 1960s, when we knew what to do. In those days, we had Thurgood Marshall! Today, we have Clarence Thomas.

In those days, we had Bull Connor. We knew what to do with the police dogs, the fire hoses, the firebombs, and the assassins. The enemy was clear. We could all see who the enemy was and what he was doing. His language was explicit. Today, the enemy wears a business suit, and in too many cases the person speaking for the enemy is black. The language he speaks is politically correct. He is against "quotas." He is for "hard work." He is against "minority set-asides."

It gives us a sense of comfort to host events in which we celebrate the victories, the heroes, and the heroines of the past. We are constantly thinking of new and more extensive honors to bestow on them. Every civil rights warrior is writing a book and receiving some kind of medal or medallion. We are engaged in an orgy of celebration of the period when we knew what to do. For all the glories and victories of the past, however, the situation for our children has changed little.

What Has Changed

Upward mobility for African American families has had to be achieved within a very short time frame. Economic slavery, in the form of sharecropping, ended as late as 1948 — rather than 1865, as we have been taught (see Hale 1994, 15). African American families have not had the gradual three-generational climb toward upward mobility that European immigrants have enjoyed. We have had to achieve upward mobility in one generation. Most African Americans who are college educated come from working-class backgrounds. Most of the African Americans in college today represent the first generation in their families to attend college. African Americans have had only a few decades in which to connect with the "culture of power" and learn the fine points and nuances of mainstream America (Comer 1988, 1997; Comer et al. 1999).

The emergence of African American families from sharecropping in 1948 coincided with the end of the industrial period in American history, during which factories began to close, and little was being done nationally to prepare African American men and women for the postindustrial economy. As a result, every indicator of positive economic, mental, and social health in the African American community began to decline from 1950 to the present. In 1950, for example, only about 20 percent of African American families were headed by a single female (Comer 1988, 213). Today, 65 percent of African American families are female headed, and 85 percent of African American children come to school from single-parent households (Schomburg 1999, 320).

The economic limitations placed on African American men has placed a heavy burden on African American women to generate income, raise children, and hold our families and communities together. Even in the cases in which a man is present (only about 40 percent of African Americans are married today), African American women have to contribute a greater percentage of family income than white women. In general, African American women do not have as much time for "parental involvement" (as it is presently conceptualized) and homeschooling as middle-class white women do. Nevertheless, schools, as they presently operate, expect children to arrive at school at a high level of development—both intellectually and socially.

Furthermore, there is little recognition on the part of members of the helping professions of the division of energy that occurs when such a large number of African American women with children are unmarried. In addition to trying to be a "good mother" at a young age, an unmarried African American mother has to give attention to trying to find a husband or at least to obtaining some element of emotional security and satisfaction in her personal life. Male-female relations in the African American community are contentious, and many women feel abused by men emotionally and physically. This instability makes it all the more difficult for African American women to shoulder the burden that is theirs in rearing children alone.

It takes a high degree of maturity and development for a young mother to give priority time to a child when there is not enough time for herself. It takes a high degree of maturity and development to devote money to a child when there is not enough money for basic necessities.

The public schools were not intended to provide equal educational opportunities for African Americans. They were created to provide upward mobility for the children of European immigrants. African Americans have been engaged in a game of hide-and-seek with white Americans for quality education: white America has been hiding quality education, and African Americans have been seeking it (Hale 1994, 17–20).

The Supreme Court's *Brown* decision was an important landmark in the game of hide-and-seek in that it precipitated the post-1954 civil rights movement and indicated to the African American community that we could look to the federal government to intervene in the way we were being treated by state government officials. Only because of this decision and the widespread use of television could bus boycotts and other protests and demonstrations be launched by civil rights activists. It was critical that the whole nation see the police dogs and fire hoses on the evening news to mold public opinion in our favor. African Americans have a distrust of what Republicans believe in so strongly: local and state control of money for education and social welfare services. Historically, local decisions were made with no sense of integrity toward African Americans. If the federal government did not step in and make white state officials act fairly, the African American community suffered. So, for all practical purposes, the cries of "states rights," "sovereignty," "outside agitators," "carpetbaggers" all sound to us like the battle cry of the Ku Klux Klan.

White Americans have become aggressive in the past thirty years in providing educational advantages for their children, even before birth and certainly before they arrive at school. White Americans created the concept of giftedness when school desegregation began. By creating an academic discipline focused on the "gifted and talented," they produced a pedagogy for educating their children on the top floor of an integrated school while African American children were trained on the bottom levels.

A few years ago, I was invited to give a keynote speech in Los Angeles on the black gifted child. In preparation for the address, I had discovered in the literature the connection between desegregation and the gifted movement. I asked my hosts why they wanted to participate in a movement that has its impetus in sidestepping desegregation. In reply, they said that the white parents who were promoting gifted education were securing public money to enrich their children. The African American parents felt that they should at least try to get African American children identified for the program, so that they could obtain their fair share of the tax dollars that were being devoted to those programs.

Over the past twenty years, while we have been busy rediscovering our African roots, many white Americans have been securing their places in college, professional schools, and the workplace. The creation of African American studies departments, the documentation of African contributions to civilization, the preservation of African and African American cultural artifacts are all important intellectual work, and I consider myself a part of the African American cultural intelligentsia. However, these areas of inquiry should not be seen as an end in themselves for educational scholars and psychologists. There are so few of us that we must challenge ourselves to apply our scholarship to the issue of raising the academic achievement levels for African American children. This is the most significant challenge for the twenty-first century.

Public schools that serve inner-city children have not produced positive educational outcomes because there is no system of instructional accountability that operates for parents who have not themselves had the benefits of advanced education. The middle-income African Americans who have the information about cutting-edge educational practices have moved to suburban and private schools and have taken their advocacy with them, leaving inner-city African Americans to fend for themselves.

We know how to train good teachers. What we have not addressed is how to erect support systems and supervisory strategies so that the teachers are motivated to do what they have been trained to do. Moreover, how do we get teachers to teach children effectively when the teachers have little stake in the achievement of the children they are teaching? We make teacher training the focus of school reform, but the real issue is teacher supervision. Is the principal providing instructional leadership for the teachers in his or her building? This issue is, or should be, on the cutting edge of school reform. The most important element in education is the activity between the teacher and the child. If the parent does not have the skills to supervise the services rendered to the child, it becomes the responsibility of the highest-ranking professional in the building to ensure that every child is taught effectively.

Recommendations for In-service Training of Teachers

It has been my pleasure for the past twenty-six years to work as a consultant with public school districts throughout the country. In that capacity, I have had the opportunity to observe the ways in which in-service training has been structured for teachers in the area of multicultural education. If schools are going to engage teachers in addressing the issues raised here to improve the education of African American children, the way in which training proceeds needs to be changed.

First of all, there needs to be a top-down strategy to truly effect change. The superintendent of schools in Charlottesville, Virginia, asked me to make a presentation to the school board, members of the city council, and community leaders before I ever addressed the teachers. That is a highly effective strategy. Many of these issues require the cooperation of the top decision makers in a school district before training begins for teachers.

I have participated in planning sessions with consultants who were designing teacher training programs, in response to a federal court order on inequality of outcomes for minority children, that did not include the principals. I asked the consultants how they expected to stimulate lasting change without involving the principals. They intended to involve one teacher from each building in the training: did they expect teachers, I asked, to notify the principal of the new direction the building would be going in? I have also participated in otherwise well-organized diversity and multicultural days at which numerous speakers were brought in but everyone in the school heard a different speech.

If change is going to be stimulated, it is now time to structure training so that everyone in the building hears the same thing. More important, after the training, time must be provided for the faculty to meet with the principal and plan how they are going to implement the strategies they have learned about. I have not yet witnessed this second step. Until we begin to train teachers and principals together and create a structure in which they engage each other around the ideas, we will continue to hold "feel-good" revival meetings and return the next school day to business as usual.

Recommendations for Civil Rights Groups, African American Controlled Public School Boards, and Advocacy Organizations

Civil rights groups must marshal the political forces of the African American community and their allies in state legislatures to equalize school financing. There is no question that there are gross inequities in school financing. In addition, civil rights leadership groups must bring in African American intellectuals to contribute to the discussion around strategies to achieve quality education for African American children. Many of our leaders are politicians, not scholars. There must be seats at the table for scholars and politicians to engage in dialogue and to formulate solutions.

In city after city, discussions of school reform essentially involve a group of local activists, politicians, and angry parents fighting it out for the microphone. The African American community now includes many intellectuals who have devoted their careers to issues related to school reform. In addition to town meetings, school boards should host "think tanks" at which papers are presented and ideas solicited from the African American intellectual community and evaluated for designing reform. I once participated in such a forum, sponsored by the Chicago Urban League and funded by the Spencer Foundation. The papers from that forum are now available to the public (Watkins, Lewis, and Chou 2001).

When a scholar launches an organization to create an agenda for the implementation of his or her ideas, the generation of ideas suffers because of the energy required to build the organization. A partnership between those who build organizations and those who generate ideas would allow a greater degree of both creative ideas and the implementation of those ideas. Think tanks should be held at conferences sponsored by professional associations. Instead of conferences consisting only of presentations given to practitioners, think tanks should also be organized so that scholars can talk with one another and with civil rights leaders, advocates, and politicians.

Achieving equal educational outcomes is key to solving the fundamental problems facing African Americans in this country, and this objective should be given top priority by civil rights and advocacy leadership groups. Recent civil rights activity has focused more on commemorating past marches and milestones than on carving out a path for our future.

Civil rights leaders have begun to operate like firefighters: in an emergency, when someone is beaten up or mistreated, the civil rights leaders all run to the scene to protest. There is a need for that in the African American community—Rev. Al Sharpton and Johnnie Cochran to the rescue! I myself have needed to be rescued several times during the course of my career. However, there is as great a need for civil rights leaders to formulate a long-term strategy for improving the situation of the African American majority. A group of people who have received a poor education cannot generate the resources to provide decent housing and quality of life for their families. It is difficult for people with low incomes to amass the economic and political power to improve the quality of education and thereby improve their fortunes. They are caught in a vicious circle.

Some of our civil rights groups focus on employment discrimination.

However, they need to realize that in the future, no one will have to discriminate against African American young people in the employment arena, because they will not be qualified for the jobs in the technologically advanced workplaces.

Leadership groups, such as the Urban League, the Children's Defense Fund, the National Black Child Development Institute, and the NAACP, need to incorporate into their agenda strategic efforts to assist African American families who are having difficulty negotiating the schools. These difficulties cut across socioeconomic levels and inner-city, suburban, and private school boundaries.

The experiences I relate in chapter 4 of this book are not unique to me and my son. A whole book could be written describing similar events experienced by people I know. Many African American parents of all income levels who are trying to guide their children's journey through school are frustrated by their interactions with teachers. Even well-educated parents feel that they are caught in a maze. The typical response for those who can afford it is to move their children from school to school. They do not have the skills or any assistance in working out problems as they occur.

In my opinion, there is a desperate need for the creation of an Educational Aide Society in African American communities throughout the country. Such an organization could be sponsored by the Urban League or by advocacy organizations such as the National Black Child Development Institute or the Children's Defense Fund. Just as the Legal Aide Society provides legal services to lower-income families, the Educational Aide Society could provide subsidized or sliding-fee-scale services for families who are having difficulty negotiating the schools. It could be a referral service through which African American families are provided with the names of psychologists, psychiatrists, counselors, educators, or social workers willing to attend parent conferences with them. It is a lonely experience for a single parent of a male child to sit alone at a parent conference opposite five staff persons with clipboards running off a list of LWBs — "learning while black" designations.

On several occasions during my son's early childhood, I observed him at school so that I might understand the context for some of the complaints about his behavior. Other parents need to have someone they can trust observe their children in the classroom. One of the biggest weapons school districts wield is the recommendation that a child be tested academically or psychologically, with the possible result being the administration of medication or special-education placement. African American parents need assistance in understanding psychological tests and their results. They also need assistance in identifying mental health professionals who can evaluate their children from a culturally sensitive frame of reference.

Educating Parents on Cutting-Edge Educational Practices

Parents and teachers in the inner city should be provided with an opportunity to visit schools in which children from the "culture of power" are educated. They should have an opportunity to attend forums and conferences so that they can use the power they amass on school boards and civic organizations to move our children into the twenty-first century.

The focus of too many school boards is upon obtaining jobs for people they know, issuing contracts for services, or amassing visibility and political clout that can lead to higher political office. An effort must be made to create a more informed constituency by elevating the awareness among African Americans in general of cutting-edge educational practices. The general citizenry is the pool from which school board members are drawn; exposing African American parents to cutting-edge educational practices will empower them to begin to construct quality educational programs in their own communities. Generally, when families have amassed sufficient resources, they either move to a more affluent community, where there are quality schools, or they enroll their children in private schools. There is no effort to broaden the horizons of those who choose the inner-city schools, or those who have no choice, to help them create a vision of how to improve the quality of education where they are. This book is written to describe strategies that can be employed in any school to raise the intellectual climate and achievement rate of the children. The children do not have to go anywhere else. We have got to put an end to this "black flight" mentality. All African American children must receive an excellent education wherever they are found. Parent activists should encourage school board members and politicians to embrace and implement the ideas presented in this book.

Support for African American Scholars

It is imperative that we raise up a cadre of African American scholars to generate research around child development and educational issues that are critical to the survival of our children. As one who has dedicated her career to this intellectual enterprise, I believe it is important to identify the many subtle forces that diminish the viability of an academic career for African Americans. Obtaining doctoral degrees is the least of the problem. The trek through academia seeking tenure and academic rank is treacherous, at best. So treacherous, in fact, that the numbers of African American men who seek the doctoral degree has declined dramatically in recent years. Over the past twenty-six years, the majority of my contemporaries who completed their doctoral work with me have left academia for "real jobs."

African American foundation executives could make a critical difference in creating support for African American academics. It is difficult for African American scholars to achieve funding for their research, which is, by definition, swimming against the current of mainstream thought and practices in America. In contrast, according to a 60 *Minutes* documentary, several of the scholars who contributed to *The Bell Curve* (Herrnstein and Murray 1994), a book that seeks to document the intellectual inferiority of African Americans, received as much as $3.5 million for their research from the Prince Foundation, a conservative private foundation that funds such efforts.

Yet those of us who dedicate our careers to the defense of African American children from such assault remain without grants. Without a grant, research can be conducted only in a scholar's free time, after working a full-time job. A close reading of the life of W. E. B. Du Bois (Lewis 1993) reveals that the premier African American scholar of this century spent sixty years trying to find funding for his work. Virtually all of the scholarship he produced was done at his own expense. It is time for African American foundation executives to take the lead and support the research careers of African American scholars so that we can generate the scholarship our community so desperately needs.

A Final Word to Parents

As we work toward the Beloved Community, it is important that African American parents impose on themselves the same standard I am setting out for white school officials in dealing with African American children. It has been disturbing to me to observe how often parents who serve as volunteers for extracurricular activities send home assignments that the children cannot do alone.

Keith joined the Cub Scouts when he was seven years old. Each year, the Cub Scouts held the Pinewood Derby car races. During his second year, when the time for the derby rolled around, I was handed a car and told that my son was to put the wheels on. We knew from previous experience that the key to winning the race is the way the wheels are put on—at least all of the leaders knew that. His Cub Scout leaders, who had sons in the pack, were automotive engineers. Many of the boys, including my son, are being raised in single-parent households. In essence, the fathers were competing with one another, and the other children were merely the vehicles for their competition.

It seems to me so much fairer for the boys to be taught to put the wheels on their own cars and for the competition to be between the boys rather than between the fathers. Of course, wanting my son to have a successful experience, I played the game (though I did not like it) and engaged one of my friends who is a mechanical engineer at Chrysler to put the wheels on my son's car. Nevertheless, my son placed third, so you can see what sort of competition we were up against. The parents of the winner probably raised Henry Ford from the dead to attach the wheels to their son's car!

The same applies to athletic teams. It is commendable that African American men donate their time to working with boys on athletic teams. However, in many cases, they need to do better, to "pull up." Often the coaches are involved because their sons are on the team, and they are far from fair and impartial in allocating playing time. Worse yet is the obsession with winning when the children are only ten years old. My sister's husband, Emanual Leaks, is a former National Basketball Association player. He has donated a great deal of his time to working on basketball skills with African American boys. He has observed that the coaches are not trying to *teach* these boys (who are as young as ten) to play basketball, they are trying to pick the ones who already know how to play.

I would add that some of the coaches act as though winning is the only thing. Rather than working with the boys on the team to develop their skills, I have observed a coach pack the team with boys who can win, allowing the boys he started with to sit on the bench with no playing time at all. There are other, wonderful programs, like the Police Athletic League, that teach ten- to twelve-year-old boys how to play the games. It defeats the whole purpose of the programs to demoralize and discourage them by placing too much emphasis on winning.

I observed a coach who was losing a game by forty-six points who would not relent in the final quarter and give the boys who had not played at all a chance to play. In another instance, I observed a coach who was winning with his first string (including his son), by a fifteen-point margin, who had to be cajoled by the parents into giving the other boys a chance to play.

I realize that most men coaching athletic teams have not had courses in child psychology and developmentally appropriate practices. However, it is important to get the message across that parents sign up their sons on sports teams for skill development and character building. It is important for African American men who work with those boys to place a premium on what is caught as well as what is taught. This concept of developing the Beloved Community needs to be discussed and disseminated throughout our community so that we exact the same standard of fairness in our dealings with our own children that we demand from white Americans.

Throughout this book, I have admonished educators to approach the education of African American children as if everything depends upon them, because in many cases it does. However, I end this book by acknowledging that unfortunately the educational system of this country operates on the concept of social Darwinism—the survival of the fittest. Until we can create the Beloved Community, parents need to realize that to a great extent, the future of a child still depends upon the parents. W. E. B. Du Bois said that "in truth, school is a desperate duel between new soul and old to pass on facts and methods and dreams from a dying world without letting either teacher or taught lose for a moment faith and interest. It is hard work. It is never wholly a success without the painstaking help of the parent" (1989, 68).

It is my intent in writing this book to engage the total community in the enterprise of parenting our children. I challenge African American parents to join advocacy groups, such as the National Black Child Development Institute. If there is not a chapter in your community, I challenge you to start one. I challenge you to attend their national conferences, to start study groups and support groups in which members share their war stories, and to organize to improve the quality of education for children in your community. Stimulate your churches to become involved in educational advocacy. No justice, no peace. No agitation, no justice.

The Church's Educational and Advocacy Mission with African American Children

Cognitive, Affective, and Religious Context

The work of instructing my dear fellow-slaves was the sweetest engagement with which I was ever blessed. . . . These dear souls came not to Sabbath School because it was popular to do so, nor did I teach them because it was reputable to be thus engaged. Every moment they spent in that school, they were liable to be taken up and given thirty-nine lashes. They came because they wished to learn. Their minds had been starved by their cruel masters. They had been shut up in mental darkness. I taught them, because it was the delight of my soul to be doing something that looked like bettering the condition of my race.

—Frederick Douglass, 1845

In chapter 7 of this book, I urge the African American church to become an advocate of change in the larger social systems that affect the socialization of black youth—particularly the public schools. The purpose of this appendix is to address internal theological issues that are related to the Christian education of African American children and youth. Nannie Helen Burroughs, an African American Baptist churchwoman, spoke of the need for black people to organize "inside," to reemphasize the moral and spiritual dimensions of life, and to teach black children "the internals and the eternals rather than the externals. Be more concerned with putting in than getting on. We have been too bothered about the externals— clothes or money. What we need are mental and spiritual giants who are aflame with a purpose" (1972, 552).

This section is designated as an appendix, separate from the body of the book, to emphasize the current separation of church and state in American society. The discussion here is designed to be an exploration of the ways in which the African American church can construct her Christian education mission internally to complement her external mission as an agent of change for all African American children in the Village.

Some elements of Christian education in the African American church are unique, and if they are not taught by the African American church, they will not be taught at all.

1. The program of Christian education must meet the needs of African Americans whatever they are. Any need or concern within the African American community, individually or collectively, falls within the scope of the Christian educational ministry. This program should contribute to political action, economic development, and training in the cultural heritage of African American people.

2. The learning theory of the curriculum should reflect a ministry relevant to the needs and growth of each stage of the life cycle: the African American child, teenager, college student, older youth, young adult, middle-aged adult, older adult, and senior adult. This education should develop naturally out of the lifestyles and experiences of African American people.

3. Christian education should enhance the development of a positive self-concept in children. People construct a self-image by seeing themselves reflected in the eyes of others in their culture. This is the concept of the "looking-glass self." If everywhere African American children look they see negative concepts of what it means to be African American, they will develop negative self-concepts.

Mission of the Sunday School

According to Robert Lynn and Elliot Wright (1971), the institution of the Sunday school was initiated in 1759, in England, by Robert Raikes, who is known as the "father" of the Sunday school. There were two purposes for establishing a church school on Sunday.

First of all, the children of the poor were required to work in factories for long hours six days a week. On Sunday, their only day of leisure, they were often unsupervised and became involved in vandalism and crime. Noting the relationship between inadequate schooling and criminal activity, Raikes established the school on Sunday as a preventative to juvenile delinquency and to help youngsters who had inadequate schooling.

The Mission of the Black Sunday School

There is an interesting parallel between the founding of the Sunday school in England and the function of the Sunday school in the African American community. Sunday school in the early African American community helped propel the African slave and those who had been freed toward literacy. It was in the Sunday school, often in secret, that African people learned to read the Bible, to do mathematics, and, eventually, to write.

According to Olivia Pearl Stokes, the Sunday school was also established for training in morals. White men used Sunday school to preach to their congregations against drinking, war, and slavery, though in America, the focus was entirely on the curse of liquor (Stokes 1972, 92). Stokes points out that after the Civil War the African American Sunday school brought literacy to the former slaves. When the historically black colleges were founded in the South, they often included Sunday schools in which the faculty were required to teach. The Sunday school was designed to reach youths who did not have the educational background to qualify for college. The Sunday school provided the chance to be educated, an opportunity denied by the larger society so that any opportunities outside of servitude to whites could be circumscribed (ibid., 92–93).

Like many a church, the Union Grove Baptist Church in Columbus, Ohio, pastored for forty-three years by my father, Rev. Phale D. Hale Sr., began as a Sunday school (in 1888) and grew into a church. At the time of its origin, the Sunday school was on the cutting edge of African American life. It met a critical need in the life of African slaves and former slaves. The theologians C. Eric Lincoln and Lawrence Mamiya have described the dynamic interactive relationship between black families and churches: "Families constituted the building blocks for black churches and the churches through their preaching and teaching, symbols, belief system, morality, and rituals provided a unity—a glue that welded families and the community to each other" (1990, 311). The authors observe that after the Civil War, black churches legitimated the informal marital relationships of freedmen and freedwomen. Parents often brought their children to church, sometimes forcing them to go because they deeply believed that the church would provide the children with a moral education. Lincoln and Mamiya note that "churches also provided Sunday school for children and adults, and for many black people for a long period of time the church was the place where they first began to learn rudimentary reading skills" (ibid., 312).

Both Carter G. Woodson and Charles S. Johnson have pointed to the molding influences of churches on rural youth. Although worship services were aimed at adult members, special Sunday services were set aside for the participation of children and children's choirs. Woodson (1969) uses the phrase "junior church," and Johnson (1967) refers to "Children's Day," to describe the special activities of rural churches for youth.

Lincoln notes that black churches also provide recreational events and sponsor athletic teams. Black churches have served as concert halls, art galleries, and public forums for African Americans. "The first public performance seen or given by many black children often occurred in the church" (Lincoln and Mamiya 1990, 312). A major problem in the programs of contemporary black churches is that there is not enough focus on black youth: "While Sunday schools continue as a traditional part of the typical black church, many perform functions more akin to babysitting than education and socialization. Too many black pastors do not concern themselves with this aspect of ministry, but tend to delegate the religious education of their youth to someone else" (ibid., 316).

In his survey and study of black churches, Lincoln has found that the vast majority of black pastors still see preaching as their major task. His findings suggest that more attention needs to be paid to the education and socialization of black youth. Black churches, he asserts, should begin with the religious education that is within their control, especially with Sunday school education and literature. "The process of identity formation is a very subtle one, and the selection and presentation of Sunday school materials, as innocuous as they seem, send messages to young children about what is important and unimportant about themselves and their society, no less than what should have religious significance in their lives" (ibid., 318).

Our task here is to consider ways of refocusing the ministry of the Sunday school so that it can continue to fulfill its mission in the future. A number of pitfalls must be avoided as we consider the Sunday school of the future.

Socioeconomic Barriers

We must remove the socioeconomic barriers that separate the church's educational ministry from the masses of African American people. Most large churches in the African American community today are overwhelmingly middle class in membership and orientation. One sometimes gets the feeling on Sunday morning that one is at a fashion show rather than worship service. The opulence on display is a deterrent to less advantaged people in the community to participate in church activities. Sunday school in these settings is not an outreach activity, it is Bible study meeting among the members. These social barriers should be removed if the Sunday school is to fulfill its mission.

My pastor, Rev. Charles G. Adams, pastor of Hartford Memorial Baptist Church, has structured a Saturday evening worship service at 7:30 P.M. that is marketed to "generation X," to which it is appropriate to wear casual attire. During the summer, casual wear is advocated for all parishioners at all services. This is a good trend for the Sunday school. I have even seen some churches with a largely middle-class membership who have Sunday school and other children's and youth activities for members' children (those in the Family) and then a separate tract of activities for the children who live in the lower-income neighborhood surrounding the church (those in the Village).

Content of Teaching Material

Attention must be given to training Sunday school teachers in child development and new trends in pedagogy as well as new trends in biblical interpretation and systematic theology. In her book, *Today's Children and Yesterday's Heritage*, Sophia Fahs (1952) discusses one problem that derives from teaching a literal interpretation of the Bible to modern children. Many children are confused by stories about God talking to people from the heavens, parting the Red Sea, striking people dead, and so forth. Modern children have been taught the laws of the universe in their science classes at school, and they are skeptical of stories relating miraculous occurrences they have never experienced in their daily lives. Fahs recommends that we bring Christian education into harmony with the rest of education.

The Bible is God's revelation of Himself to a particular people. We draw inspiration in our lives by reading about His activity in their lives. The Bible is art. The Bible is history. The Bible is literature. The question of whether to interpret the Bible literally is not important. Much of the Bible was transmitted across generations through the oral tradition, centuries before it was written down, and consequently the stories told were colored by the beliefs and worldview of the people who preserved and transmitted them. That makes them no less inspiring. However, the message is the important element in the Bible stories, not the debate about whether it is literature or fact.

We must help children read the Bible in such a way that it helps them to understand the nature of the universe. God has created a world that has order and principles that govern it. These principles are relevant to science and religion. In science we teach children the physical laws of nature so that they can understand how to function in the world. These same laws are important in religion.

We need to dispel the Santa Claus image of God that unfortunately we disseminate in Sunday school. We teach children to pray to God to help them win an athletic contest, but why should God help them and not the other team? We should help them to see that God does not operate like that. Prayer is not the same as sitting on Santa's lap and telling him what you want for Christmas. Prayer is a process of meditation wherein one is still, communes with God, focuses the God within oneself, and harnesses one's ability to perform maximally in all of life's contests. A person wins because he or she understands the laws of the universe and functions in harmony with the universe, not because God passes out favors. A correct prayer in an athletic contest is to ask God to help the team members to do their best. They will win if their best is good enough to defeat the other team. Our task in the Sunday school is to enrich our children's conceptualization of the universe by combining the insights of our religion with the theories of science.

In the Sunday school, we have a responsibility to teach the history of the African American church and the history of the African American people. We must help African Americans understand their role in the struggle for liberation and justice in America and the world. We have a responsibility to include illustrations of African American people in the Sunday school literature as well as content that reflects the culture and experience of African Americans.

It is critical that the Sunday school address the economic practices that accompany Protestant Christianity. Our children must understand the manner in which capitalism and Protestantism go hand in hand. White Anglo-Saxon Protestants read the same Bible we read, sing the same hymns we sing, and pray to the same God we pray to. However, they interpret the oppression they have perpetrated against African people to amass their fortune as a blessing from God for hard work. A survey published in *Newsweek* reveals the disparity between the "religious" beliefs of mainstream Christians and the priority they assign to applying the principles of Christianity to matters of social justice. Respondents were asked, "In the next millennium, which one of the following do you think should be organized Christianity's top priority?" Thirty-eight percent answered "Returning to traditional moral values," 32 percent "Spreading the faith," 13 percent "Increasing tolerance," and a mere 7 percent "Righting social ills" ("Christianity across the Ages" 1999, 62).

It is clear that the Christians who responded to this survey see little correlation between embracing moral values and righting social ills. This is one of the reasons that 11:00 A.M. at Sunday morning worship services can be the most segregated hour of the week.

In discussions of Christian missionary activities, we must correct the misconceptions about Africa that are perpetuated by white denominations. First of all, we must dispel the notion that Africans are primitive, cannibalistic heathens who need to be converted to Christianity in order to be civilized. This notion was at the root of African enslavement and is a cloak for present-day colonialism and economic exploitation.

Africa should be presented in all of its complexity. Crises in Africa, such as famines and civil wars over resources, including oil, gold, and diamonds, should be presented in the context of Western domination and exploitation and not from the perspective of African poverty. In the words of Olivia Pearl Stokes, "Christian education in the Black churches is that ministry of the church which provides the educational undergirding for mission as seen from the Black perspective—meaning, the struggle for liberation and equal justice in the spirit of the teachings of Jesus Christ in our worship, relationships with all men, our witness, and daily work in the American society" (1972, 100).

Elements of a Black Youth Ministry

Charles Foster has pointed out that a primary purpose of black youth ministry is to call youth into discipleship. This purpose embodies the identity and vocation central to the experience of adolescence. Identity has to do with allegiance and commitment—not only "Who am I?" but also "Whose am I?" The first task is to clarify one's relationship to Jesus Christ and the church that was formed in loyalty to Him. The second task involves clarifying one's relationship to one's cultural heritage   the heritage of African Americans. In the interplay of call and commitment to Christ, heard and responded to through the medium of the African American experience, the identity of black youth takes form. Vocation has to do with the expression of that commitment to Christ in service to the community as an agent of Christ. Vocation is political activity. Vocation engages the values and ideals of Christ shaped in the crucible of the African American experience for the sake of that community and the welfare of all humankind (Foster 1989, 103).

Discipleship is, consequently, both the aim and the means of African American youth ministry. There should be no confusion about whether youth are viewed as the church of tomorrow or participants in the church's ministry today. The call to discipleship is lifelong. Both new disciples and old disciples are disciples (Foster 1989, 103–4).

Jacquelyn Grant (1989) has set as a goal for youth ministry the nurturing of a sense of "somebodiness" in youth. The youth ministry must be evangelical. When youth are confronted with many options for their commitments, churches are faced with the task of presenting the gospel of Jesus Christ in a way that makes it relevant to their experience. We must reach out to youth wherever they are.

The creation of a coffeehouse ministry is a vehicle for involving the youth of a church in reaching out to other youth in the community. Lyman Coleman (1969) has proposed that a room in the church (with a direct entrance) be set aside for the young people, which they can decorate with posters, graffiti, small tables for intimate conversations, dim lighting, contemporary music, and a general atmosphere inviting to their peers, as a place of ministry by high school and college students to the community. The real value of a coffeehouse ministry is the opportunity it affords to bridge the gap between the church and the secular world. Many young people today have turned off the church because they think that it has nothing to offer them, and they will not come to church. They will, however, come to a coffeehouse, and this neutral "marketplace" affords the chance to sit down around a cup of coffee and pizza and talk about the common concerns and issues in their lives. This stretches the arms of the church out into the community and allows it to touch the lives of youth who would not otherwise participate in traditional church functions. A contemporary update on the coffeehouse ministry is the "gospel nightclub," a church-sponsored ministry wherein hip-hop gospel music is played, allowing the church, again, to reach out to the community (Carter 2000).

Foster insists that the call to discipleship must reveal the viability of the gospel for the lives of African American children and youth, and that viability is most evident in ministries that are hope filled. Especially for African American youth trapped in cycles of poverty and frustration, the call to discipleship is essentially a call to hope in the face of what often appears to be an absolutely hopeless situation. A gospel of otherworldly escape does not serve these youth well. The call to discipleship comes as a call to liberation. Liberation is experienced as respect, dignity, freedom, and responsibility (Foster 1989, 105–6).

Three Tasks of African American Youth Ministry

Foster suggests three tasks of African American youth ministry:

1. African American youth ministry involves connecting youth to Christ and the mission of the church. The goal of ministries to African American youth is to incorporate them into a lifestyle of discipleship. The congregation must help youth become so familiar with the stories, symbols, and traditions of the African American Christian experience that they become the means for understanding and articulating their identities and responsibilities as African American Christians. The elders must model for them what it means to live as disciples. The responsibilities of the youth ministry include reading the scripture, supported by the elders; contributing to music and worship leadership; supervision of younger children; and participation in community projects that provide care for people with special needs.

Foster identifies the central role youth played in the civil rights movement — integrating schools, restaurants, and other places of public accommodation is an example of the wider possibilities for youth ministry (1989, 112). Teenagers and college students were freer economically to become involved in demonstrations. Many college students in historically black colleges attended college out of town, so their families were not known to members of the power structure. Economic sanctions could have been more easily directed toward their parents if these demonstrations had occurred in their hometowns.

2. African American youth ministry involves advocating a viable future for African American youth. Advocacy ministry draws upon the historic emphasis upon the liberation of the oppressed in the African American Christian experience (ibid., 113). Advocacy ministry should call attention to "the seeming preference of communities for prisons rather than crime prevention or rehabilitation programs, lower taxes rather than quality schools, roads rather than parks or playgrounds, or medical programs that feature the heroic rather than the everyday needs of families." Furthermore, the church needs to speak for children and youth when they have no voice, representing them when they have little influence, as well as training them to speak and to represent themselves when and where that might be possible (ibid., 114).

Ministries of advocacy depend upon an accurate understanding of the situations in which African American youth find themselves. This step makes possible the development of appropriate strategies to equip youth to combat the forces limiting their futures. A ministry of advocacy does not end with providing youth with coping skills, however. It must ultimately involve an encounter with the institutional structures of government, industry, business, and the church at the points where the futures of African American youth are circumscribed.

> The involvement of church leaders in the movement to desegregate schools provides one example of an advocacy ministry that led to systematic changes. Similar efforts are needed to alter the conditions contributing to unemployment, drug use, teenage pregnancy, ineffective schooling, lack of enrichment experiences, and problems of self-esteem among many young people.
>
> A ministry advocating a viable future for African American youth consequently includes adults who speak out and negotiate for youth at the points of their powerlessness. It also encompasses ministries that equip youth with the skills to influence their own futures. It also engages in political and legal activities to improve the systemic conditions for the creation of a viable future for youth. (ibid., 116)

3. African American youth ministry involves training young people for leadership in Christ's ministry. Foster addresses a typical misunderstanding in the

way people view discipleship: Discipleship has little to do with nurturing in people the passive emulation of some great figure—even Jesus. Instead, it emphasizes the kind of training in the teachings and life of the master that culminates in the liberation of the disciple. "The transformational character of this process may be traced to Peter as he changed from the awestruck and awkward fisherman into the powerful leader of the early church under the influence of Jesus. Discipleship in this sense is the activity of the *empowered for the sake of the powerless that they too might be empowered for ministries of service*" (ibid., 117).

Four Elements of Transforming Leadership

Foster sets forth four elements of transforming leadership for African American youth: identity, visioning, biculturality, and leadership.

In the relationship of a young person to Jesus, the "somebodiness" of a person is determined by the grace of God rather than the structures of society. The source of one's identity and vocation transcends the expectations of those around us. African American children must be taught to transcend the circumstances of their situation in the United States as they try to build the lives they envision. Foster suggests that we must imbue youth with the freedom to walk around within the structures of this society in much the same way that Daniel wandered around the lion's den. They must be taught to view the events and circumstances of this world from God's perspective rather than from a human perspective that seeks to circumscribe their possibilities (ibid., 118).

Transforming leadership must enable African American youth to transcend their situations and envision a bright and fulfilling future. Foster sees vision as crucial to the continuity of a community. Slaves drew inspiration from the promises of liberation described in Exodus and from the freedom of the early church faith implicit in the resurrection of Christ. Those stories inspired and guided the actions of countless men and women through the years of servitude and bondage.

The task of visioning for African American Christians today is more difficult than it was for our ancestors. "The forms of oppression are more subtle. The structures of society are more complex. The dangers for all of humanity are more comprehensive" (ibid., 119). African American youth face a future characterized by the growing disparity between those who have and those who have not. Similarly, the playing field has been increasingly stratified to give an advantage to the children connected to the culture of power. African American youth will not be connected to employment in our rapidly changing world unless they have the ability to adjust to changing technologies and institutional structures. "They are faced with the threat of fragmenting communities, an environment so polluted as to be dangerous to their health and welfare, and the specter of nuclear annihilation. The future for youth is a fragile one. It could easily become a hopeless future" (ibid.). It is therefore essential that the African American youth ministry provide practice in envisioning in the face of these forces.

A third element of transforming leadership involves the ability to act with meaning and power in more than one cultural milieu. One of the most crucial challenges faced by those who are involved in the socialization of African American children and youth is to assist them in synthesizing the meaning of their existence in America, where their very physical appearance subjects them to the judgments of European Americans. They must understand that their very presence on this continent identifies them with bondage and servitude.

W. E. B. Du Bois pointed out at the turn of the twentieth century the "two-ness" of being African and American (1989, 3). Foster maintains that African American youth need to be guided into the process of accenting this double consciousness to achieve cross-cultural and global ecumenical conversations with other young people so they can discern and respond to God's liberating activity from more than one cultural perspective (ibid., 120). African American youth need to be guided to view the limitations and hypocrisy of the societal structures that circumscribe their fortunes and future from a transcendent perspective. In other words, they need to understand what they are up against, with a view to overcoming those obstacles.

A goal for African American youths must always be the refinement of biculturality. They must be confident in the beauty of their heritage, culture, and lifestyles. But they also must keep an eye on the skills and abilities they will need to function creatively in the American mainstream.

Finally, African American youth need explicit training in practicing skills central to transactional leadership. Foster emphasizes that this leadership is crucial to the tasks of "initiating ideas and programs, negotiating options, exercising power to implement decisions, mobilizing people, and promoting common values and concerns." African American churches must continue their work in helping youth work on many of these skills—public speaking and reading, parliamentary procedure, and attention to the interpersonal dynamics of leadership (ibid., 121–22).

In the complexity of our modern world, these skills alone are insufficient to the task of training transforming leaders. "It is also important to help youth develop skills to function effectively in the institutions that give form to modern living—schools, jobs, etc. These organizational skills include the ability to discern patterns of power and authority, recruit volunteers, identify the needs of people and programs, set goals, develop strategies to accomplish those goals, and . . . evaluate the consequences of their efforts and the faithfulness of their participation in the ministry of Christ" (ibid., 122). Members of the helping professions need an insight into the missing pieces in the experiences of children who are not raised in middle-class families.

It is sometimes difficult for those who are offering help to fully grasp the areas in which help is needed. Several years ago, I was invited to give a lecture on child development to teenaged African American girls who had given birth to a child out of wedlock. The intent of the program was to give the girls job training and support so that they would not bear additional children without the support of marriage.

I prepared and delivered an hour-long address about child development and early-childhood education to assist them in raising their children. When the time came for the question-and-answer period, I was amazed that the girls did not ask me one question about the topic of my address. Every question had to do with how to handle conflict and stressful situations with supervisors and co-workers at their jobs. As I answered their questions, it occurred to me that when I was their age, I had found the answers to those types of questions around the dinner table in discussions with my parents. Later in life, I found the answers in long-distance telephone calls to them. One of the problems of growing up in a disadvantaged environment is that you do not have access to people who can guide you, advise you, and offer strategies for success.

Foster maintains that the youth ministry needs to develop the skills for articulating the meanings of the events in which people find themselves from the stories, symbols, and traditions of the African American Christian heritage. To help people find meaning in their own heritage is to help them find power. It also helps them to name the implications of their experience for the future. In that act they begin to help people discover meaning and hope in their experience. They become agents in God's liberating activity (ibid., 122–23). The school and the church can play a critical role in providing children and youth with close, nurturant mentoring by adults connected to the "culture of power," who can imbue them with strategies for negotiating people and societal structures that will lead to upward mobility and creative, productive lives.

References

Adams, John Hurst. 1972. "Saturday Ethnic School." *Spectrum*, July–August, 8–9.

Akbar, Na'im. 1976. Paper presented at the annual meeting of the Black Child Development Institute, October, San Francisco.

Anderson, Claud. 1994. *Black Labor, White Wealth: The Search for Power and Economic Justice*. Edgewood, Md.: Duncan and Duncan.

Asante, Molefi K. 1988. *Afrocentricity*. Trenton, N.J.: Africa World Press.

Association for Supervision and Curriculum Development. 1996. "Schools as Partners in Character Development." Press release. Arlington, Va.

Avery, Gordon F. 1998. "Globalism and the Prison Industrial Complex: An Interview with Angela Davis." *Race and Class* 40, no. 2–3: 145–57.

Banks, James. 1976. "Crucial Issues in the Education of Afro-American Children." *Journal of Afro-American Issues* 4, no. 3–4: 392–407.

Barrett, Leonard. 1974. "African Religions in the Americas." In *The Black Experience in Religion*, edited by C. Eric Lincoln. New York: Anchor.

Barrett, Paul. 1999. *The Good Black: A True Story of Race in America*. New York: Dutton.

Berry, Mary Frances. 1999. "The Forgotten Prisoners of a Disastrous War." *Essence* 30, no. 6: 194.

Billingsley, Andrew. 1992. *Climbing Jacob's Ladder: The Enduring Legacy of African-American Families*. New York: Simon and Schuster.

Boykin, A. Wade. 1978. "Psychological Behavioral Verve in Academic/Task Performance: Pretheoretical Considerations." *Journal of Negro Education* 47, no. 4: 343–54.

——. 1986. "The Triple Quandary and the Schooling of Afro-American Children." In *The School Achievement of Minority Children*, edited by Ulric Neisser. Hillsdale, N.J.: Lawrence Erlbaum Associates.

——. 1994. "A Talent Development Approach to School Reform." Paper presented at the annual meeting of the American Educational Research Association, April, New York.

Boykin, A. Wade, and O. A. Miller. 1997. "In Search of Cultural Themes and Their Expression in the Dynamics of Classroom Life." Paper presented at the annual meeting of the American Educational Research Association, March, Chicago.

Bredekamp, Sue, and Lorrie Shepard. 1989. "How Best to Protect Children from Inappropriate School Expectations, Practices, and Policies." *Young Children* 44, no. 3: 14–24.

Burroughs, Nannie Helen. 1972. "Unload Your Uncle Toms" (1927). In *Black Women in White America: A Documentary History*, edited by Gerda Lerner. New York: Vintage.

Campbell, Bebe M. 1994. *Brothers and Sisters.* New York: G. P. Putnam's Sons.

Carter, Kelley. 2000. "Heavenly Hip-Hop." *Detroit Free Press,* July 18, C-1.

Cartwright, Madeline, and Michael D'Orso. 1993. *For the Children: Lessons from a Visionary Principal.* New York: Doubleday.

Chisholm, Shirley. 1970. *Unbought and Unbossed.* New York: Avon.

"Christainity across the Ages." 1999. *Newsweek,* March 29, 52–58, 62.

Coleman, Lyman. 1969. *The Coffee House Itch.* Scottsdale, Pa.: Halfway House.

Comer, James P. 1988. *Maggie's American Dream: The Life and Times of a Black Family.* New York: New American Library.

———. 1997. *Waiting for a Miracle: Why Schools Can't Solve Our Problems—and How We Can.* New York: Dutton.

Comer, James P., Michael Ben-Avie, Norris M. Haynes, and Edward T. Joyner, eds. 1999. *Child by Child: The Comer Process for Change in Education.* New York: Teachers College Press.

Comer, James P., N. M. Haynes, E. T. Joyner, and Michael Ben-Avie. 1996. *Rallying the Whole Village: The Comer Process for Reforming Education.* New York: Teachers College Press.

Conley, Dalton. 1999. *Being Black, Living in the Red: Race, Wealth, and Social Policy in America.* Berkeley: University of California Press.

Cose, Ellis. 1993. *The Rage of a Privileged Class.* New York: HarperCollins.

———. 1998. "Living with the Test: Why Do Certain Black Students Succeed?" *Newsweek,* September 14, 65.

———. 1999. "The Good News about Black America (and Why Blacks Aren't Celebrating)." *Newsweek,* June 7, 28–40.

DeBarros, K., and Claudette Bennett. 1998. "The Black Population in the United States: March 1997 (Update)." In *Current Population Reports,* Series P-20, no. 508. Washington, D.C.: U.S. Government Printing Office.

Delpit, Lisa D. 1988. "The Silenced Dialogue: Power and Pedagogy in Educating Other People's Children." *Harvard Educational Review* 58, no. 3: 280–98.

———. 1995. *Other People's Children.* New York: New Press.

Dickerson, Brian. 2000. "Bad Schools: The Case for Low Standards." *Detroit Free Press,* August 30, 1B.

Dixon, Vernon. 1976. "Worldviews and Research Methodology." In *African Philosophy: Assumptions and Paradigms for Research on Black Persons,* edited by Lewis King, Vernon Dixon, and Wade Nobles. Los Angeles: Fanon Center.

Du Bois, W. E. B. 1968. *The Autobiography of W. E. B. Du Bois: A Soliloquy on Viewing My Life from the Last Decade of Its First Century.* New York: International Publishers.

———. 1989. *The Souls of Black Folk.* 1903. New York: Bantam.

Elkind, David. 1987. *Miseducation: Preschoolers at Risk.* New York: Alfred A. Knopf.

Ellison, Constance M., A. W. Boykin, D. P. Towns, and A. Stokes. 2000. "Classroom Cultural Ecology: The Dynamics of Classroom Life in Schools Serving Low-Income African American Children." Report 44 (May). Washington, D.C.: Howard University, Center for Research on the Education of Students Placed at Risk.

Ellison, Ralph. 1986. *Going to the Territory.* New York: Random House.

Eversley, Melanie. 1998. "Rising Tide of Young Blacks behind Bars." *Detroit Free Press,* February 21, 1A and 10A.

Fahs, Sophia. 1952. *Today's Children and Yesterday's Heritage.* Boston: Beacon.

Feagin, Joe, and Melvin P. Sikes. 1994. *Living with Racism: The Black Middle-Class Experience.* Boston: Beacon.

Foster, Charles R. 1989. "Elements of a Black Youth Ministry." In *Working with Black Youth: Opportunities for Christian Ministry,* edited by Charles R. Foster and Grant S. Shockley. Nashville, Tenn.: Abingdon.

Franklin, V. P. 1992. *Black Self-determination: A Cultural History of African American Resistance.* Westport, Conn.: Lawrence Hill.

Fuller, Mary Lou, and Glenn Olsen. 1998. *Home-School Relations: Working Successfully with Parents and Families.* Boston: Allyn and Bacon.

Gardner, Howard. 1983. *Frames of Mind: The Theory of Multiple Intelligences.* New York: Basic Books.

———. 1999. *Intelligence Reframed: Multiple Intelligences for the Twenty-first Century.* New York: Basic Books.

Gaskill, Peggy. 1993. "Research on Kindergarten Practices: Age of Entrance, Delayed Entry, Extra Year Programs, Assessing Readiness, and Retention." *Beacon* (newsletter of the Michigan Association for the Education of Young Children) 12, no. 2: 1–5.

Gay, Geneva, and Willie L. Baber. 1987. *Expressively Black.* New York: Praeger.

Goldman, Ronald, and J. W. Sanders. 1969. "Cultural Factors and Hearing." *Exceptional Children* 35, no. 6: 489–90.

Grant, Jacquelyn. 1989. "A Theological Framework." In *Working with Black Youth: Opportunities for Christian Ministry*, edited by Charles R. Foster and Grant S. Shockley. Nashville, Tenn.: Abingdon.

Gutman, Herbert G. 1976. *The Black Family in Slavery and Freedom, 1750–1925.* New York: Pantheon.

Hacker, Andrew. 1992. *Two Nations: Black and White, Separate, Hostile, and Unequal.* New York: Ballantine.

Hale, Janice E. 1986. *Black Children: Their Roots, Culture, and Learning Styles.* Baltimore: Johns Hopkins University Press.

——. 1994. *Unbank the Fire: Visions for the Education of African American Children.* Baltimore: Johns Hopkins University Press.

Herrnstein, Richard J., and Charles Murray. 1994. *The Bell Curve: Intelligence and Class Structure in American Life.* New York: Free Press.

Hilliard, Asa G., III. 1995. *The Maroon within Us.* Baltimore: Black Classics Press.

——. 1997. *SBA: The Reawakening of the African Mind.* Gainesville, Fla.: Makare Publishing.

Holt, John. 1964. *How Children Fail.* New York: Dell.

Huitt, William. 1997. "The SCANS Report Revisited." Paper presented to the fifth annual Gulf Youth Business and Vocational Education Conference, April 18, Valdosta State University, Valdosta, Georgia.

——. 1998. "Educational Psychology Interactive: Moral and Character Development." http://chiron.valdosta.edu/whuitt/col/morchr/morchr.html (April 6, 2000).

Jackson, Jesse. 1998. Address to the National Urban League Annual Conference. In "National Urban League Holds Annual Conference in Philadelphia." *Jet*, September 7, 46–48.

Jennings, Peter. 1993. "Common Miracles: The New American Revolution in Learning." ABC News documentary, aired January 23.

Johnson, Charles S. 1967. *Growing Up in the Black Belt: Negro Youth in the Rural South.* 1941. New York: American Council on Education. Reprint, New York: Schocken.

Johnston, Robert C., and Debra Viadero. 2000. "Unmet Promise: Raising Minority Achievement." *Education Week*, March 15, 18–21.

Jones, J. M. 1983. Conceptual and Strategic Issues in the Relationship of Black Psychology to American Social Science. In *Research Directions of Black Psychologists*, edited by A. W. Boykin, A. J. Franklin, and J. R. Yates. New York: Russell Sage Foundation.

Kantrowitz, Barbara, and Claudia Kalb. 1998. "Boys Will Be Boys." *Newsweek*, May 11, 1998, 55–60.

King, Martin Luther, Jr. 1964. "Letter from Birmingham Jail." In *Why We Can't Wait*. New York: Harper and Row.

Kohlberg, Lawrence. 1984. *The Psychology of Moral Development*. San Francisco: Harper and Row.

Kohn, Alfie. 1993. *Punished by Rewards*. Boston: Houghton Mifflin.

Kozol, Jonathan. 1991. *Savage Inequalities*. New York: Crown.

Kunjufu, Jawanza. 1984. *Developing Positive Self-images and Discipline in Black Children*. Chicago: African American Images.

——. 1985. *Countering the Conspiracy to Destroy Black Boys*. Chicago: African American Images.

——. 1986. *Motivating and Preparing Black Youth for Success*. Chicago: African American Images.

Langway, Lynn, Tenley Ann Jackson, Marsha Zabarsky, Don Shirley, and James Whitmore. 1983. "Bringing Up Superbaby: Parents Are Pushing Their Kids to Learn Earlier Than Ever." *Newsweek*, March 28, 62–68.

Leadership Conference on Civil Rights. 2000. *Justice on Trial: Racial Disparities in the American Criminal Justice System*. Washington, D.C.

Levine, Lawrence W. 1977. *Black Culture and Black Consciousness*. New York: Oxford University Press.

Lewis, Barbara A. 1991. *The Kid's Guide to Social Action: How to Solve the Social Problems You Choose—and Turn Creative Thinking into Positive Action*. Minneapolis: Free Spirit Publishing.

——. 1995. *The Kid's Guide to Service Projects: Over Five Hundred Service Ideas for Young People Who Want to Make a Difference*. Minneapolis: Free Spirit Publishing.

Lewis, David Levering. 1993. *W. E. B. Du Bois: Biography of a Race, 1868–1919*. New York: Henry Holt.

Lienert, Anita. 2000. "Medical Access for Minorities Lag." *Detroit News*, June 25, 8A.

Lincoln, C. Eric, and Lawrence Mamiya. 1990. *The Black Church in the African American Experience*. Durham: Duke University Press.

Loscocco, Laurie. 1994. "It's Tough to Convince Black Men That Prostate Cancer Test Is Vital." *Columbus (Ohio) Dispatch*, April 17, 1C–2C.

Lynn, Robert W., and Elliot Wright. 1971. *The Little Big Sunday School*. New York: Harper and Row.

Malinowski, Bronislaw. 1954. *Magic, Science, and Religion, and Other Essays*. Garden City, N.Y.: Doubleday.

Marans, A., and R. Lourie. 1967. "Hypotheses Regarding the Effects of Child-Rearing Patterns on the Disadvantaged Child." In *The Disadvantaged Child*, vol. 1, edited by Jerome Hellmuth. New York: Brunner/Mazel.

Massey, Douglas, and Nancy Denton. 1993. *American Apartheid: Segregation and the Making of the Underclass*. Cambridge: Harvard University Press.

Mays, Benjamin, and Joseph Nicholson. 1969. *The Negro's Church*. New York: Arno.

McCarthy, D. A. 1972. *Manual for the McCarthy Scales of Children's Abilities*. New York: Psychological Corporation.

McDermott, Ray. 1987. "Achieving School Failure: An Anthropological Approach to Literacy and Social Stratification." In *Education and Cultural Process: Anthropological Approaches*, 2d ed., edited by George Spindler. Prospect Heights, Ill.: Waveland.

McWhorter, John H. 2000. *Losing the Race: Self-sabotage in Black America*. New York: Free Press.

Miller, D. W. 1999. "The Black Hole of Education Research: Why Do Academic Studies Play Such a Minimal Role in Efforts to Improve the Schools?" *Chronicle of Higher Education: Research and Publishing Section* 45, no. 48: A17–A18.

Miller, Jerome. 1997. *Search and Destroy: African American Males in the Criminal Justice System*. New York: Cambridge University Press.

Mintz, Sidney W., and Richard Price. 1976. *The Birth of African-American Culture: An Anthropological Perspective*. Boston: Beacon.

National Urban League. 2000. *The State of Black America*. New York.

Northwest Regional Educational Laboratory. 1998. *Catalog of School Reform Models*. Washington, D.C.: U.S. Department of Education.

Peck, J. T., Ginny McCaig, and M. E. Sapp. 1988. *Kindergarten Policies: What Is Best for Children?* Washington, D.C.: National Association for the Education of Young Children.

Perry, Theresa, and Lisa Delpit, eds. 1998. *The Real Ebonics Debate*. Boston: Beacon.

Piaget, Jean. 1962. *The Moral Judgment of the Child*. 1932. New York: Collier.

Raboteau, Albert. 1995. *A Fire in the House: Reflections on African-American Religious History*. Boston: Beacon.

Roeper City and Country School Curriculum Guide. 1993. Bloomfield Hills, Mich.

Royce, Josiah. 1914. *The Problem of Christianity*. 2 vols. New York: Macmillan.

Schneider, Iris. 1992. "Refuge and Strength: Black Church Life in Southern California." *Los Angeles Times*, February 9, E-1.

Schomburg Center for Research in Black Culture, New York Library. 1999. *African American Desk Reference*. New York: John Wiley and Sons.

Shepard, L. A., and M. L. Smith. 1986. "Synthesis of Research on School Readiness and Kindergarten Retention." *Educational Leadership* 44, no. 3: 78–86.

Shepard, Paul. 2000. "Black America Making Gains." *Detroit Free Press*, July 26, 3A.

Silberman, Charles. 1970. *Crisis in the Classroom.* New York: Vintage.

Smitherman, Geneva. 1977. *Talking and Testifying: The Language of Black America:* Boston: Houghton Mifflin.

Spencer, Margaret Beale. 1999. "Identity, Achievement Orientation, and Race: Lessons Learned about the Normative Developmental Experiences of African American Males." Paper presented at the Urban League's Conference on Race and Education, University of Illinois, Chicago, March 12–14.

Staples, Robert. 1985. "Black Male/Female Relationships." In *Conference on the Black Family Proceedings*, edited by Janice Hale-Benson. Cleveland, Ohio: Cleveland State University.

Stokes, Olivia Pearl. 1972. "The Black Perspective: Christian Education in Today's Church." In *To You Who Teach in the Black Church*, edited by Riggins R. Earl Jr. Nashville, Tenn.: National Baptist Convention Publishing Board.

Thurman, Howard. 1980. "Get in Touch with the Genuine in You." Baccalaureate sermon at Spelman College, Atlanta, Georgia, May.

Toppo, Greg. 2000. "Wages Rise, but Families Work More: Blacks, Hispanics, Put in Longer Hours Than White Counterparts to Earn Same." *Detroit News*, September 3, 17A.

U.S. Bureau of Justice Statistics. 2000. *Jail Inmates Annual.* Washington, D.C.

U.S. Bureau of the Census. 2000. *Current Population Reports*, *Series P20-487. Washington, D.C.

Vail, Patricia. 1989. "The Hole in Whole Language." *New York ODS Branch Newsletter*, August, 2–3.

Vincent, Philip F. 1996. *Developing Character in Students: A Primer.* Chapel Hill, N.C.: New View Publications.

Wachs, Theodore, I. Uzgiris, and J. M. Hunt. 1971. "Cognitive Development in Infants of Different Age Levels and from Different Environmental Backgrounds: An Explanatory Investigation." *Merrill Palmer Quarterly* 17, no. 4: 283–317.

Watkins, William H., James H. Lewis, and Victoria Chou. 2001. *Race and Education: The Roles of History and Society in Educating African American Students.* Boston: Allyn and Bacon.

Wilson, Thomasyne. 1972. "Notes toward a Process of Afro-American Education." *Harvard Educational Review* 42, no. 3: 374–89.

Wilson, William Julius. 1978. *The Declining Significance of Race: Blacks and Changing American Institutions.* Chicago: University of Chicago Press.

——. 1987. *The Truly Disadvantaged: The Inner City, the Underclass, and Public Policy.* Chicago: University of Chicago Press.

Woodson, Carter G. 1969. *The Rural Negro.* 1930. New York: Russell and Russell.

Yinger, J., G. Galster, B. Smith, and F. Eggers. 1978. *The Status of Research into Racial Discrimination and Segregation in American Housing Markets.* Washington, D.C.: U.S. Department of Housing and Urban Development.

Young, Virginia H. 1970. "Family and Childhood in a Southern Negro Community." *American Anthropologist* 72, no. 2: 269–88.

Index

Kohlberg, Lawrence, 160
Kohn, Alfie, 123
Kozol, Jonathan, 35, 38, 111, 176
Ku Klux Klan battle cry, 181
Kunjufu, Jawanza, 82

labor market, inequalities in, 27
Lawrence, Martin, 39
leadership: training for youth, 199–200; transforming, elements of, 200; transactional, elements of, 201; visioning, as element of transforming leadership, 200–201; vocation, 197. See also Foster, Charles
Leadership Conference on Civil Rights, 40–41
Leaks, Marna Amoretti Hale (sister), 6, 64
learning: of African American children, 119; while black, xi, xii, xiv, xix, 10, 185; cherished beliefs about, 150
Legal Aide Society, 184
Lemann, Nicholas, 3
Levine, Lawrence, 116, 165–166
Lewis, David Levering, 187
Lewis, James, 184
liberation, 198, 199, 200
Lincoln, C. Eric, 155, 193–194
literacy, 114, 148; orientation, 119
Losing the Race (John H. McWhorter), 128
Louis, Joe (black hero), 168
Lynn, Robert, 192

magnet schools, xvii, xix, 176
Malinowski, Bronislaw, 166
Mamiya, Lawrence, 193
mantras (deeply held beliefs of educators), xv, xvi, 47; "there is something wrong with African American children," 44
Marshall, Thurgood, 52, 178

Martin Luther King Jr. Center for Non-Violent Social Change, xxvi
Massey, Douglas, 33
mastery, xxii; of criterion-referenced material, 131; grading practices, xx, 151
Math Pentathlon, 134
Mays, Benjamin, 154
McCarthy Scales of Children's Abilities, 46, 102
McDermott, Ray, 41, 54, 56, 63, 69, 73
McWhorter, John H., 128
medication of children, 186
mentoring, xiv, 161; of children, 96–97; of children and youth by school and church, 202; and being "cool," 162; of males, 142–144, 149; role models, for males, 162; role models, for younger children, 161
Michigan Association for the Education of Young Children, 72
Miller, D. W., 150
Miller, James, 38, 94–95
Miller, O. A., 119, 120
Miller, Reggie, and burning of home of, 175
minorities: hiring goals, 11; minority top-off, 11; set-aside programs, 11, 179
Mintz, Sidney, 116
Moore, Evelyn, xxii
morals: character issues for young people, 159; education, 159; moral values, Christian beliefs about, 196; moral thinking, development of, in children, 160. See also values
Morehouse College, 38
Moss, Rev. Otis, Jr., 168
Mother Bethel AME Church, 154
motivation, xiii; intrinsic, 44, 123, 128, 145
multicultural education, 63, 182
multiple intelligences. See Gardner, Howard
Mungin, Lawrence D., 18–20